WORKBOOK to Accompany

Understanding
Health Insurance

A Guide to Professional Billing

WORKBOOK to Accompany

Understanding Health Insurance

A Guide to Professional Billing

7TH EDITION

JoAnn C. Rowell

Founder and Former Chairperson, Medical Assisting Department
Anne Arundel Community College, Arnold, MD
Adjunct Faculty
Community College of Baltimore County—Catonsville Campus, Catonsville, MD

Michelle A. Green, MPS, CMA

Professor, Department of Physical & Life Sciences
Alfred State College
Alfred, NY

WORKBOOK WRITTEN BY

Ruth M. Burke

Medical Billing and Coding Program Specialist at
The Community College of Baltimore County, MD
Adjunct Faculty, The Community College of Baltimore County, MD
Adjunct Faculty, Harford Community College, MD
Consultant on Administrative Procedures to Health Care Practices in Maryland and Virginia
President of the Independent Medical Billers Alliance (IMBA)
Member of the Maryland Medical Group Management Association (MGMA)

THOMSON

DELMAR LEARNING   Australia   Canada   Mexico   Singapore   Spain   United   Kingdom   United States

THOMSON

DELMAR LEARNING

Workbook to Accompany Understanding Health Insurance, A Guide to Professional Billing, 7th Edition
by Ruth M. Burke

Vice President, Health Care
William Brottmiller

Editorial Director:
Cathy L. Esperti

Acquisitions Editor:
Rhonda Dearborn

Developmental Editor:
Marjorie A. Bruce

Marketing Director:
Jennifer McAvey

Marketing Coordinator:
Mona Caron

Editorial Assistant:
Natalie Wager

Technology Project Manager:
Laurie Davis

Production Director:
Karen Leet

Art/Design Coordinator:
Connie Lundberg-Watkins

Project Editor:
Mary Ellen Cox

Production Coordinator:
Catherine Ciardullo

Library of Congress Cataloging-in-Publication Data

ISBN 1-4018-8435-0

International Divisions List

Asia (Including India):
Thomson Learning
60 Albert Street, #15-01
Albert Complex
Singapore 189969
Tel 65 336-6411
Fax 65 336-7411

Australia/New Zealand:
Nelson
102 Dodds Street
South Melbourne
Victoria 3205
Australia
Tel 61 (0)3 9685-4111
Fax 61 (0)3 9685-4199

Latin America:
Thomson Learning
Seneca 53
Colonia Polanco
11560 Mexico, D.F. Mexico
Tel (525) 281-2906
Fax (525) 281-2656

Canada:
Nelson
1120 Birchmount Road
Toronto, Ontario
Canada M1K 5G4
Tel (416) 752-9100
Fax (416) 752-8102

UK/Europe/Middle East/Africa:
Thomson Learning
Berkshire House
1680-173 High Holborn
London WC1V 7AA
United Kingdom
Tel 44 (0)20 497-1422
Fax 44 (0)20 497-1426

Spain (includes Portugal):
Paraninfo
Calle Magallanes 25
28015 Madrid
España
Tel 34 (0)91 446-3350
Fax 34 (0)91 445-6218

Notice to the Reader

Contents

Chapter 1

Health Insurance Specialist—
Roles and Responsibilities 1

Chapter 2

Introduction to Health Insurance 5

Chapter 3

Managed Health Care 11

Chapter 4

Life Cycle of an Insurance Claim 17

Chapter 5

Legal and Regulatory Considerations 23

Chapter 6

ICD-9-CM Coding 31

Chapter 7

CPT Coding 45

Chapter 8

HCPCS Coding System 61

Chapter 9

CMS Reimbursement Issues 67

Chapter 10

Coding for Medical Necessity 71

Chapter 11

Essential CMS-1500 Claim Instructions 79

Chapter 12

Filing Commercial Claims 93

Chapter 13

Blue Cross and Blue Shield Plans 119

Chapter 14

Medicare 145

Chapter 15

Medicaid 185

Chapter 16

Tricare 201

Chapter 17

Workers' Compensation 217

Chapter 1
Health Insurance Specialist—
Roles and Responsibilities

HEALTH INSURANCE OVERVIEW

1. Define the following health care terms:

   a. health insurance claim _____

   _____

   b. preauthorization _____

   _____

   c. health care provider _____

   _____

   d. Centers for Medicare and Medicaid Services (CMS) _____

   _____

   e. hold harmless clause _____

   _____

   f. electronic claims processing _____

   _____

   g. coding _____

   _____

2. List six career opportunities open to health insurance specialists.

   a. _____

   b. _____

   c. _____

   d. _____

   e. _____

   f. _____

3. A consumer claim assistance professional helps private individuals _____

   _____

BASIC SKILL REQUIREMENTS

4. List six basic skills anyone who aspires to become a health insurance specialist must possess.

   a. _____

   b. _____

   c. _____

   d. _____

   e. _____

   f. _____

5. Health insurance specialists must draw on their knowledge of medical ____ to assign codes to the written narratives documented by the health care provider. (Circle the correct answer.)

   a. descriptions

   b. requirements

   c. terminology

   d. all of the above

6. Working with coded information requires an understanding of the ____ of these coding systems to ensure proper selection of individual codes. (Circle the correct answer.)

   a. application

   b. conventions

   c. rules

   d. all of the above

7. Misreading or misinterpreting any word or diagnosis may result in assignment of incorrect code numbers and the possibility of a _____ or _____ of a claim.

8. Insurance specialists must be comfortable discussing insurance concepts and regulations with ____. (Circle the correct answer.)

   a. health care providers

   b. insurance company personnel

   c. patients

   d. all of the above

9. Most insurance companies use Web sites to release _____ and

   _____ _____ prior to adoption.

HEALTH INSURANCE SPECIALIST RESPONSIBILITIES

Critical Thinking

10. Write a paragraph describing the responsibilities of an insurance specialist.

   _____

   _____

   _____

   _____

PROFESSIONAL CREDENTIALS

11. List three professional organizations dedicated to serving health insurance specialists.

   a. _____

   b. _____

   c. _____

Know Your Acronyms

12. Define the following acronyms:

   a. ACAP _____

   b. AAPC _____

   c. AHIMA _____

   d. CMS _____

   e. CPT _____

   f. EDI _____

   g. EOB _____

   h. HCPCS _____

   i. ICD-9-CM _____

Chapter 2
Introduction to Health Insurance

HEALTH INSURANCE, DISABILITY INSURANCE, AND LIABILITY INSURANCE

1. Define the following terms:

   a. health insurance _____

   _____

   b. medical care _____

   _____

   c. health care _____

   _____

   d. preventive services _____

   _____

   e. disability insurance _____

   _____

   f. liability insurance _____

   _____

MAJOR DEVELOPMENTS IN HEALTH INSURANCE

2. An insurance program that requires employers to cover medical expenses and loss of wages for workers who are injured on the job is called ____. (Circle the correct answer.)
   a. workers' compensation
   b. workers' health care
   c. workers' reimbursement
   d. none of the above

3. The first Blue Shield plan was founded in ____. (Circle the correct answer.)
   a. California
   b. Oklahoma
   c. Texas
   d. none of the above

4. Health care coverage available through employers is called ____. (Circle the correct answer.)
   a. employers health insurance
   b. group health insurance
   c. workers' health insurance
   d. none of the above

5. Three or more health care providers sharing equipment, supplies, and personnel is called a ____. (Circle the correct answer.)
   a. combined medical practice
   b. group medical practice
   c. large medical practice
   d. none of the above

6. The International Classification of Diseases was developed by the _____
   _____ _____.

7. Inpatients are admitted to the hospital for treatment with the expectation that the patient will remain in the hospital for a period of ____ hours or more. (Circle the correct answer.)
   a. 12
   b. 24
   c. 48
   d. 64

8. Coverage for catastrophic or prolonged illnesses and injuries is known as ____. (Circle the correct answer.)
   a. intermediate medical insurance
   b. maximum medical insurance
   c. major medical insurance
   d. none of the above

9. The amount for which the patient is financially responsible before an insurance policy provides coverage is called the _____.

10. Describe a *lifetime maximum amount*. _____
    _____
    _____
    _____

11. What act was signed into law providing health care to dependents of active military personnel?
    _____
    _____

12. Match the term in the first column with the description in the second column. Write the correct letter in each blank.

_____ Medicare   a. health care to low-income Americans

_____ Medicaid   b. benefits for dependents of armed forces personnel

_____ TRICARE   c. health care to Americans over the age of 65

13. Current Procedural Terminology (CPT) was developed by _____. (Circle the correct answer.)
    a. AMA
    b. CMS
    c. WHO
    d. none of the above

14. Legislation designed to protect all employees against injuries from occupational hazards in the work place is known as _____.

15. A chronic kidney disorder that requires long-term hemodialysis or kidney transplantation is termed

_____.

16. Describe the responsibility of an HMO. _____

_____

17. Describe *copayment (copay)*. _____

_____

18. The Health Care Financing Administration is now called ____. (Circle the correct answer.)
    a. CMS
    b. HCFA
    c. HHS
    d. none of the above

19. Match the health care term or acronym in the first column with the description in the second column. Write the correct letter in each blank.

_____ BCBSA   a. association of independent Blue Cross and Blue Shield plans

_____ CLIA   b. system that issues a predetermined payment for services

_____ CMS-1500 claim   c. issues payment based on daily rates

_____ COBRA   d. reimburses hospitals for inpatient stays

_____ DRGs   e. used to submit all government claims

_____ fee schedule   f. allows employees to continue health care coverage beyond the benefit termination date

_____ HEDIS

_____ per diem   g. established quality standards for all laboratory testing

_____ PPS   h. created standards to assess managed care systems

_____ RBRVS   i. payment system based on physician work, practice expense, and malpractice insurance expense

      j. list of predetermined payments for health care services

20. Why was the National Correct Coding Initiative developed? _____

_____

21. Describe the primary intent of HIPAA. _____

_____

22. What issues does the Balanced Budget Act of 1997 address? _____

_____

23. Why was the Outpatient Prospective Payment System implemented? _____

_____

Know Your Acronyms

24. Define the following acronyms:

a. ACP _____

b. BBA _____

c. BCA _____

d. BCBSA _____

e. CRI _____

f. CHAMPVA _____

g. CHAMPUS _____

h. CLIA _____

i. COBRA _____

j. CCI _____

k. DRG _____

l. ERISA _____

m. ESRD _____

n. E/M _____

o. FECA _____

p. HIPAA _____

q. HMO _____

r. HEDIS _____

s. HH PPS _____

t. IRF PPS _____

u. ICD _____

v. MDS _____

w. OSHA _____

x. OBRA _____

y. OASIS _____

z. OPPS _____

aa. PSRO _____

bb. PPS _____

cc. RUGs _____

dd. RBRVS _____

ee. SNF PPS _____

ff. TEFRA _____

gg. WHO _____

Chapter 3
Managed Health Care

HISTORY OF MANAGED HEALTH CARE

1. Managed health care was developed to provide ____ health care services to enrollees. (Circle the correct answer.)
   a. affordable
   b. comprehensive
   c. prepaid
   d. all of the above

2. The HMO Act of 1973 required most employers with more than ____ employees to offer HMO coverage if local plans were available. (Circle the correct answer.)
   a. 15
   b. 20
   c. 25
   d. 30

3. For each item, enter **T** for a true statement or **F** for a false statement on the line provided.

   _____ a. ERISA mandated reporting and disclosure requirements for group life and health plans, excluding managed care plans.

   _____ b. TEFRA defined risk contract as an arrangement among providers to provide fee-for-service health care services to Medicare beneficiaries.

   _____ c. OBRA provided states with the flexibility to establish HMOs for Medicare and Medicaid programs.

   _____ d. The Preferred Provider Health Care Act of 1985 allowed subscribers to seek health care from providers inside the PPO.

   _____ e. COBRA established an employee's right to continue health care coverage beyond the scheduled benefit termination date.

   _____ f. HEDIS created standards to assess managed care systems.

   _____ g. HCFA's Office of Managed Care was established to facilitate innovation and competition among Medicare HMOs.

_____ h. HIPAA created federal standards for insurers, HMOs, and employer plans, including those who self-insure.

_____ i. The Balanced Budget Act of 1997 *discouraged* formation of provider service networks and provider service organizations.

MANAGED CARE ORGANIZATIONS

4. A managed care organization is responsible for the health care of a group of _____. (Circle the correct answer.)
   a. employers
   b. enrollees
   c. physicians
   d. all of the above

5. Define *capitation*. _____

_____

6. Describe the role of the primary care provider. _____

_____

7. HEDIS consists of performance measures used to evaluate _____. (Circle the correct answer.)
   a. grievance procedures
   b. health care providers
   c. managed care plans
   d. none of the above

8. What does case management involve? _____

_____

_____

9. Why do managed care plans often require a second surgical opinion? _____

_____

_____

10. What do gag clauses prevent? _____

_____

_____

11. Physician incentives include payments made directly or indirectly to health care providers to serve as encouragement to _____ or _____ services.

SIX MANAGED CARE MODELS

12. Why were MCOs created? _____

_____

13. List six major MCO models available in this country today.

    a. _____

    b. _____

    c. _____

    d. _____

    e. _____

    f. _____

14. An exclusive provider organization is a managed care plan that provides benefits to subscribers if they receive services from _____ providers.

15. Describe a *network provider*. _____

_____

_____

16. An integrated delivery system is an organization of affiliated provider sites that offers joint health care services to subscribers. List some examples of these affiliated provider sites.

    a. _____

    b. _____

    c. _____

17. What type of service does an MSO provide? _____

18. Traditional health insurance coverage is usually provided on a ____ basis. (Circle the correct answer.)
    a. capitation
    b. fee-for-service
    c. prepaid
    d. all of the above

19. HMOs provide preventive care services to promote ____. (Circle the correct answer.)
    a. easy access to medical care
    b. emergency services
    c. wellness
    d. all of the above

20. HMOs assign each subscriber to a ____ responsible for coordination of health care services and referrals to other health care providers. (Circle the correct answer.)
    a. primary care provider
    b. specialist
    c. surgeon
    d. all of the above

21. HMOs often require a copayment from _____. (Circle the correct answer.)
   a. patients
   b. physicians
   c. providers
   d. all of the above

22. Define *deductible*. _____

   _____

23. Match the HMO model in the first column with the description in the second column. Write the correct letter in each blank.

   _____ direct contract model   a. services provided to subscribers by physicians
   _____ group model   employed by the HMO
   _____ IPA   b. intermediary that negotiates the HMO contract
   _____ network model   c. the HMO reimburses the physician group
   _____ staff model   d. services delivered to subscribers by
                                            individual physicians in the community
                                         e. services provided to subscribers by two or more
                                            physician multi-specialty group practices

24. What have some HMOs and PPOs implemented to create flexibility in managed care plans?

   _____

25. In a POS plan, patients have the freedom to use what type of providers?

   a. _____

   b. _____

26. A PPO is a network of physicians and hospitals that have joined together to contract with insurance companies, employers, or other organizations to provide health care to subscribers for a _____. (Circle the correct answer.)
   a. premium fee
   b. discounted fee
   c. standard fee
   d. all of the above

27. PPO premiums, deductibles, and copayments are usually _____ than those paid for HMOs. (Circle the correct answer.)
   a. higher
   b. lower
   c. same
   d. all of the above

28. A _____ _____ _____ provides subscribers with a choice of HMO, PPO, or traditional health insurance plans.

ACCREDITATION OF MANAGED CARE ORGANIZATIONS

29. List two organizations that evaluate (and accredit) managed care organizations.

    a. _____

    b. _____

30. Why would a health care facility undergo NCQA accreditation? _____

    _____

EFFECTS OF MANAGED CARE ON A PHYSICIAN'S PRACTICE

31. Managed care programs have tremendous impact on a practice's administrative procedures. List procedures that must be in place in a medical office.

    a. _____

    b. _____

    c. _____

    d. _____

    e. _____

    f. _____

Know Your Acronyms

32. Define the following acronyms:

    a. CMP _____

    b. EPO _____

    c. EQRO _____

    d. GPWW _____

    e. IPA _____

    f. IDS _____

    g. IPO _____

    h. JCAHO _____

    i. MCO _____

    j. MSO _____

    k. NCQA _____

l. PHO _____

m. POS _____

n. PAC _____

o. PPO _____

p. PCP _____

q. QAPI _____

r. QISMC _____

s. TPA _____

t. URO _____

Chapter 4
Life Cycle of an Insurance Claim

DEVELOPMENT OF THE CLAIM

1. The development of an insurance claim begins when _____

_____

2. List three parts of insurance claim development.

    a. _____

    b. _____

    c. _____

3. Define *new patient*. _____

_____

4. Define *established patient.* _____

_____

NEW PATIENT INTERVIEW AND CHECK-IN PROCEDURES

5. Match the term in the first column with the definition in the second column. Write the correct letter in each blank.

    _____ beneficiary

    _____ birthday rule

    _____ encounter form

    _____ guarantor

    _____ nonparticipating provider

    _____ participating provider

    _____ patient registration form

    _____ policyholder

    _____ primary insurance

    a. person responsible for paying the charges

    b. person whose name the insurance policy is issued

    c. patient is not expected to pay the difference between the insurance payment and the provider's fee

    d. patient is expected to pay the difference between the insurance payment and the provider's fee

    e. used to create the patient's financial and medical records

    f. person eligible to receive health care benefits

    g. insurance plan responsible for paying claims first

    h. policyholder whose birth month and day occurs earlier in the calendar year holds the primary policy

    i. used to record treated diagnoses and services

POSTCLINICAL CHECK-OUT PROCEDURES

6. Place in chronological order the following postclinical check-out procedures.

   a. Collect payment from the patient

   b. Assign CPT and ICD-9-CM codes

   c. Post charges to the patient's ledger/account record

   d. Complete the insurance claim

   e. Post payment to the patient's account

   f. Enter charges for procedures and/or services performed and total the charges

   Step 1: _____

   Step 2: _____

   Step 3: _____

   Step 4: _____

   Step 5: _____

   Step 6: _____

7. The _____ _____ is the permanent record of all financial transactions between the patient and practice.

8. The manual daily accounts receivable journal, also known as the _____ _____, is a chronological summary of all transactions posted to individual patient ledgers/accounts on a specific day.

9. What is a *copay*? _____

   _____

10. What is a *coinsurance payment*? _____

    _____

11. State the name of the insurance claim form used to report professional and technical services. _____

    _____

INSURANCE COMPANY PROCESSING OF A CLAIM

12. Use each of the following terms in a statement.

    noncovered procedure _____

    _____

    unauthorized service _____

    _____

common data file _____

_____

allowed charge _____

_____

deductible _____

_____

explanation of benefits (EOB) _____

_____

13. For each item, enter **T** for a true statement or **F** for a false statement on the line provided.

_____ a. Patients may not be billed for uncovered or noncovered procedures.

_____ b. Patients may be billed for unauthorized services.

_____ c. If a procedure or service does not match an appropriate diagnosis, it is considered medically unnecessary and may be disallowed.

_____ d. The allowed charge is the maximum amount the insurance company will pay for each procedure or service, according to the patient's policy.

_____ e. Payment may sometimes be greater than the fee submitted by the provider if the allowed amount is greater than the charge.

14. List five items the explanation of benefits (EOB) may contain.

a. _____

b. _____

c. _____

d. _____

e. _____

15. If a check is mailed to the patient by the insurance company, whose responsibility is it to obtain payment from the patient? _____

MAINTAINING INSURANCE CLAIM FILES

16. The federal Omnibus Budget Reconciliation Act of 1987 requires providers to retain copies of any government insurance claims and all attachments filed by the provider for a period of _____. (Circle the correct answer.)
    a. 1 year
    b. 3 years
    c. 6 years
    d. forever

17. The federal Privacy Act of 1974 prohibits _____. (Circle the correct answer.)
    a. a patient from notifying the provider regarding payment or rejections of unassigned claims
    b. payers from notifying providers about payments on or rejections of unassigned claims
    c. the provider from appealing processing errors on unassigned claims
    d. payers from notifying the patient regarding payment or rejections of unassigned claims

Critical Thinking

18. Write a paragraph explaining the six steps that should be taken when an error in claims processing is found.

_____

_____

_____

_____

_____

_____

19. Define the following *reasons for denials* that may be indicated on the transmittal notice.

a. Procedure or service not medically necessary _____

_____

b. Pre-existing condition _____

_____

c. Noncovered benefit _____

_____

d. Termination of coverage _____

_____

e. Failure to obtain preauthorization _____

_____

f. Out-of-network provider used _____

_____

g. Lower level of care could have been provided _____

_____

DELINQUENT CLAIMS

20. What is the best way to deal with delinquent claims? _____

_____

21. What is the name of the report that shows the status of outstanding claims from each payer?

_____

22. Define a *clean claim.* _____

_____

23. What type of company would the Fair Debt Collection Practices Act regulate? _____

_____

24. When might a medical practice use litigation to recover a debt? _____

_____

25. Insurance is regulated by the ____. (Circle the correct answer.)
    a. CMS
    b. individual states
    c. federal government
    d. none of the above

Know Your Acronyms

26. Define the following acronyms:

   a. EOB _____

   b. FDCPA _____

   c. MSN _____

   d. nonPAR _____

   e. OBRA _____

   f. PAR _____

Chapter 5
Legal and
Regulatory Considerations

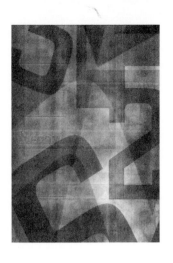

INTRODUCTION TO LEGAL AND REGULATORY CONSIDERATIONS

1. Match the term in the first column with the description in the second column. Write the correct letter in each blank.

_____	civil law	a. legal notice to providers published by CMS
_____	criminal law	b. areas of the law not classified as criminal
_____	subpoena	c. legal newspaper published by the NARA
_____	deposition	d. areas of the law that deal with crimes and their prosecution
_____	interrogatory	e. requires a witness to appear at a particular time and place to testify
_____	*Federal Register*	f. document containing a list of questions to be answered in writing
_____	*Medicare Bulletin*	g. testimony under oath taken outside of court

2. What should health care organizations do with the *Medicare Bulletin?* (Circle the correct answer.)

   a. Appoint one individual to review the Bulletin, update the manual, and educate staff about changes.

   b. Ignore it.

   c. Wait for another health care organization to contact you regarding any changes.

   d. None of the above.

CONFIDENTIALITY OF PATIENT INFORMATION

3. Match the term in the first column with the description in the second column. Write the correct letter in each blank.

_____	privacy	a. restricting patient information access to those with proper authorization
_____	confidentiality	b. the right of individuals to keep their information from being disclosed to others
_____	security	c. the safekeeping of patient information

4. Breach of confidentiality is often unintentional and involves the _____ release of patient information to a third party. (Circle the correct answer.)

    a. authorized

    b. intentional

    c. unauthorized

    d. none of the above

5. Match the insurance terms in the first column with the definitions in the second column. Write the correct letter in each blank.

    _____ first party

    _____ second party

    _____ third party

    _____ contract

    _____ guardian

    a. the person or organization who is providing the service

    b. an agreement between two or more parties to perform specific services or duties

    c. the person designated in a contract to receive a contracted service

    d. the person who is legally designated to be in charge of a patient's affairs

    e. the one who is not involved in the patient/provider relationship

6. For each item, enter **T** for a true statement or **F** for a false statement on the line provided.

    _____ a. Accessing patient information without a job-related reason would be considered a breach of confidentiality.

    _____ b. Prior to completing a patient's claim you must have the patient sign an authorization for the release of medical information statement.

    _____ c. A dated, signed special release form is generally considered valid for five years.

    _____ d. Computerized practices do not need to obtain the patient's signature on an authorization for the release of medical information statement.

    _____ e. To release medical information to an individual other than the payer, the patient must complete an authorization to release medical information statement.

    _____ f. When health care providers agree to treat either a Medicaid or workers' compensation case, they agree to accept the program's payment as payment in full for covered procedures rendered to these patients.

    _____ g. Patients who undergo screening for HIV or AIDS should not be asked to sign an additional authorization statement releasing information regarding the patient's HIV/AIDS status.

7. List the three exceptions to the required authorization for release of medical information allowed by the federal government.

    a. _____

    b. _____

    c. _____

CLAIMS INFORMATION TELEPHONE INQUIRIES

Critical Thinking

8. It is very simple for a curious individual to place a call to a physician's office and claim to be an insurance company benefits clerk. Write a paragraph explaining how a physician's office can verify insurance company telephone inquiries.

_____

_____

_____

_____

_____

_____

_____

9. Great care should be taken when attorneys request information over the telephone. Write a paragraph explaining how a physician's office can verify attorneys' inquiries.

_____

_____

_____

_____

_____

_____

_____

FACSIMILE TRANSMISSION

10. Each facsimile transmission (FAX) of sensitive material should have a cover sheet that includes the following information:

   a. _____

   b. _____

   c. _____

   d. _____

   e. _____

   f. _____

RETENTION OF PATIENT INFORMATION AND HEALTH INSURANCE RECORDS

11. OBRA of 1987 requires patient information and health insurance records to be maintained for ____ years. (Circle the correct answer.)
    a. five
    b. six
    c. seven
    d. none of the above

12. Patient information and health insurance records must be available as references for use by ____. (Circle the correct answer.)
    a. DHHS
    b. fiscal intermediaries
    c. CMS
    d. all of the above

13. It is acceptable to microfilm patient information and insurance records if the microfilm _____

_____ .

FEDERAL FALSE CLAIMS ACT

14. The practice of assigning an ICD-9-CM code that does not match patient record documentation for the purpose of illegally increasing reimbursement is called _____ .

15. Describe *self-referral*. _____

_____

HEALTH INSURANCE PORTABILITY AND ACCOUNTABILITY ACT OF 1996

16. List four ways HIPAA provisions improve the portability and continuity of health care coverage.
    a. _____
    b. _____
    c. _____
    d. _____

17. Define *fraud*. _____

_____

18. Define *abuse*. _____

_____

19. Indicate whether each of the following applies to **fraud (f)** or **abuse (a)** on the line provided.

_____ a. violations of participating provider agreements

_____ b. billing for services not furnished

_____ c. falsifying medical records to justify payment

_____ d. excessive charges for services

_____ e. unbundling codes

_____ f. submitting claims that include services not medically necessary to treat the patient's stated condition

_____ g. improper billing practices that result in a payment by a government program when the claim is the legal responsibility of another third-party payer

_____ h. receiving a kickback

_____ i. misrepresenting the diagnosis to justify payment

20. A person found guilty of Medicare fraud faces _____, _____, and/or _____ penalties.

21. Civil penalties for committing Medicare fraud are ____ per false claim. (Circle the correct answer.)
    a. $1,000 to $2,000
    b. $4,000 to $8,000
    c. $5,000 to $10,000
    d. $10,000 to $20,000

22. The civil False Claims Act covers only offenses that are committed with ____. (Circle the correct answer.)
    a. actual knowledge of the falsity of the claim
    b. deliberate ignorance of the truth or falsity of a claim
    c. reckless disregard
    d. all of the above

23. Which of the following is a compliance risk area for physicians? (Circle the correct answer.)
    a. ensuring that services are reasonable and necessary
    b. proper coding and billing
    c. proper documentation
    d. all of the above

24. The Payment Error Prevention Program requires facilities to ____. (Circle the correct answer.)
    a. discuss HIPAA regulations
    b. ensure hospital claims are submitted electronically
    c. identify improper Medicare payments
    d. all of the above

25. Funds a provider or beneficiary has received in excess of amounts due and payable under Medicare and Medicaid statutes and regulations are called _____.

26. The Correct Coding Initiative was developed to reduce Medicare program expenditures by detecting _____ coding.

27. Match the term in the first column with the description in the second column. Write the correct letter in each blank.

_____ CCI edits

_____ component code

_____ comprehensive code

_____ mutually exclusive codes

a. the lesser procedure or service when reported with another code

b. procedures or services that could not reasonably be performed at the same session by the same provider on the same beneficiary

c. pairs of CPT and/or HCPCS level II codes that are not payable separately

d. the major procedure or service when reported with another code

28. A tax-exempt trust for the purpose of paying medical expenses is known as a

_____ _____ _____.

29. No policy can be sold as a long-term care insurance policy if it limits or excludes coverage by type of

_____, _____ _____, or _____.

30. The process of sending data from one party to another via computer linkages is known as

_____ _____ _____.

31. Does HIPAA require payers to implement uniform language for EDI? _____

32. Are computer-generated paper claims categorized as EDI? _____

33. Should ICD-9-CM be used to report diagnosis and inpatient hospital services? _____

34. Should ICD-9-CM be used to report physician services? _____

35. What must physicians use to report their services? _____

36. What must institutional and professional pharmacies use to report their transactions? _____

37. What must retail pharmacies use to report their transactions? _____

38. What does the Privacy Rule protect? _____

39. The Privacy Rule ____ to their own medical records. (Circle the correct answer.)
    a. gives patients greater access
    b. limits patient access
    c. does not change patient access
    d. all of the above

40. Covered entities are ____. (Circle the correct answer.)
    a. health care clearinghouses
    b. health care providers
    c. health care plans
    d. all of the above

41. The Privacy Rule compliancy date for covered entities is ____. (Circle the correct answer.)
    a. April 14, 2002
    b. April 14, 2003
    c. December 28, 2000
    d. none of the above

42. Describe a *business associate*. _____

_____

43. Does the Privacy Rule preempt state laws that are more restrictive than federal regulations? _____

44. Does the Privacy Rule require physicians to inform patients of their privacy rights and how their information can be used? _____

45. Does the Privacy Rule allow employees to go untrained regarding privacy procedures? _____

46. Does the Privacy Rule require covered entities to designate an individual to ensure that the privacy procedures are adopted and followed? _____

47. Does the Privacy Rule allow pharmacists to fill prescriptions phoned in by a physician before obtaining the patient's written consent? _____

48. Does the Privacy Rule require employees to use identifying numbers instead of patient names to locate them in waiting areas? _____

49. Does the Privacy Rule allow physician offices to use sign-in sheets? _____

50. Does the Privacy Rule require patient records to be secured at all times? _____

Know Your Acronyms

51. Define the following acronyms:

a. CCI _____

b. CDT _____

c. EDI _____

d. EIN _____

e. EMC _____

f. FI _____

g. HIPAA _____

h. MSA _____

i. NDC _____

j. NPI _____

k. NSF _____

l. OCR   _____

m. OIG   _____

n. PHI   _____

o. NSF   _____

p PEPP   _____

q. TPO   _____

Chapter 6
ICD-9-CM Coding

INTRODUCTION TO ICD-9-CM

1. Match the acronyms in the first column with their function in the second column. Write the correct letter in each blank.

_____ ICD   a. creates annual procedure classification updates for ICD-9-CM

_____ WHO   b. used to code and classify mortality data

_____ CMS   c. official system for assigning codes to diagnoses

_____ NCHS   d. publishes ICD

_____ ICD-9-CM   e. coordinates official disease classification activities for ICD-9-CM

2. The ICD-9-CM is organized into _____ volumes. (Circle the correct answer.)
   a. two
   b. three
   c. four
   d. five

3. Define *medical necessity*. _____

_____

4. If a service or procedure is found "medically unnecessary" by Medicare the patient must sign a(n)
   _____ _____ _____.

5. New diagnosis codes officially go into effect on _____ of each year. (Circle the correct answer.)
   a. January 1
   b. March 1
   c. July 1
   d. October 1

OUTPATIENT CODING GUIDELINES

6. Explain when codes that describe symptoms and signs, as opposed to definitive diagnoses, are acceptable for reporting. _____

_____

7. For each item, enter **T** for a true statement or **F** for a false statement on the line provided.

      _____ a. There are ICD-9-CM codes to describe symptoms and problems.

      _____ b. Always begin searching for a code in the Tabular List.

      _____ c. ICD-9-CM is composed of codes that contain 3 or 4 digits.

      _____ d. A three-digit code is used only if it is not further subdivided.

      _____ e. Do not code diagnoses documented as "probable."

      _____ f. Code conditions that were previously treated and no longer exist.

8. Describe when historical codes (V10–V19) may be used. _____

_____

_____

PRIMARY AND PRINCIPAL DIAGNOSES

9. List three general classifications of facilities in which an outpatient is treated.

    a. _____

    b. _____

    c. _____

10. Define *inpatient*. _____

_____

11. Who stipulates the inpatient admission status? _____

12. Which diagnosis is reported on physician office claims? (Circle the correct answer.)

    a. primary

    b. principal

13. Which diagnosis is reported on inpatient hospital claims? (Circle the correct answer.)

    a. primary

    b. principal

14. Which claim is used to report physician office services and procedures? (Circle the correct answer.)

    a. CMS-1500

    b. UB-92

15. Which claim is used to report inpatient admissions and outpatient and emergency department services and/or procedures? (Circle the correct answer.)

    a. CMS-1500

    b. UB-92

16. Which diagnosis is the most significant condition for which services and/or procedures were provided? (Circle the correct answer.)

    a. primary

    b. principal

17. Which diagnosis is the condition determined after study that resulted in the patient's admission to the hospital? (Circle the correct answer.)

    a. primary

    b. principal

18. Why is the CMS-1500 claim printed in red ink? _____

PRIMARY AND PRINCIPAL PROCEDURES

19. Hospitals are required to code all inpatient procedures using the _____

_____

20. Outpatient procedures performed in the hospital are coded using the ____. (Circle the correct answer.)

    a. CPT and HCPCS level II

    b. ICD-9-CM Volume III

    c. ICD-9-CM Volumes I & II

    d. any of the above

21. The definition of a *principal procedure* is ____. (Circle the correct answer.)

    a. a procedure performed to treat a complication

    b. a procedure performed for definitive treatment

    c. a procedure performed which is most closely related to the principal diagnosis

    d. any of the above

CODING QUALIFIED DIAGNOSES

22. Define *qualified diagnosis.* _____

_____

23. List five examples of qualified diagnoses. (Do not use examples found in the textbook.)

    a. _____

    b. _____

    c. _____

    d. _____

    e. _____

24. Are qualified diagnoses routinely coded on claims submitted from health care practitioners' offices?

_____

25. What do CMS regulations permit on the CMS-1500 claim in place of qualified diagnoses?

_____

ICD-9-CM CODING SYSTEM

26. Match the coding terms in the first column with the definitions in the second column. Write the correct letter in each blank.

_____ Volume 1   a. Index to Procedures and Tabular List

_____ Volume 2   b. Tabular List

_____ Volume 3   c. Index to Diseases

27. Match the coding terms in the first column with the definitions in the second column. Write the correct letter in each blank.

_____ V codes   a. external causes of injury and poisoning

_____ E codes   b. tissue type of neoplasms

_____ M codes   c. factors influencing health status

28. List three sections of the Index to Diseases (Volume 2).

a. _____

b. _____

c. _____

29. Describe Tabular List and the Index (Volume 3).

_____

_____

ICD-9-CM INDEX TO DISEASES

30. Main terms are printed in _____ type and followed by the

_____   _____ .

31. A list of _____ is indented two spaces under the main term.

32. Secondary qualifying conditions are indented two spaces under a _____ .

33. Always consult the code description in the _____ _____ before assigning a code.

BASIC STEPS FOR USING THE INDEX TO DISEASES

34. What is the first step for using the Index to Diseases? _____

_____

35. Underline the main term in each of the following:

a. Newborn anoxia

b. Insect bite

c. Radiation sickness

d. Allergic bronchitis

e. Infarction of brain stem

f. Cranial nerve compression

g. Erosion of the cornea

h. Abdominal cramp

36. Assign codes to the following:

    a. Tension headache _____

    b. Bronchial croup _____

    c. Chronic conjunctivitis _____

    d. Acute confusion _____

    e. Car sickness _____

    f. Rosacea _____

37. Define *coding conventions*. _____

    _____

38. Match the coding conventions in the first column with the definitions in the second column.
    Write the correct letter in each blank.

    _____ nonessential modifiers   a. not elsewhere classifiable

    _____ NEC   b. diseases (or procedures) named for an individual

    _____ essential modifiers   c. listed as secondary codes because they are
                                              manifestations of other conditions
    _____ eponyms
                                           d. subterms that are enclosed in parentheses following
    _____ codes in slanted brackets   the main term

                                           e. clarifies the main term and must be contained in the
                                              diagnostic statement

39. Assign codes to the following:

    a. Pneumonia with influenza _____

    b. Maxillary sinusitis _____

    c. Hiatal hernia _____

40. Assign codes to the following:

    a. Blindness due to injury NEC _____

    b. Erythema, infectional NEC _____

    c. Spontaneous hemorrhage NEC _____

    d. Herpes zoster without mention of complication _____

    e. Eruption due to other chemical products _____

41. Assign codes to the following:

    a. Parkinson's disease _____

    b. Skene's gland abscess _____

    c. Stokes-Adams syndrome _____

    d. Sprengel's deformity _____

    e. Haglund's disease _____

42. Match the coding conventions in the first column with the definitions in the second column. Write the correct letter in each blank.

_____ *See Category*

_____ *See also*

_____ Notes

_____ *See*

a. directs the coder to a more specific term

b. contained in boxes to define terms, clarify index entries, and list choices for additional digits

c. refers the coder to an index entry that may provide additional information

d. refers the coder directly to the Tabular List category

43. Assign codes to the following (remember fifth digits):

a. Polydactyly of fingers _____

b. Sickle-cell crisis, NOS _____

c. Closed lateral dislocation of elbow _____

d. Grand mal epilepsy without mention of intractable epilepsy _____

e. Classical migraine, intractable _____

ICD-9-CM TABULAR LIST OF DISEASES

44. ICD-9-CM codes for Chapters 1 through 17 are organized according to _____ _____ category codes.

45. How is specificity achieved? _____

46. List the six basic steps for using the Tabular List.

Step 1: _____

Step 2: _____

Step 3: _____

Step 4: _____

Step 5: _____

Step 6: _____

47. Define the coding convention term *brackets.* _____

48. Assign codes to the following:

a. Abnormal electroencephalogram (EEG) _____

b. Pyogenic arthritis, upper arm _____

c. Pediculus corporis _____

d. Dermatitis due to poison ivy _____

49. Assign codes to the following:

a. Osteoarthrosis, generalized, hand _____

b. Allergic arthritis, multiple sites _____

    c. Loose body in joint, shoulder region   _____

    d. Loose body in knee   _____ _____

50. Define the coding convention term *includes*. _____

51. Assign codes to the following:

    a. Coccidioidomycosis, unspecified   _____

    b. Splinter, cheek, without major open
       wound, infected   _____

    c. Sliding inguinal hernia, with gangrene,
       bilateral   _____

52. Define the coding convention term *excludes*. _____

53. Assign codes to the following:

    a. Smokers' cough   _____

    b. Acute gingivitis   _____

    c. Anal and rectal polyp   _____

    d. Obstruction of gallbladder   _____

    e. Situs inversus   _____

54. Define the coding convention term *braces*. _____

55. Assign codes to the following:

    a. Hypertrophy of tonsils with adenoids   _____

    b. Cirrhosis of lung   _____

    c. Rupture of appendix with generalized
       peritonitis   _____

    d. Hiatal hernia with gangrene   _____

    e. Diverticulum of appendix   _____

56. Define the coding convention term *colon*. _____

57. Assign codes to the following:

    a. Chronic tracheobronchitis   _____

    b. Bronchopneumonia with influenza   _____

    c. Dermatitis due to acids   _____

58. What does the abbreviation NOS indicate? _____

59. Assign codes to the following:

    a. Acute sore throat NOS   _____

    b. Femoral hernia, unilateral NOS   _____

    c. Transfusion reaction NOS   _____

    d. Acute cerebrovascular insufficiency NOS   _____

    e. Unspecified peritonitis NOS   _____

60. When does a *code first underlying disease* appear? _____

61. Assign codes to the following case studies, giving special attention to the words "code first underlying disease" and assign codes in the correct order.

	First Code	Second Code
a. Patient presents with myotonic cataract resulting from Thomsen's disease	_____	_____
b. Patient presents with post-infectious encephalitis resulting from post-measles	_____	_____
c. Patient presents with cerebral degeneration in generalized lipidoses resulting from Fabry's disease	_____	_____
d. Patient presents with parasitic infestation of eyelid caused by pediculosis	_____	_____
e. Patient presents with xanthelasma of the eyelid resulting from lipoprotein deficiencies	_____	_____

62. Assign codes to the following case studies, giving special attention to the word "and." (Some cases may require two codes; other cases require only one code.)

	First Code	Second Code
a. Patient presents with degenerative disorders of eyelid and periocular area, unspecified	_____	_____
b. Patient presents with acute and chronic conjunctivitis	_____	_____
c. Patient presents with cholesteatoma of middle ear and mastoid	_____	_____
d. Patient presents with psoriatic arthropathy and parapsoriasis	_____	_____
e. Patient presents with nausea and vomiting	_____	_____
f. Patient presents with headache and throat pain	_____	_____

63. Assign codes to the following, giving special attention to the word "with."

a. Rheumatic fever with heart involvement _____

b. Diverticulosis with diverticulitis _____

c. Acute lung edema with heart disease _____

d. Emphysema with acute and chronic bronchitis _____

e. Fracture fibula (closed) with tibia _____

f. Varicose vein with inflammation and ulcer _____

ICD-9-CM INDEX TO DISEASES TABLES

64. For each item, enter **T** for a true statement or **F** for a false statement on the line provided.

_____ a. The Hypertension/Hypertensive Table contains a complete listing of hypertension codes and other conditions associated with hypertension.

_____ b. It is not always necessary to check the Tabular List before assigning a final code for hypertension/hypertensive conditions.

_____ c. When "with" separates two conditions in the diagnostic statement only one code is needed.

_____ d. Secondary hypertension is a unique and separate condition listed on the table.

_____ e. The fourth digit 9 should be used sparingly.

65. Assign codes to the following:

a. Hypertension, benign _____

b. Chronic hypertension, malignant _____

c. Hypertension due to brain tumor, unspecified _____

d. Malignant hypertension with congestive heart failure _____

e. Newborn affected by maternal hypertension _____

66. Define the following terms:

a. neoplasms _____

b. benign _____

c. malignant _____

d. lesion _____

67. List five examples of benign lesions.

a. _____

b. _____

c. _____

d. _____

e. _____

68. Match the neoplasm classifications in the first column with the definitions in the second column. Write the correct letter in each blank.

_____ primary malignancy   a. a malignant tumor that is localized

_____ secondary malignancy   b. there is no indication of the histology or nature of the tumor

_____ carcinoma *in situ*

_____ uncertain behavior   c. it is not possible to predict subsequent behavior from the submitted specimen

_____ unspecified nature

      d. the tumor has spread

      e. the original tumor site

69. Assign codes to the following:

a. Hodgkin's sarcoma _____

b. Ovarian fibroma _____

c. Bronchial adenoma _____

d. Carcinoma of oral cavity and pharynx _____

e. Chronic lymphocytic leukemia _____

f. Reticulosarcoma, intrathoracic _____

g. Adenocarcinoma of rectum and anus _____

h. Benign lymphoma of breast _____

i. Carcinoid small intestine _____

j. Multiple myeloma _____

k. Lipoma, right kidney _____

70. What is the Table of Drugs and Chemicals used for? _____

_____

71. Define *adverse effect* or *reaction.*

_____

_____

72. What are E codes used for in regard to poisoning? _____

_____

73. Describe when an E code might be used as the primary code for poisoning. _____

_____

74. Assign codes to the following, using E codes where applicable.

	First Code	Second Code
a. Poisoning due to isopropyl alcohol	_____	_____
b. Poisoning due to amino acid	_____	_____
c. Suicide attempt, overdose of tranquilizers	_____	_____
d. Accidental methadone poisoning	_____	_____
e. Poisoning due to therapeutic use of codeine	_____	_____
f. Brain damage due to allergic reaction to penicillin	_____	_____

75. V codes are contained in a supplementary classification of factors influencing the patient's
_____ _____.

76. List the three V code categories.

a. _____

b. _____

c. _____

77. Assign codes to the following:

a. Exercise counseling _____

b. History of alcoholism _____

c. Counseling for parent/child conflict, unspecified _____

d. Screening, cancer, unspecified _____

e. Follow-up exam, post-surgery _____

f. Health check, not pediatric _____

g. Routine child health check _____

h. Fitting of artificial eye _____

i. Flu shot _____

j. Family history of breast cancer _____

k. Observation for suspected tuberculosis _____

CODING SPECIAL DISORDERS

78. What precautions should a coder take before entering the HIV/AIDS code on a claim?

_____

79. If the diagnostic statement does not specify whether a fracture is opened or closed, which one should

the coder select? _____

80. Assign codes to the following:

a. Fracture of base of skull with cerebral contusion _____

b. Open fracture of nasal bones _____

c. Fifth cervical vertebra fracture, closed _____

d. Open fracture coccyx with other spinal cord injury _____

e. Closed fracture of three ribs _____

f. Closed fracture of clavicle _____

g. Open finger fracture _____

h. Bennett's fracture, closed _____

i. Fracture of head of tibia _____

j. Heel bone fracture, closed _____

81. Define *late effect.* _____

82. When coding a late effect, the primary code is the _____ condition and the
secondary code represents the _____ condition or etiology of the late effect.

83. Assign codes to the following in the correct order:

	First Code	Second Code
a. Scarring due to third-degree burn of left arm	_____	_____
b. Nonunion fracture of neck of femur	_____	_____
c. Esophageal stricture due to old lye burn of esophagus	_____	_____
d. Hemiplegia due to old CVA	_____	_____

84. The percentage of total body area or surface affected by burns follows the

" _____ _____ _____ ."

85. Assign codes to the following:

	First Code	Second Code	Third Code
a. Second-degree burn, right upper arm and shoulder	_____	_____	_____
b. Third-degree burn, trunk, 35% body surface	_____	_____	_____
c. Burn of mouth, pharynx, and esophagus	_____	_____	_____
d. Blisters on back of hand and palm	_____	_____	_____
e. Erythema on forearm and elbow	_____	_____	_____
f. Deep third-degree burn with loss of thumb	_____	_____	_____

86. Describe why a coder might report E codes on physician claims. _____

_____

_____

87. Assign E codes to the following, adding a second code when the place of occurrence is provided.

	First Code	Second Code
a. Assault by hanging and strangulation	_____	_____
b. Unarmed fight	_____	_____
c. Self-inflicted injury by crashing of motor vehicle, highway	_____	_____
d. Exposure to noise at nightclub	_____	_____
e. Struck accidentally by falling rock at quarry	_____	_____
f. Struck by thrown ball at baseball field	_____	_____
g. Caught accidentally in escalator at amusement park	_____	_____
h. Dog bite	_____	_____
i. Accidental poisoning from shellfish at restaurant	_____	_____
j. Foreign object left in body during surgical operation	_____	_____
k. Fall from ladder at home	_____	_____
l. Accident caused by hunting rifle at rifle range	_____	_____

88. Codes are to be selected according to the highest level of _____.

89. Indicate which of the following codes need to be carried out to the highest level of specificity by writing the correct code in the space provided.

_____ a. 464.2 Acute laryngotracheitis without mention of obstruction

_____ b. 393 Chronic rheumatic pericarditis

_____ c. 690 Cradle cap

_____ d. 574.2 Calculus of gallbladder without mention of cholecystitis, without obstruction

_____ e. 570 Acute and subacute necrosis of liver

_____ f. 571.4 Chronic persistent hepatitis

_____ g. 914 Infected blister of the hand

90. Describe how diagnoses documented as "probable," "suspected," "questionable," or "ruled out" should be coded. _____

_____

91. A 45-year-old patient presents with polyuria and polydipsia. The physician documents "suspected diabetes mellitus." Circle the correct diagnoses to be coded.

    a. diabetes mellitus type II (adult-onset)

    b. diabetes mellitus with other specified manifestations

    c. polyuria; polydipsia; diabetes mellitus

    d. polyuria; polydipsia

92. A patient presents with a blood pressure of 150/90 and is asked to rest for 10 minutes. Upon re-evaluation the blood pressure is 130/80. The patient is asked to return to the office in two weeks to rule out hypertension. Circle the correct diagnosis to be coded.

    a. hypertension

    b. elevated blood pressure

    c. observation for suspected cardiovascular disease

    d. personal history of other specified circulatory disorder

93. A patient presents with wheezing and a productive cough. The physician recorded "probable bronchitis, pending chest X-ray results." X-ray results confirmed bronchitis. During this visit the patient's glucose was checked to determine the status of his diabetes. The patient reported that his previous indigestion and diarrhea were currently not a problem. Circle the correct diagnoses to be coded.

    a. productive cough

    b. productive cough; indigestion; diarrhea

    c. bronchitis; diabetes mellitus

    d. bronchitis; diabetes mellitus; indigestion; diarrhea

94. A patient presents complaining of tenderness in the left breast and a family history of breast cancer. Upon examination, the physician discovers a small lump in the left breast. The patient is referred to a breast surgeon and X-ray for a mammogram. The physician records "questionable breast cancer of the left breast." Circle the correct diagnosis to be coded.

    a. breast cancer

    b. family history of breast cancer

    c. breast pain; breast cancer

    d. breast lump; breast pain; family history of breast cancer

CONSIDERATIONS TO ENSURE ACCURATE ICD-9-CM CODING

95. For each item, enter **T** for a true statement or **F** for a false statement on the line provided.

_____ a. M codes should be reported on the CMS-1500 claim.

_____ b. Code books should be purchased every other year.

_____ c. Providers and insurance specialists should be kept informed of annual coding changes.

_____ d. Preprinted diagnosis codes on encounter forms should be reviewed to verify inclusion of fifth and sixth digits.

_____ e. The postoperative diagnosis should be coded.

_____ f. Diagnosis codes should be reviewed for accuracy when updates are installed in office management software.

_____ g. Diagnosis codes should be proofread to ensure proper entry in the permanent record.

Know Your Acronyms

96. Define the following acronyms:

a. ICD-9-CM _____

b. NCHS _____

c. NEC _____

d. NOS _____

Chapter 7
CPT Coding

CPT CODING SYSTEM

1. CPT is a listing of descriptive terms and identifying codes for reporting _____ _____ and _____.

2. CPT is updated _____. (Circle the correct answer.)
   a. annually
   b. semiannually
   c. every two years
   d. none of the above

3. The updated version of CPT is released in _____. (Circle the correct answer.)
   a. January
   b. late spring
   c. late fall
   d. none of the above

4. Federal programs generally implement the new codes on _____. (Circle the correct answer.)
   a. January 1
   b. June 1
   c. September 1
   d. none of the above

5. What must each procedure submitted on a claim be linked to? _____
   _____

6. List the six sections of Category I procedures and services. (List in the order in which they appear.)

   a. _____
   b. _____
   c. _____
   d. _____
   e. _____
   f. _____

7. Where are the Evaluation and Management codes located? _____

8. Describe the contents of the following:

Appendix A _____

Appendix B _____

Appendix C _____

Appendix D _____

Appendix E _____

9. A ____ code number and a narrative description identify each procedure and service listed in CPT. (Circle the correct answer.)

a. three-digit

b. four-digit

c. five-digit

d. none of the above

10. How many symbols are located throughout the CPT coding book? (Circle the correct answer.)

a. six

b. seven

c. eight

d. none of the above

11. Match the CPT symbol in the first column with the definition in the second column. Write the correct letter in each blank.

_____ bullet	a. the code is not to be used with modifier -51
_____ triangle	b. a new code added to CPT
_____ horizontal triangles	c. add-on codes
_____ asterisk	d. indicates variable preoperative and postoperative services
_____ circle with slash	e. surround revised guidelines and notes
_____ plus symbol	f. code description revision

CPT CATEGORIES, SUBCATEGORIES, AND HEADINGS

12. Describe the function of the guidelines located at the beginning of each section in the CPT code book. _____

13. When would an unlisted procedure or service code be assigned? _____

_____

CPT INDEX

14. The CPT index is organized by _____.

15. Describe what *main terms* represent. _____

_____

16. Match the CPT term in the first column with the description in the second column. Write the correct letter in each blank.

_____ boldface type   a. used for the cross reference term, *See*, in the CPT Index

_____ *See*   b. main terms in the CPT

_____ italicized type   c. directs coders to an index entry

_____ inferred words   d. used to save space in the CPT Index

CPT MODIFIERS

17. CPT modifiers indicate that the description of the service or procedure performed has been ____. (Circle the correct answer.)
    a. altered
    b. deleted
    c. converted
    d. none of the above

18. CPT modifiers are reported as ____ numeric codes added to the 5-digit CPT code. (Circle the correct answer.)
    a. 1-digit
    b. 2-digit
    c. 3-digit
    d. none of the above

19. Where is a list of all CPT modifiers with brief descriptions located? _____

20. Assign codes and modifiers to the following:

    a. bilateral partial mastectomy   _____

    b. vasovasostomy discontinued after anesthesia due to heart arrhythmia, hospital outpatient   _____

    c. decision for surgery during initial office visit, comprehensive   _____

    d. expanded office visit for follow-up mastectomy, new onset diabetes was discovered and treated   _____

    e. cholecystectomy, postoperative management only   _____

    f. difficult and complicated resection of external cardiac tumor   _____

    g. hemorrhoidectomy by simple ligature discontinued prior to anesthesia due to severe drop in blood pressure, hospital outpatient   _____

    h. assistant surgeon, modified radical mastectomy   _____

    i. total abdominal hysterectomy, preoperative management only   _____

    j. total urethrectomy, including cystostomy, female, surgical care only   _____

    k. simple repair of a 2-inch laceration on the right foot discontinued due to severe dizziness, physician's office   _____

21. Assign codes to the following:

	First Code	Second Code

a. tonsillectomy and adenoidectomy, age 10, and a wart removed from the patient's neck while in the OR _____ _____

b. excision, malignant lesion 0.6 to 1.0 cm, face and layer closure of wounds of face, 2.0 cm _____ _____

c. incision and drainage, perianal abscess, superficial and puncture aspiration of abscess, hematoma, cyst _____ _____

d. muscle repair of forearm and suture of major peripheral nerve, arm, without transposition _____ _____

BASIC STEPS FOR CODING PROCEDURES

22. List seven basic steps for coding procedures.

Step 1: _____

_____

Step 2: _____

_____

Step 3: _____

_____

Step 4: _____

_____

Step 5: _____

_____

Step 6: _____

_____

Step 7: _____

_____

23. Using only the index, write the code or range of codes to be investigated. In addition, underline the main term you referenced in the index.

a. ankle amputation _____

b. lower arm biopsy _____

c. artery angioplasty _____

d. bone marrow aspiration _____

e. bladder aspiration _____

f. bladder neck resection _____

g. rib resection _____

h. salivary duct dilation _____

i. wrist disarticulation _____

j. drinking test for glaucoma _____

k. Dwyer procedure _____

l. new patient office visit _____

m. well-baby care _____

n. wound repair of pancreas _____

o. inpatient hospital discharge _____

p. house calls _____

SURGERY SECTION

24. The surgery section is organized by _____ _____.

25. What are three questions that must be asked to code surgeries properly?

    a. _____

    b. _____

    c. _____

26. CPT divides surgical procedures into which two main groups? _____

27. List three services/procedures included in a surgical package.

    a. _____

    b. _____

    c. _____

28. On what basis are minor surgical procedures to be billed? _____
    _____

29. Briefly describe *unbundling.* _____

30. Assign codes to the following. (If an asterisk appears, include it in your answer.)

    a. removal of foreign body in tendon sheath, simple _____

    b. puncture aspiration of cyst of breast _____

    c. incision and drainage of thyroid gland cyst _____

    d. abrasion, single lesion _____

    e. destruction of four flat warts _____

    f. incision and drainage of ankle abscess _____

    g. incision and drainage of wrist hematoma _____

    h. aspiration thyroid cyst _____

    i. laparoscopy with bilateral total pelvic
       lymphadenectomy and periaortic lymph node biopsy _____

31. The parenthetical note, *separate procedure,* follows a code description that identifies what?
    _____

32. Assign codes to the following, giving special attention to "separate procedure."

    a. removal of impacted vaginal foreign body _____

    b. dilation of cervical canal, instrumental _____

    c. pleurectomy, parietal _____

d. thoracentesis with insertion of tube   _____

  e. laryngoscopy endoscopy, indirect   _____

  f. biopsy of testis, incisional   _____

33. Define *multiple surgical procedures.* _____

_____

34. What is added to the CPT number for each lesser surgical procedure that does not have the symbol
    Ⓞ in front of the code?

_____

Critical Thinking

35. Write a paragraph describing why multiple surgical procedures are ranked into major and lesser procedures.

_____

_____

_____

_____

CODING SPECIAL SURGERY CASES

36. Define the following terms:

  a. skin lesion _____

  b. excision of a lesion _____

  c. destruction of a lesion _____

37. List five things you must know when reporting the excision or destruction of lesions.

  a. _____

  b. _____

  c. _____

  d. _____

  e. _____

38. Layered closure requires the use of two codes: one for the _____, and one for an

_____ _____.

39. If a physician reports the size of a lesion in inches what must the coder do? _____

_____

40. When converting the size of a lesion, one inch equals _____

41. When there are multiple lacerations, which repair should be listed first? _____

_____

42. Assign codes to the following; then convert inches to centimeters.

	First Code	Second Code
a. excision, 1-inch benign lesion, left leg	_____	_____
b. excision, 1/2-inch malignant lesion, finger	_____	_____
c. simple repair of a 2-inch laceration on the right foot	_____	_____
d. intermediate repair of a 5-inch laceration of the back	_____	_____
e. layer closure of a 3-inch wound of the neck	_____	_____
f. repair of laceration, 2.0-cm, anterior two-thirds of tongue	_____	_____

43. What are six questions that must be asked to code fractures/dislocations correctly?

a. _____

b. _____

c. _____

d. _____

e. _____

f. _____

44. Match the fracture terms in the first column with the definitions in the second column. Write the correct letter in each blank.

_____ closed fracture treatment

_____ open fracture treatment

_____ manipulation of a fracture

_____ reduction of a fracture

_____ ORIF

a. the application of manually applied forces to restore normal anatomical alignment

b. open reduction with internal fixation

c. the fracture site was not surgically opened

d. the fracture site was surgically opened, bone ends visualized, aligned, and internal fixation may have been applied

e. a fixation device has been applied

45. When is arthrotomy considered the primary procedure? _____

_____

46. Assign codes to the following:

a. open treatment of fracture great toe, phalanx, with external fixation   _____

b. closed treatment of nasal bone fracture with stabilization   _____

c. treatment of closed elbow dislocation; without anesthesia   _____

d. closed treatment of ulnar fracture, proximal end; with manipulation   _____

e. open treatment of maxillary fracture   _____

f. closed treatment of shoulder dislocation, with manipulation; requiring anesthesia   _____

g. surgical elbow arthroscopy, with removal of loose body   _____

h. diagnostic hip arthroscopy, with synovial biopsy   _____

47. Endoscopy codes in CPT are classified according to (list four):

    a. _____

    b. _____

    c. _____

    d. _____

48. Complete the following sentences:

    a. Endoscopies of the digestive system are always coded to the furthest site accessed by the

       _____ .

    b. Endoscopic guide-wire dilation involves the passage of a guide-wire through an endoscope into
       the _____ .

    c. Indirect laryngoscopy means the larynx is visualized by using a warm laryngeal

       _____ .

    d. Direct laryngoscopy is performed by passing a rigid or fiberoptic endoscopy into the

       _____ .

49. Assign codes to the following:

    a. surgical wrist endoscopy with release of
       transverse carpal ligament   _____

    b. flexible esophagoscopy with single biopsy   _____

    c. direct operative laryngoscopy with foreign body removal   _____

    d. flexible colonoscopy with biopsy   _____

    e. rigid proctosigmoidoscopy with dilation   _____

MEDICINE SECTION

50. The medicine section starts with what code? _____

51. Invasive procedures of the heart and pericardium are located in which section of CPT? (Circle the
    correct answer.)

    a. medicine section

    b. surgery section

52. Cardiac catheterizations are located in which section of CPT? (Circle the correct answer.)

    a. medicine section

    b. surgery section

53. Define *professional component.* _____

_____

54. Define *technical component.* _____

_____

55. When a physician performs only one component of a test, what modifier should be added to the
    global code to indicate the full procedure was not performed? _____

56. The special services and reports section is a miscellaneous section which covers services considered to be _____ as _____ to basic services provided to the patient.

57. How are psychiatric consultations reported? _____

_____

58. Are psychiatric codes reserved for use only by psychiatrists? _____

59. Assign codes to the following:

    a. right heart cardiac catheterization, for congenital cardiac anomalies   _____

    b. medical testimony   _____

    c. services requested between 10:00 P.M. and 8:00 A.M. in addition to basic service   _____

    d. acupuncture; one or more needles, with electrical stimulation   _____

    e. wheelchair management/propulsion training, 15 minutes   _____

    f. massage therapy, 45 minutes   _____

    g. extended medical report preparation   _____

    h. family psychotherapy without the patient present   _____

    i. hypnotherapy   _____

    j. nonpressurized inhalation treatment for acute airway obstruction   _____

    k. educational video tapes for the patient   _____

    l. one hour of psychological testing with interpretation and report   _____

RADIOLOGY SECTION

60. Define *radiologic views*. _____

61. Describe the professional component of a radiologic examination. _____

_____

62. Describe the technical component of a radiologic examination. _____

_____

63. Assign codes to the following:

    a. complete radiologic examination of the mandible   _____

    b. urography, retrograde   _____

    c. pelvimetry   _____

    d. orthoroentgenogram, scanogram   _____

    e. chest X-ray, two views, with fluoroscopy   _____

    f. X-ray of facial bones, four views   _____

g. CAT scan of the abdomen, with contrast   _____

h. gastroesophageal reflux study   _____

i. X-ray of the cervical spine, two views   _____

j. barium enema   _____

k. cardiac shunt detection   _____

l. splenoportography   _____

m. X-ray of the scapula, complete   _____

n. X-ray of the forearm   _____

o. hip X-ray, three views   _____

PATHOLOGY/LABORATORY SECTION

64. How would a coder locate the list of panel options? _____

_____

65. Describe the use of the following sections:

a. drug testing _____

_____

b. therapeutic drug assays _____

_____

c. evocative/suppression testing _____

_____

d. consultations (clinical pathology) _____

_____

e. urinalysis, chemistry, hematology and coagulation, and immunology _____

_____

f. transfusion medicine _____

_____

g. microbiology_____

_____

h. anatomic pathology _____

_____

i. cytopathology and cytogenic studies _____

_____

j. surgical pathology _____

_____

k. transcutaneous procedures _____

_____

l. other procedures _____

_____

66. Assign codes to the following:

a. red blood cell count   _____

b. blood gases pH only   _____

c. glucose-6-phosphate dehydrogenase screen   _____

d. glucose tolerance test, three specimens   _____

e. KOH prep   _____

f. HIV antibody confirmatory test   _____

g. leptospira   _____

h. HDL cholesterol   _____

i. glucose reagent strip   _____

j. occult blood, feces   _____

k. PKU   _____

l. rapid test for infection, screen, each antibody   _____

m. pregnancy test, urine   _____

n. herpes simplex virus, quantification   _____

o. urinary potassium   _____

p. urine dip, non-automated, without microscopy   _____

q. triglycerides   _____

r. cholesterol, serum, total   _____

s. TSH   _____

EVALUATION AND MANAGEMENT SECTION

67. Why is the Evaluation and Management Section located at the beginning of CPT?

_____

68. The E/M _____ refers to the physical location where health care is provided. (Circle the correct answer.)

a. level of service
b. place of service
c. type of service
d. none of the above

69. The E/M _____ reflects the amount of work involved in providing health care to patients. (Circle the correct answer.)

a. level of service
b. place of service
c. type of service
d. none of the above

70. The E/M _____ refers to the kind of health care services provided to patients.
(Circle the correct answer.)
    a. level of service
    b. place of service
    c. type of service
    d. none of the above

71. A new patient is one who has not received any professional services from the physician or another physician of the same specialty who belongs to the same group practice within the past _____ years.
(Circle the correct answer.)
    a. two
    b. three
    c. four
    d. none of the above

72. List the three key components on which E/M code selection is based.
    a. _____
    b. _____
    c. _____

73. _____ key component(s) must be considered when assigning codes for established patients. (Circle the correct answer.)
    a. One
    b. Two
    c. Three
    d. Four

74. _____ key component(s) must be considered when assigning codes for new patients. (Circle the correct answer.)
    a. One
    b. Two
    c. Three
    d. Four

75. _____ is an assessment of the patient's organ and body systems. (Circle the correct answer.)
    a. A history
    b. Medical decision making
    c. A physical examination
    d. All of the above

76. _____ is an interview of the patient that includes an HPI, a ROS, and a PFSH. (Circle the correct answer.)
    a. A history
    b. Medical decision making
    c. A physical examination
    d. All of the above

77. ____ refers to the complexity of establishing a diagnosis and/or selecting a management option. (Circle the correct answer.)

    a. A history

    b. Medical decision making

    c. A physical examination

    d. All of the above

78. List the four types of medical decision making.

    a. _____

    b. _____

    c. _____

    d. _____

79. List four contributory components.

    a. _____

    b. _____

    c. _____

    d. _____

80. Describe *coordination of care.* _____

_____

81. List five types of presenting problems.

    a. _____

    b. _____

    c. _____

    d. _____

    e. _____

EVALUATION AND MANAGEMENT CATEGORIES

82. For each item, enter **T** for a true statement or **F** for a false statement on the line provided.

    _____ a. The hospital is required to establish a physical area of observation.

    _____ b. Inpatient hospital care services cover the first hospital inpatient encounter the admitting/attending physician has with the patient for each admission.

    _____ c. Subsequent hospital care includes the review of the patient's chart, the results of diagnostic studies, and/or reassessment of the patient's condition since the last assessment performed by the physician.

    _____ d. Hospital discharge services do not include the final examination of the patient.

    _____ e. Consultants may not initiate diagnostic and/or therapeutic services as necessary during the consultative encounter.

    _____ f. A preoperative clearance is not considered a consultation when the referring physician is the patient's primary care physician.

    _____ g. A confirmatory consultation is an E/M service requested by the patient.

_____ h. Nursing facility services do not include services performed at long-term care facilities.

_____ i. Domiciliary care covers E/M services provided to patients who live in custodial care or boarding home facilities that do not provide 24-hour nursing care.

83. Assign codes to the following:

a. follow-up inpatient consult, expanded _____

b. subsequent nursing facility care, problem focused _____

c. initial office visit, problem focused _____

d. follow-up office visit, comprehensive _____

e. initial observation care, detailed _____

f. initial hospital care, low severity _____

g. subsequent hospital care, expanded _____

h. initial home visit, detailed _____

i. follow-up home visit, comprehensive _____

j. observation care discharge _____

k. initial inpatient consult, detailed _____

l. initial confirmatory consult, problem focused _____

m. emergency department. visit, comprehensive _____

n. physician direction of EMS emergency care _____

o. nursing facility assessment, comprehensive _____

p. new patient rest home visit, expanded _____

q. follow-up rest home visit, expanded _____

r. office consult, problem focused _____

84. Fill in the blanks using the definitions provided.

a. _____ are reported when a physician directly delivers medical care for a critically ill or critically injured patient.

b. _____ is used for reporting services performed by physicians for critically ill newborns.

c. _____ codes are assigned in addition to other E/M services when treatment exceeds, by 30 minutes or more, the time included in the CPT description of the service.

d. _____ allows for the reporting of cases in which the physician spends a prolonged period of time without patient contact waiting for an event to occur that will require the physician's services.

e. _____ is the process by which an attending physician coordinates and supervises the care provided to a patient by other health care providers.

f. _____ covers the physician's time spent supervising a complex and multidisciplinary care treatment program for a specific patient who is under the care of a home health agency, hospice, or nursing facility.

g. Routine examinations or risk management counseling for children and adults exhibiting no overt signs or symptoms of a disorder while presenting to the medical office for a preventive medical physical are _____ .

h. Examination of normal or high-risk neonates in the hospital or other locations, subsequent newborn care in a hospital, and resuscitation of high-risk babies is _____ .

85. Assign codes to the following:

a. operative physician standby, 30 minutes   _____

b. critical care, first hour   _____

c. established well-child check-up, age 7   _____

d. prolonged office care with direct patient contact, one hour   _____

e. complex telephone call with a distraught patient   _____

f. initial inpatient history and examination of normal newborn   _____

g. periodic preventive medicine, age 52   _____

h. initial well-baby check-up, 6 months old   _____

i. telephone call to discuss test results in detail   _____

Know Your Acronyms

86. Define the following acronyms:

a. CPT _____

b. E/M _____

c. HCPCS _____

d. HPI _____

e. ORIF _____

f. PFSH _____

g. ROS _____

Chapter 8
HCPCS Coding System

HCPCS CODING SYSTEM

1. How many code levels are associated with HCPCS? (Circle the correct answer.)
   a. two
   b. three
   c. four
   d. none of the above

2. Level I codes are developed and published by _____. (Circle the correct answer.)
   a. AMA
   b. HCFA
   c. LMC
   d. CMS

3. J codes are found in which level? (Circle the correct answer.)
   a. level I
   b. level II
   c. level III
   d. level IV

4. Level II codes identify the services of _____. (Circle the correct answers.)
   a. nurse practitioners
   b. speech therapists
   c. durable medical equipment
   d. all of the above

5. J codes list _____. (Circle the correct answer.)
   a. pathology and laboratory
   b. durable medical equipment
   c. medications
   d. all of the above

6. Who is responsible for the annual updates to HCPCS level II? (Circle the correct answer.)
   a. AMA
   b. CMS
   c. LMC
   d. none of the above

7. Level III codes are assigned by _____. (Circle the correct answer.)
   a. AMA
   b. CMS
   c. LMC
   d. none of the above

HCPCS LEVEL II CODES

8. For each item, enter **T** for a true statement or **F** for a false statement on the line provided.

   _____ a. HCPCS level II is a comprehensive and standardized coding system that classifies similar medical products and services according to category for the purpose of efficient claims processing.

   _____ b. HCPCS is a reimbursement system and coverage is guaranteed.

   _____ c. HCPCS level II codes are organized into type, depending on the purpose for the codes and the entity responsible for establishing and maintaining them.

   _____ d. HCPCS level II permanent codes are used for only private health insurers.

   _____ e. HCPCS level II dental codes are contained in the CPT.

   _____ f. HCPCS level II miscellaneous codes include miscellaneous/not otherwise classified codes.

   _____ g. Whenever a permanent code is established by the HCPCS National Panel to replace a temporary code, the temporary code is not deleted.

9. Is CMS responsible for errors that might occur in or from the use of private printings of HCPCS level II codes? _____

10. Which professional organization updates codes in the level II D Series? _____

11. Describe the function of HCPCS code modifiers. _____
_____

12. Match the HCPCS level II modifier in the first column with the description in the second column. Write the correct letter in each blank.

   _____ AH   a. left hand, thumb
   _____ E4   b. technical component
   _____ FA   c. nurse midwife
   _____ GX   d. RN
   _____ NU   e. left foot, great toe
   _____ RC   f. lower right eyelid
   _____ SB   g. new equipment
   _____ TA   h. clinical psychologist
   _____ TC   i. services not covered by Medicare
   _____ TD   j. right coronary artery

13. Assign codes to the following. (Be sure to add the correct HCPCS modifier to each code.)

   a. family psychotherapy without the patient present, by a clinical psychologist _____

   b. psychoanalysis, by a clinical social worker _____

c. initial office visit, problem focused, by a nurse practitioner in a rural area _____

d. new three-prong cane _____

e. tooth reimplantation of accidentally displaced tooth, emergency treatment _____

f. emergency ambulance transport (BLS), all inclusive from physician's office to hospital _____

g. dental radiographs, bitewing, single film, left side _____

h. portable whirlpool, new when rented _____

i. chemotherapy administration by infusion technique only, physician providing service in a rural HMSA _____

j. rented loop heel wheelchair _____

k. initial well-adult check-up, age 67, waiver of liability statement on file _____

l. initial home visit, detailed, changed to initial home visit, expanded because it was incorrect on the original claim _____

m. non-emergency ambulance transport (BLS), all inclusive from hospital to skilled nursing home _____

n. anesthesia for amputation of upper 2/3 of femur complicated by total body hypothermia _____

o. expanded follow-up inpatient consult provided by a substitute physician under a reciprocal billing arrangement _____

p. custom made plastic prosthetic right eye _____

q. left ankle splint for foot drop _____

r. second opinion language screening ordered by a professional review organization _____

s. five-minute follow-up BP check by a physician assistant _____

14. Because of the wide variety of services and procedures described in HCPCS level II, the _____ _____ is very helpful in finding the correct code.

15. When looking up a code in the level II index, it is important to verify the code in the _____ section of the codebook.

16. Assign codes to the following:

a. injection, aminophylline, up to 250 mg _____

b. elbow orthosis; elastic with metal joints _____

c. ambulance service; BLS, non-emergency transport _____

d. alcohol wipes, two boxes _____

e. amputee adapter, wheelchair _____

f. wound cleanser _____

g. artificial larynx _____

h. ultrasonic generator filter _____

i.   IPD supply kit   _____

j.   infusion pump, insulin   _____

k.   hypertonic saline solution   _____

l.   ambulance oxygen   _____

m. rocking bed   _____

n.   complete upper dentures   _____

o.   breast prosthesis, adhesive skin support   _____

p.   culture sensitivity study   _____

q.   nasogastric tubing, with stylet   _____

r.   pinworm examination   _____

s.   plasma, single donor, fresh frozen   _____

t.   frames purchases   _____

u.   hearing aid, monaural, behind the ear   _____

v.   routine venipuncture for collection of specimens _____

w. assessment for hearing aid   _____

x.   transportation of X-ray to nursing home, one patient _____

y.   speech screening   _____

z.   noncoring needle   _____

DETERMINING CARRIER RESPONSIBILITY

17. HCPCS level II codes beginning with D, G, M, P, or R fall under the jurisdiction of the _____. (Circle the correct answer.)
   a. DMERC
   b. LMC
   c. DMEPOS
   d. all of the above

18. Which is responsible for level II codes beginning with B, E, K, and L? (Circle the correct answer.)
   a. DMERC
   b. LMC
   c. DMEPOS
   d. all of the above

19. Codes beginning with A, J, Q, and V may be assigned to the_____. (Circle the correct answers.)
   a. DMERC
   b. LMC
   c. DMEPOS
   d. all of the above

20. For each item, enter **T** for a true statement or **F** for a false statement on the line provided.

   _____   a.   Because DME billings were out of control, CMS decided to have all DME claims processed by only four regional carriers, the DMERCs.

_____ b. Providers dispensing medical equipment and supplies must register with a DMERC.

_____ c. When a Medicare patient is treated for a fractured leg and supplied with crutches, only one claim is generated.

_____ d. If the doctor is not registered with the DMERC, the patient is billed directly for the medical equipment.

_____ e. Most dental procedures are included as Medicare benefits.

_____ f. New medical and surgical services may first be assigned a level II code because the review procedures for adding new codes to level II is a much shorter process.

Know Your Acronyms

21. Define the following acronyms:

a. CDT-3 _____

b. CIM _____

c. DME _____

d. DMEPOS _____

e. DMERC _____

f. HCPCS _____

g. LMC _____

h. MCM _____

i. OPPS _____

j. SADMERC _____

Chapter 9
CMS Reimbursement Issues

CMS PAYMENT SYSTEMS

1. List six health care programs administered by the federal government.

   a. _____

   b. _____

   c. _____

   d. _____

   e. _____

   f. _____

AMBULANCE FEE SCHEDULE

2. For each item, enter **T** for a true statement or **F** for a false statement on the line provided.

   _____ a. Starting in April 2002 the ambulance fee schedule was phased in over a five-year period.

   _____ b. Ambulance suppliers do not need to accept Medicare assignment.

   _____ c. HCPCS codes may not be reported on claims for ambulance services.

   _____ d. Medicare pays for beneficiary transportation services when other means of transportation are contraindicated.

AMBULATORY SURGICAL CENTERS (ASC)

3. Describe an *ambulatory surgical center (ASC)*. _____

   _____

CLINICAL LAB DIAGNOSTIC FEE SCHEDULE

4. Medicare reimburses laboratory services according to the _____. (Circle the correct answer.)

   a. local fee schedule

   b. national limitation amount

   c. submitted charge

   d. all of the above

5. The local fee schedules are developed by _____. (Circle the correct answer.)
   a. Medicaid carriers
   b. Medicare carriers
   c. TRICARE carriers
   d. none of the above

6. Clinical laboratory codes are currently listed in the _____ CPT code series. (Circle the correct answer.)
   a. 50010–59899
   b. 70010–79999
   c. 80048–89399
   d. none of the above

DURABLE MEDICAL EQUIPMENT, PROSTHETICS, ORTHOTICS, AND SUPPLIES FEE SCHEDULE

7. How often is the DMEPOS fee schedule updated? _____

8. Who legislates the DMEPOS fee schedule? _____

9. HH PPS uses HHRGs to establish prospective reimbursement rates for each _____ episode of home health care. (Circle the correct answer.)
   a. 30-day
   b. 45-day
   c. 60-day
   d. none of the above

HOSPITAL INPATIENT PROSPECTIVE PAYMENT SYSTEM

10. DRG is based on the patient's _____ and _____ diagnoses/procedures.

11. The DRG determines _____.

MEDICARE PHYSICIAN FEE SCHEDULE

12. List the three components of RVUs.
    a. _____
    b. _____
    c. _____

13. Anesthesia services payments are based on the _____. (Circle the correct answer.)
    a. actual time spent with a patient
    b. number of patients served
    c. place of service
    d. none of the above

14. Radiology services payments vary according to the _____. (Circle the correct answer.)
    a. actual time spent with a patient
    b. number of patients served
    c. place of service
    d. all of the above

15. Pathology services payments vary according to the _____. (Circle the correct answer.)
    a. actual time spent with a patient
    b. number of patients served
    c. place of service
    d. all of the above

16. What is the intent of Medicare's limiting charge policy? _____
    _____

17. Define *balance billing*. _____
    _____

18. List four examples of when Medicare would be considered the secondary payer.
    a. _____
    b. _____
    c. _____
    d. _____

19. Who defines the NP's and PA's scope of practice? (Circle the correct answer.)
    a. state law
    b. federal law

20. Define *scope of practice*. _____
    _____

21. What has Medicare issued to NPs and PAs so that their services can be billed directly to Medicare?
    (Circle the correct answer.)
    a. special billing address
    b. special provider numbers
    c. special TOS codes
    d. all of the above

22. The global period for each surgery includes _____. (Circle the correct answer.)
    a. suture removal
    b. postoperative office visits
    c. dressing changes
    d. all of the above

23. During the global period, if a patient has an office visit not related to the surgery, an appropriate
    _____ must be attached.

Know Your Acronyms

24. Define the following acronyms:

    a. APCs _____

    b. ASC _____

    c. DMEPOS _____

    d. DRG _____

    e. EGHP _____

    f. HAVEN _____

    g. HH PPS _____

    h. HHRGs _____

    i. IPPS _____

    j. IRFs _____

    k. LGHP _____

    l. MCOs _____

    m. MSN _____

    n. MSP _____

    o. NP _____

    p. OASIS _____

    q. OPPS _____

    r. PA _____

    s. PPS _____

    t. PFS _____

    u. RVUs _____

Chapter 10
Coding for Medical Necessity

APPLYING CODING GUIDELINES

1. For each item, enter **T** for a true statement or **F** for a false statement on the line provided.

   _____ a. Code and report conditions and procedures even if they are not documented in the record as treated or medically managed.

   _____ b. Use the full range of ICD codes from 001 through 999.9 and V01 through V82.9, and E codes when warranted by circumstances.

   _____ c. Code and report all conditions that are stated as questionable or suspected or are to be ruled out.

   _____ d. Code to the highest level of specificity any disorder or injury that is known and documented at the time of the encounter.

   _____ e. Documented symptoms should be coded and reported when they are manifestations of a reported disorder or injury.

   _____ f. V codes are assigned when there is justification for the patient to seek health care but no disorder currently exists.

   _____ g. Code only those conditions treated during the encounter or that affect the treatment rendered.

   _____ h. Up to six diagnoses can be reported on one CMS-1500 claim.

   _____ i. Report all past conditions even if they are not currently active problems.

   _____ j. Link each procedure or service provided to a condition that proves the medical necessity for performing that procedure/service.

2. Match the procedure/service in the first column with the diagnosis in the second column. Write the correct letter in each blank.

   _____ EKG   a. impacted cerumin

   _____ urinalysis   b. jaundice

   _____ strep test   c. hay fever

   _____ wrist X-ray   d. bronchial asthma

   _____ venipuncture   e. chest pain

(continues)

_____ removal of ear wax   f. strep throat

_____ sigmoidoscopy   g. fractured wrist

_____ inhalation treatment   h. hematuria

_____ allergy test   i. rectal bleeding

CODING FROM CASE SCENARIOS

3. List six steps for selecting diagnoses/procedures from case scenarios.

a. _____

b. _____

c. _____

d. _____

e. _____

f. _____

4. Assign ICD-9 and CPT codes to the following scenarios. Be sure to include all necessary CPT and/or HCPCS modifiers.

a. A 35-year-old established patient came to the office for excessive menstruation and irregular menstrual cycle. The physician performed an expanded problem focused evaluation and cervical biopsy.

CPT Codes   **ICD-9 Codes**

_____   _____

b. Patient was referred to me by his primary care physician, Dr. Pearson, because of severe back pain. Dr. Pearson feels he should have surgery but the patient states the pain is relieved by regular chiropractic care and doesn't want to have back surgery. After a problem focused examination and a complete radiologic examination of the lumbosacral spine, including bending views, I consulted with Dr. Pearson and concluded the patient's degenerative disc disease is probably doing as well with a chiropractor as with orthopedic treatment. I did not recommend surgery at this time.

CPT Codes   **ICD-9 Codes**

_____   _____

c. Patient underwent a barium enema which included air contrast. The request form noted severe abdominal pain and diarrhea for the past two weeks. The radiology impression was diverticulitis of the colon.

CPT Codes   **ICD-9 Codes**

_____   _____

d. Patient presented for follow-up of COPD. At this time the patient is experiencing no significant cough, no sputum, no fever, and no respiratory distress. However, there is dyspnea only with exertion, which is accompanied by angina. A detailed examination was performed and the physician spent approximately 25 minutes with the patient. Chest is clear, no wheeze or rales. Chest X-rays, frontal and lateral, were taken to determine status of COPD. No additional treatment is required at this time.

CPT Codes   **ICD-9 Codes**

_____   _____

e. A surgeon is called to the hospital by the emergency department physician to see a 59-year-old male who presented with an abdominal mass, left lower quadrant. The surgeon performed a comprehensive examination, admitted the patient, and scheduled an exploratory laparotomy.

CPT Codes   **ICD-9 Codes**

_____   _____

f. On 08/12/YYYY the patient underwent an exploratory laparotomy, a left partial hepatic resection for a malignant hepatoma, and a cholecystectomy.

CPT Codes   **ICD-9 Codes**

_____   _____

g. On 04/01/YYYY a 65-year-old patient underwent a bronchoscopy and biopsy for a left lower lobe lung mass. The biopsy revealed adenocarcinoma of the left lower lobe lung. On 04/05/YYYY the same surgeon performed a left lower lobe lobectomy and thoracic lymphadenectomy.

CPT Codes   **ICD-9 Codes**

_____   _____

_____   _____

h. On 04/01/YYYY a 39-year-old female presents to her GYN office with a mass and pain in the right breast. Her mother and sister died of breast cancer. A detailed history and examination was performed. The patient was referred to a surgeon for consultation.

CPT Codes   **ICD-9 Codes**

_____   _____

i. On 04/03/YYYY the patient presents to the surgeon's office for consultation. The patient is experiencing pain in her right breast and has noticed a lump there. She also has a family history of breast cancer. The surgeon performs a level III consultation and two breast aspirations of the right breast.

CPT Codes   **ICD-9 Codes**

_____   _____

j. On 04/09/YYYY the patient underwent an excision of the right breast mass in the outpatient surgery center. The pathology report revealed a malignant neoplasm, central portion of the right breast. On 04/13/YYYY the patient underwent a right modified radical mastectomy by the same surgeon.

CPT Codes   **ICD-9 Codes**

_____   _____

_____   _____

k. On 07/23/YYYY a four-month-old patient returned to the office for her routine well-baby check-up. The following vaccines were administered by the medical assistant: inactivated poliovirus (IPV), hepatitis B, diphtheria, tetanus toxoids, and acellular pertussis. The patient is to return to the office in two months for her six-month check-up and vaccinations.

CPT Codes   **ICD-9 Codes**

_____   _____

l. Patient returned to the office, after a five-year absence, because of abdominal pain, diarrhea, and rectal bleeding which began three weeks ago. A detailed examination revealed a tense abdomen with some guarding at the right upper quadrant. Patient to be scheduled for a flexible sigmoidoscopy to R/O colon cancer.

CPT Codes   **ICD-9 Codes**

_____   _____

CODING FROM CLINIC NOTES AND DIAGNOSTIC TEST RESULTS

5. List two major formats health care providers use for documenting clinic notes.

   a. _____

   b. _____

6. Match the SOAP terms in the first column with the definitions in the second column. Write the correct letter in each blank.

   _____ subjective data   a. diagnostic statement

   _____ objective data   b. how treatment will proceed

   _____ assessment data   c. chief complaint and description of problem

   _____ plan   d. information not relevant to treatment

                                    e. observations made during the physical examination and diagnostic testing

7. Assign diagnostic codes to the following SOAP notes:

   a. S Patient complains of one week of severe epigastric pain and burning especially after eating.

      O On examination there is extreme guarding and tenderness, epigastric region, no rebound. Bowel sounds normal. BP 110/70.

      A R/O gastric ulcer.

      P Patient to have upper gastrointestinal series. Start on Zantac and eliminate alcohol, fried foods, and caffeine. Return to office in one week.

      ICD-9 Codes _____

   b. S Patient returns after undergoing an upper gastrointestinal series. She states she is still experiencing epigastric pain.

      O Upper gastrointestinal series revealed areas of ulceration.

      A Acute gastric ulcer.

      P Omeprazole 10 mg qd. Return for follow-up visit in three weeks.

      ICD-9 Codes _____

   c. S Patient was walking up his driveway when he slipped and fell, landing on his left arm and striking his head against his car. He was unconscious for less than ten minutes, experienced dizziness and vomiting, and felt severe pain in his left arm.

      O Examination reveals restriction of motion of his left arm and a laceration on his head.

      A Mild concussion. Laceration occipital region of scalp. Undisplaced fracture proximal left humerus (greater tuberosity).

      P Laceration repair occipital region of scalp. Patient sent to Dr. Smith for fracture care.

      ICD-9 Codes _____

   d. S Patient complains of rectal discomfort, rectal bleeding, and severe itching.

      O Examination reveals multiple soft external hemorrhoids.

      A Multiple external hemorrhoids.

      P Suppositories after each bowel movement. Return to office in four weeks.

      ICD-9 Codes _____

e. S   Patient presents complaining of polyuria, polydipsia, and weight loss.

O   Urinalysis by dip, automated, with microscopy reveals elevated glucose.

A   Possible diabetes.

P   Patient to have a glucose tolerance test and return in three days for blood work results.

ICD-9 Codes _____

CODING OPERATIVE REPORTS

8. List five items contained in an operative report.

a. _____

b. _____

c. _____

d. _____

e. _____

9. Explain why you should make a copy of the operative report before assigning codes.

_____

10. Explain why it is important to compare the postoperative diagnosis with the biopsy report on all excised neoplasms. _____

11. For each item, enter **T** for a true statement or **F** for a false statement on the line provided.

_____ a. Because there is a monetary value for each CPT code, be sure to assign multiple, separate codes to describe a procedure even if CPT has a single code that classifies all the individual components of the procedure described by the physician.

_____ b. Never assign a code number described in CPT as a "separate procedure" when it is performed within the same incision site as the primary procedure and is an integral part of a greater procedure.

_____ c. The postoperative diagnosis should explain the medical necessity for performing the procedure(s).

_____ d. When working in a medical practice you should code an excision even if the pathology report has not been received.

12. Assign ICD-9 and CPT codes to the following operative reports:

a. PREOPERATIVE DIAGNOSIS: Pterygium of the right eye

POSTOPERATIVE DIAGNOSIS: Pterygium of the right eye

PROCEDURE PERFORMED: Pterygium excision with conjunctival autograft of the right eye

ANESTHESIA: General endotracheal anesthesia

PROCEDURE: After the patient was prepped and draped in the usual sterile fashion, attention was directed to his right eye under the operating microscope. The area of the pterygium was viewed and an injection of lidocaine with Marcaine was placed subconjunctivally to infiltrate area of the pterygium and surrounding conjunctiva. Then, using a combination of sharp and blunt dissection with 57 Beaver blade Westcott scissors, the pterygium was lifted away from the cornea, making a plane to the cornea to achieve clarity to the cornea. Next, an area was marked with a hand-held cautery nasally through the conjunctiva. A muscle hook was inserted to identify the medial rectus muscle. Then, using Westcott scissors and .12, the head and body of the pterygium were removed noting where the medial rectus muscle was at all times. Cautery was used to achieve hemostasis.

An area of conjunctiva superior to the area of the prior pterygium under the lid was isolated and an incision was made through the conjunctiva. This section of conjunctiva was then transposed and placed into position over the area of the prior pterygium, thus forming an autograft. This was sutured into place with multiple single 8-0 Vicryl sutures. The autograft was noted to be in good position. Hemostasis was noted to be well achieved. The cornea was noted to be smooth and clear in the area of the prior pterygium with the epithelial defect secondary to removal of the pterygium. Maxitrol drops were placed. The patient's eye was patched. The patient tolerated the procedure well without complications and is to follow up in our office tomorrow.

CPT Codes   **ICD-9 Codes**

_____   _____

b. PREOPERATIVE DIAGNOSIS: Subcutaneous mass, posterior scalp

POSTOPERATIVE DIAGNOSIS: Subcutaneous mass, posterior scalp

PROCEDURE PERFORMED: Excision, subcutaneous mass, posterior scalp

ANESTHESIA: General

PROCEDURE: After instillation of 1% Xylocaine, a transverse incision was made directly over this elongated posterior scalp lesion. Hemostasis was obtained with electrocautery and suture ligature. A fatty tumor was encountered and sharp dissection used in completely excising this lesion. Hemostasis was obtained with ties, suture ligatures, and electrocautery. The 3-cm lesion was removed in its entirety. The wound was irrigated and the incision closed in layers. The skin was closed with a running nylon suture for hemostasis.

CPT Codes   **ICD-9 Codes**

_____   _____

c. PREOPERATIVE DIAGNOSIS: Ventral hernia

POSTOPERATIVE DIAGNOSIS: Ventral hernia

PROCEDURE PERFORMED: Repair of ventral hernia with mesh

ANESTHESIA: General

PROCEDURE: The vertical midline incision was opened. Sharp and blunt dissection was used in defining the hernia sac. The hernia sac was opened and the fascia examined. The hernia defect was sizable. Careful inspection was utilized to uncover any additional adjacent fascial defects. Small defects were observed on both sides of the major hernia and were incorporated into the main hernia. The hernia sac was dissected free of the surrounding subcutaneous tissues and retained. Prolene mesh was then fashioned to size and sutured to one side with running #0 Prolene suture. Interrupted Prolene sutures were placed on the other side and tagged untied. The hernia sac was then sutured to the opposite side of the fascia with Vicryl suture. The Prolene sutures were passed through the interstices of the Prolene mesh and tied into place, insuring that the Prolene mesh was not placed under tension. Excess mesh was excised. Jackson-Pratt drains were placed, one on each side. Running subcutaneous suture utilizing Vicryl was placed, after which the skin was stapled.

CPT Codes   **ICD-9 Codes**

_____   _____

d. PREOPERATIVE DIAGNOSIS: Intermittent exotropia, alternating

Fusion with decreased stereopsis

POSTOPERATIVE DIAGNOSIS: Intermittent exotropia, alternating

Fusion with decreased stereopsis

PROCEDURE PERFORMED: Bilateral lateral rectus recession of 7.0 mm

ANESTHESIA: General endotracheal anesthesia

PROCEDURE: The patient was brought to the operating room and placed in supine position where she was prepped and draped in the usual sterile fashion for strabismus surgery. Both eyes were exposed to the surgical field. After adequate anesthesia, one drop of 2.5% Neosynephrine was placed in each eye for vasoconstriction. Forced ductions were performed on both eyes and the lateral rectus was found to be normal. An eye speculum was placed in the right eye and surgery was begun on the right eye. An inferotemporal fornix incision was performed. The right lateral rectus muscle was isolated on a muscle hook. The muscle insertion was isolated and checked ligaments were dissected back. After a series of muscle hook passes using the Steven's hook and finishing with two passes of a Green's hook, the right lateral rectus was isolated. The epimesium, as well as Tenon's capsule, was dissected from the muscle insertion and the checked ligaments were lysed. The muscle was imbricated on a 6-0 Vicryl suture with an S29 needle with locking bites at either end. The muscle was detached from the globe and a distance of 7.0 mm posterior to the insertion of the muscle was marked. The muscle was then reattached 7.0 mm posterior to the original insertion using a cross-swords technique. The conjunctiva was closed using two buried sutures. Attention was then turned to the left eye where an identical procedure was performed. At the end of the case the eyes seemed slightly exotropic in position in the anesthetized state. Bounce back tests were normal. Both eyes were dressed with Tetracaine drops and Maxitrol ointment. There were no complications. The patient tolerated the procedure well, was awakened from anesthesia without difficulty, and sent to the recovery room. The patient was instructed in the use of topical antibiotics and detailed postoperative instructions were provided. The patient will be followed up within a 48-hour period in my office.

CPT Codes   **ICD-9 Codes**

_____   _____

Chapter 11
Essential CMS-1500
Claim Instructions

GENERAL BILLING GUIDELINES

1. The development of an insurance claim begins when the ___. (Circle the correct answer.)
   a. patient presents to the medical facility
   b. patient schedules an appointment
   c. services are delivered to the patient
   d. all of the above

2. Inpatient medical cases are billed on ___. (Circle the correct answer.)
   a. a fee-for-service basis
   b. a global fee basis
   c. an additional procedure basis
   d. none of the above

3. Inpatient or outpatient major surgery cases are billed on ___. (Circle the correct answer.)
   a. a fee-for-service basis
   b. a global fee basis
   c. an additional procedure basis
   d. none of the above

4. Postoperative complications requiring a return to the operating room for surgery related to the original procedure are billed on ___. (Circle the correct answer.)
   a. a fee-for-service basis
   b. a global fee basis
   c. an additional procedure basis
   d. none of the above

5. Minor surgery cases are billed on ___. (Circle the correct answer.)
   a. a fee-for-service basis
   b. a global fee basis
   c. an additional procedure basis
   d. none of the above

6. Some claims require attachments such as ___. (Circle the correct answer.)
   a. clinic notes
   b. operative reports
   c. discharge summaries
   d. all of the above

7. List four circumstances in which a letter should be used.
   a. _____
   b. _____
   c. _____
   d. _____

8. Data on paper-generated claims that run into the adjacent data blocks or appear in the wrong block will cause _____ of _____ .

9. Before printing a claim, a _____ _____ should be printed to assist with paper alignment in the printer.

OPTICAL SCANNING GUIDELINES

10. For each item, enter **T** for a true statement or **F** for a false statement on the line provided.

    _____ a. The CMS-1500 claim was designed to accommodate optical scanning of paper claims.

    _____ b. The processing time for claims prepared for optical character readers (OCR) is a little slower than for claims that must be manually entered into the insurance company's computer system.

    _____ c. The OCR guidelines are now used by all payers that process claims using the official CMS-1500 claim.

    _____ d. When completing a claim, pica type (12 characters per inch) should be used.

    _____ e. When completing a claim, all alpha characters should be typed in uppercase (capital letters).

    _____ f. When completing a claim, a zero and the alpha character O should not be interchanged.

11. List five key strokes that can be substituted by a space when completing a claim.
    a. _____
    b. _____
    c. _____
    d. _____
    e. _____

12. Enter one _____ _____ between the patient's/policyholder's last name, first name, and middle initial.

13. Do not use any _____ in a patient's/policyholder's or provider's name, except for a hyphen in a compound name.

14. Do not use a person's title or other designations such as Sr., Jr., II, or III on a claim unless they appear on the patient's _____ _____ _____ .

15. Describe how the name on the claim should be typed for the following patients:

    a. The name on the ID card reads: James M. Apple, II   _____

    b. The name on the ID card reads: Charles T. Treebark, Jr.   _____

    c. The name on the ID card reads: David J. Hurts, III   _____

    d. The name on the ID card reads: Jake R. Elbow, Sr.   _____

16. Describe how the birth date on the claim should be typed for the following dates of birth:

    a. January 5, 1954:   _____

    b. March 11, 1971:   _____

    c. August 31, 1985:   _____

    d. December 2, 1994:   _____

17. The borders of pin-fed claims should be _____.

REPORTING DIAGNOSES: ICD-9-CM CODES

18. Diagnosis codes are entered in ___. (Circle the correct answer.)
    a. Block 24
    b. Block 33
    c. Block 21
    d. none of the above

19. The maximum number of ICD-9-CM codes that may appear on a single claim is ___. (Circle the correct answer.)
    a. four
    b. six
    c. two
    d. none of the above

20. The first code reported on a claim should be the ___. (Circle the correct answer.)
    a. qualified diagnosis
    b. possible diagnosis
    c. primary diagnosis
    d. any of the above

21. If a diagnosis not treated or addressed during an encounter is stated on the patient's record, you should ___. (Circle the correct answer.)
    a. not list the diagnosis
    b. list the diagnosis as secondary
    c. list the diagnosis as probable
    d. none of the above

22. Until a definitive diagnosis is determined, which of the following diagnoses should be used? (Circle the correct answer.)
    a. rule out
    b. suspicious for
    c. possible
    d. none of the above

23. Match the blocks in the first column with the definitions in the second column. Write the correct letter in each blank.

    _____ Block 24A   a. Procedure Codes and Modifiers

    _____ Block 24B   b. Charges

    _____ Block 24C   c. COB

    _____ Block 24D   d. Dates of Service

    _____ Block 24E   e. Days/Units

    _____ Block 24F   f. EMG

    _____ Block 24G   g. Reserved for Local Use

    _____ Block 24H   h. Place of Service

    _____ Block 24I   i. EPSDT Family Plan

    _____ Block 24J   j. Diagnosis Code

    _____ Block 24K   k. Type of Service

24. The maximum number of CPT codes that may appear on a single claim is ___. (Circle the correct answer.)
    a. four
    b. six
    c. two
    d. none of the above

25. When reporting more than one code on a CMS-1500 claim, the first code entered in line 1 of Block 24 should be the ___. (Circle the correct answer.)
    a. primary code
    b. code that took the longest
    c. code with the highest fee
    d. any of the above

26. Identical procedures or services can be reported on the same line if the following circumstances apply. (Circle the correct answer.)
    a. Procedures were performed on consecutive days in the same month.
    b. The same code is assigned to the procedures.
    c. Identical charges apply to the assigned code.
    d. all of the above

27. The maximum number of modifiers that can be entered in Block 24D is ___. (Circle the correct answer.)
    a. four
    b. six
    c. two
    d. none of the above

Critical Thinking

28. Write a paragraph describing how to use diagnosis reference numbers.

_____

_____

_____

_____

REPORTING THE BILLING ENTITY

29. The billing entity is the _____ _____ _____ of the practice.

30. If the billing entity has a group practice identification number required by the insurance carrier, this number should be typed in Block _____ on the claim.

PROCESSING SECONDARY CLAIMS

31. The secondary insurance claim is filed ___. (Circle the correct answer.)
    a. after the EOB from the primary claim has been received
    b. at the same time the primary claim is filed
    c. after the patient has paid his/her co-pay
    d. any of the above

32. As a general rule the secondary claim cannot be filed electronically because ___. (Circle the correct answer.)
    a. a report must always accompany a secondary claim
    b. secondary insurance carriers do not accept claims electronically
    c. the primary EOB must be attached to the secondary claim
    d. all of the above

33. Supplemental plans usually cover the ___. (Circle the correct answer.)
    a. secondary procedures billed
    b. deductible and copay/coinsurance
    c. non-allowed amount
    d. none of the above

COMMON ERRORS THAT DELAY PROCESSING

34. List five common errors that delay processing of a claim.
    a. _____
    b. _____
    c. _____
    d. _____
    e. _____

FINAL STEPS IN PROCESSING PAPER CLAIMS

35. List the six final processing steps of paper claims.

a. _____

b. _____

c. _____

d. _____

e. _____

f. _____

MAINTAINING INSURANCE CLAIM FILES FOR THE PRACTICE

36. The federal Omnibus Budget Reconciliation Act of 1987 requires physicians to keep copies of any ___. (Circle the correct answer.)

a. Blue Cross/Blue Shield insurance claims

b. commercial insurance claims

c. government insurance claims

d. all of the above

37. How do providers and billing services filing claims electronically comply with the federal regulation?

_____

_____

_____

38. List four examples of the way paper claim files should be organized.

a. _____

b. _____

c. _____

d. _____

Critical Thinking

39. Write a paragraph describing steps that should be taken when an error in processing is found.

_____

_____

_____

_____

_____

_____

Know Your Acronyms

40. Define the following acronyms:

a. ASC _____

b. EIN _____

c. EMC _____

d. EOB _____

e. GRP# _____

f. OCR _____

g. PIN _____

h. POS _____

i. SSN _____

j. TOS _____

EXERCISES

41. Using Optical Scanning Guidelines, circle the errors found in Stanley L. Fruit's claim on the following page.

42. Using the information provided on Stanley L. Fruit's claim, complete the blank claim correctly.

(SAMPLE ONLY - NOT APPROVED FOR USE)

CARRIER

| | PICA | | **HEALTH INSURANCE CLAIM FORM** | PICA | | |

1. MEDICARE	MEDICAID	CHAMPUS	CHAMPVA	GROUP HEALTH PLAN	FECA BLK LUNG	OTHER	1a. INSURED'S I.D. NUMBER	(FOR PROGRAM IN ITEM 1)
☐ (Medicare #)	☐ (Medicaid #)	☐ (Sponsor's SSN)	☐ (VA File #)	☐ (SSN or ID)	☐ (SSN)	☒ (ID)	017-09-1234	

2. PATIENT'S NAME (Last Name, First Name, Middle Initial)
STANLEY L. FRUIT JR.

3. PATIENT'S BIRTH DATE   MM | DD | YY   SEX
7 | 15 | 1964   M ☒   F ☐

4. INSURED'S NAME (Last Name, First Name, Middle Initial)
SAME

5. PATIENT'S ADDRESS (No. Street)
25 S. HANSON ST.

6. PATIENT RELATIONSHIP TO INSURED
Self ☒ Spouse ☐ Child ☐ Other ☐

7. INSURED'S ADDRESS (No. Street)
SAME

CITY
ANYWHERE

STATE
US

8. PATIENT STATUS
Single ☒ Married ☐ Other ☐

Employed ☒   Full-Time Student ☐   Part-Time Student ☐

CITY

STATE

ZIP CODE
12345

TELEPHONE (Include Area Code)
(101) 112-2222

ZIP CODE

TELEPHONE (INCLUDE AREA CODE)
( )

9. OTHER INSURED'S NAME (Last Name, First Name, Middle Initial)
None

10. IS PATIENT'S CONDITION RELATED TO:

11. INSURED'S POLICY GROUP OR FECA NUMBER
FED 101

a. OTHER INSURED'S POLICY OR GROUP NUMBER

a. EMPLOYMENT? (CURRENT OR PREVIOUS)
☐ YES ☒ NO

a. INSURED'S DATE OF BIRTH   MM | DD | YY   SEX
M ☐   F ☐

b. OTHER INSURED'S DATE OF BIRTH   MM | DD | YY   SEX
M ☐   F ☐

b. AUTO ACCIDENT?   PLACE (State)
☐ YES ☒ NO

b. EMPLOYER'S NAME OR SCHOOL NAME
U.S. POSTAL SERVICE

c. EMPLOYER'S NAME OR SCHOOL NAME

c. OTHER ACCIDENT?
☐ YES ☒ NO

c. INSURANCE PLAN NAME OR PROGRAM NAME
MAILHANDLERS

d. INSURANCE PLAN NAME OR PROGRAM NAME

10d. RESERVED FOR LOCAL USE

d. IS THERE ANOTHER HEALTH BENEFIT PLAN?
☐ YES ☒ NO   If yes, return to and complete item 9 a – d.

READ BACK OF FORM BEFORE COMPLETING & SIGNING THIS FORM.
12. PATIENT'S OR AUTHORIZED PERSON'S SIGNATURE I authorize the release of any medical or other information necessary to process this claim. I also request payment of government benefits either to myself or to the party who accepts assignment below.

SIGNED   SIGNATURE ON FILE   DATE

13. INSURED'S OR AUTHORIZED PERSON'S SIGNATURE I authorize payment of medical benefits to the undersigned physician or supplier for services described below.

SIGNED   SIGNATURE ON FILE

PATIENT AND INSURED INFORMATION

14. DATE OF CURRENT: MM | DD | YY   ◄ ILLNESS (First symptom) OR INJURY (Accident) OR PREGNANCY (LMP)

15. IF PATIENT HAS HAD SAME OR SIMILAR ILLNESS, GIVE FIRST DATE   MM | DD | YY

16. DATES PATIENT UNABLE TO WORK IN CURRENT OCCUPATION
FROM MM | DD | YY   TO MM | DD | YY

17. NAME OF REFERRING PHYSICIAN OR OTHER SOURCE

17a. I.D. NUMBER OF REFERRING PHYSICIAN

18. HOSPITALIZATION DATES RELATED TO CURRENT SERVICES
FROM MM | DD | YY   TO MM | DD | YY

19. RESERVED FOR LOCAL USE

20. OUTSIDE LAB? $ CHARGES
☐ YES ☒ NO

21. DIAGNOSIS OR NATURE OF ILLNESS OR INJURY. (RELATE ITEMS 1, 2, 3, OR 4 TO ITEM 24E BY LINE)

1. 782 . 0
2. 788 . 41
3. ___ . ___
4. ___ . ___

22. MEDICAID RESUBMISSION CODE   ORIGINAL REF. NO.

23. PRIOR AUTHORIZATION NUMBER

24. A	DATE(S) OF SERVICE				B	C	D		E	F	G	H	I	J	K
	From MM DD YY	To MM DD YY			Place of Service	Type of Service	PROCEDURES, SERVICES, OR SUPPLIES (Explain Unusual Circumstances) CPT/HCPCS | MODIFIER		DIAGNOSIS CODE	$ CHARGES	DAYS OR UNITS	EPSDT Family Plan	EMG	COB	RESERVED FOR LOCAL USE
1	6 7 YYYY				11		99213		782.0	$ 60 00	1				
2															
3	6 7 YYYY				11		81001		788.41	$ 10 00	1				
4															
5															
6															

25. FEDERAL TAX I.D. NUMBER	SSN EIN	26. PATIENT'S ACCOUNT NO.	27. ACCEPT ASSIGNMENT? (For govt. claims, see back)	28. TOTAL CHARGE	29. AMOUNT PAID	30. BALANCE DUE
11-123456	☐ ☒	123	☐ YES ☒ NO	$ 70 00	$	$ 70 00

31. SIGNATURE OF PHYSICIAN OR SUPPLIER INCLUDING DEGREES OR CREDENTIALS (I certify that the statements on the reverse apply to this bill and are made a part thereof.)

R.K. PAINFREE, M.D.

SIGNED   DATE MMDDYYYY

32. NAME AND ADDRESS OF FACILITY WHERE SERVICES WERE RENDERED (If other than home or office)

33. PHYSICIAN'S, SUPPLIER'S BILLING NAME, ADDRESS, ZIP CODE & PHONE #
GOODMEDICINE CLINIC

PIN#   GRP#

PHYSICIAN OR SUPPLIER INFORMATION

(SAMPLE ONLY - NOT APPROVED FOR USE)   *PLEASE PRINT OR TYPE*   SAMPLE FORM 1500
SAMPLE FORM 1500 SAMPLE FORM 1500

PLEASE
DO NOT
STAPLE
IN THIS
AREA

HEALTH INSURANCE CLAIM FORM

| | | PICA

PICA | | |

| | | PICA |

1. MEDICARE ☐ (Medicare #) MEDICAID ☐ (Medicaid #) CHAMPUS ☐ (Sponsor's SSN) CHAMPVA ☐ (VA File #) GROUP HEALTH PLAN ☐ (SSN or ID) FECA BLK LUNG ☐ (SSN) OTHER ☐ (ID)

1a. INSURED'S I.D. NUMBER   (FOR PROGRAM IN ITEM 1)

2. PATIENT'S NAME (Last Name, First Name, Middle Initial)

3. PATIENT'S BIRTH DATE MM | DD | YY   SEX M ☐ F ☐

4. INSURED'S NAME (Last Name, First Name, Middle Initial)

5. PATIENT'S ADDRESS (No. Street)

6. PATIENT RELATIONSHIP TO INSURED Self ☐ Spouse ☐ Child ☐ Other ☐

7. INSURED'S ADDRESS (No. Street)

CITY   STATE

8. PATIENT STATUS Single ☐ Married ☐ Other ☐

Employed ☐ Full-Time Student ☐ Part-Time Student ☐

CITY   STATE

ZIP CODE   TELEPHONE (Include Area Code) (   )

ZIP CODE   TELEPHONE (INCLUDE AREA CODE) (   )

9. OTHER INSURED'S NAME (Last Name, First Name, Middle Initial)

10. IS PATIENT'S CONDITION RELATED TO:

11. INSURED'S POLICY GROUP OR FECA NUMBER

a. OTHER INSURED'S POLICY OR GROUP NUMBER

a. EMPLOYMENT? (CURRENT OR PREVIOUS) YES ☐ NO ☐

a. INSURED'S DATE OF BIRTH MM | DD | YY   SEX M ☐ F ☐

b. OTHER INSURED'S DATE OF BIRTH MM | DD | YY   SEX M ☐ F ☐

b. AUTO ACCIDENT?   PLACE (State) YES ☐ NO ☐

b. EMPLOYER'S NAME OR SCHOOL NAME

c. EMPLOYER'S NAME OR SCHOOL NAME

c. OTHER ACCIDENT? YES ☐ NO ☐

c. INSURANCE PLAN NAME OR PROGRAM NAME

d. INSURANCE PLAN NAME OR PROGRAM NAME

10d. RESERVED FOR LOCAL USE

d. IS THERE ANOTHER HEALTH BENEFIT PLAN? YES ☐ NO ☐ If yes, return to and complete item 9 a – d.

READ BACK OF FORM BEFORE COMPLETING & SIGNING THIS FORM.
12. PATIENT'S OR AUTHORIZED PERSON'S SIGNATURE I authorize the release of any medical or other information necessary to process this claim. I also request payment of government benefits either to myself or to the party who accepts assignment below.

SIGNED _____   DATE _____

13. INSURED'S OR AUTHORIZED PERSON'S SIGNATURE I authorize payment of medical benefits to the undersigned physician or supplier for services described below.

SIGNED _____

14. DATE OF CURRENT: MM | DD | YY ◄ ILLNESS (First symptom) OR INJURY (Accident) OR PREGNANCY (LMP)

15. IF PATIENT HAS HAD SAME OR SIMILAR ILLNESS, GIVE FIRST DATE MM | DD | YY

16. DATES PATIENT UNABLE TO WORK IN CURRENT OCCUPATION MM | DD | YY FROM   TO MM | DD | YY

17. NAME OF REFERRING PHYSICIAN OR OTHER SOURCE

17a. I.D. NUMBER OF REFERRING PHYSICIAN

18. HOSPITALIZATION DATES RELATED TO CURRENT SERVICES MM | DD | YY FROM   TO MM | DD | YY

19. RESERVED FOR LOCAL USE

20. OUTSIDE LAB? YES ☐ NO ☐ $ CHARGES

21. DIAGNOSIS OR NATURE OF ILLNESS OR INJURY. (RELATE ITEMS 1, 2, 3, OR 4 TO ITEM 24E BY LINE)

1. |___.___| 3. |___.___|

2. |___.___| 4. |___.___|

22. MEDICAID RESUBMISSION CODE   ORIGINAL REF. NO.

23. PRIOR AUTHORIZATION NUMBER

24. A			B	C	D		E	F	G	H	I	J	K
DATE(S) OF SERVICE			Place of Service	Type of Service	PROCEDURES, SERVICES, OR SUPPLIES (Explain Unusual Circumstances)		DIAGNOSIS CODE	$ CHARGES	DAYS OR UNITS	EPSDT Family Plan	EMG	COB	RESERVED FOR LOCAL USE
From MM DD YY		To MM DD YY			CPT/HCPCS	MODIFIER							
1													
2													
3													
4													
5													
6													

25. FEDERAL TAX I.D. NUMBER   SSN ☐ EIN ☐

26. PATIENT'S ACCOUNT NO.

27. ACCEPT ASSIGNMENT? (For govt. claims, see back) YES ☐ NO ☐

28. TOTAL CHARGE $

29. AMOUNT PAID $

30. BALANCE DUE $

31. SIGNATURE OF PHYSICIAN OR SUPPLIER INCLUDING DEGREES OR CREDENTIALS (I certify that the statements on the reverse apply to this bill and are made a part thereof.)

SIGNED _____   DATE _____

32. NAME AND ADDRESS OF FACILITY WHERE SERVICES WERE RENDERED (If other than home or office)

33. PHYSICIAN'S, SUPPLIER'S BILLING NAME, ADDRESS, ZIP CODE & PHONE #

PIN#   GRP#

(SAMPLE ONLY - NOT APPROVED FOR USE)

PLEASE PRINT OR TYPE

SAMPLE FORM 1500
SAMPLE FORM 1500 SAMPLE FORM 1500

CASE STUDIES

43. Using Optical Scanning Guidelines, complete the blank claim for Jane Normal. Use the step-by-step instructions provided in the textbook to properly fill out the claim.

DONALD L. GIVINGS, M.D.

11350 Medical Drive ■ Anywhere US 12345 ■ (101) 111-5555

EIN: 11-123456   SSN: 123-12-1234   MEDICARE: D1234
PIN: DG1234   GRP DG: 12345   MEDICAID: DLG1234
BCBS: 12345

Encounter Form

PATIENT INFORMATION:

Name:	Jane Normal
Address:	534 Robin St.
City:	Anywhere
State:	US
Zip Code:	12345
Telephone:	(410) 123-1234
Gender:	Female
Date of Birth:	02-07-1953
Occupation:	
Employer:	Dress Barn
Spouse's Employer:	

INSURANCE INFORMATION:

Patient Number:	121-01-2179
Place of Service:	Office
Primary Insurance Plan:	Metropolitan
Primary Insurance Plan ID #:	121-01-2179
Group #:	C26
Primary Policyholder:	Jane Normal
Policyholder Date of Birth:	02-07-1953
Relationship to Patient:	Self
Secondary Insurance Plan:	
Secondary Insurance Plan ID #:	
Secondary Policyholder:	

Patient Status   ☒ Married   ☐ Divorced   ☐ Single   ☐ Student   ☐ Other

DIAGNOSIS INFORMATION

Diagnosis	Code	Diagnosis	Code
1. Sinusitis, frontal	461.1	5.	
2.		6.	
3.		7.	
4.		8.	

PROCEDURE INFORMATION

Description of Procedure or Service	Date	Code	Charge
1. Established patient OV level II	02-05-YYYY	99212	$65.00
2.			
3.			
4.			
5.			

SPECIAL NOTES:

   Return visit: PRN

(SAMPLE ONLY - NOT APPROVED FOR USE)

CARRIER

HEALTH INSURANCE CLAIM FORM

☐☐ PICA   PICA ☐☐☐

1. MEDICARE MEDICAID CHAMPUS CHAMPVA GROUP HEALTH PLAN FECA BLK LUNG OTHER	1a. INSURED'S I.D. NUMBER (FOR PROGRAM IN ITEM 1)
☐ (Medicare #) ☐ (Medicaid #) ☐ (Sponsor's SSN) ☐ (VA File #) ☐ (SSN or ID) ☐ (SSN) ☐ (ID)	

2. PATIENT'S NAME (Last Name, First Name, Middle Initial)	3. PATIENT'S BIRTH DATE SEX	4. INSURED'S NAME (Last Name, First Name, Middle Initial)
	MM ¦ DD ¦ YY M ☐ F ☐	

5. PATIENT'S ADDRESS (No. Street)	6. PATIENT RELATIONSHIP TO INSURED	7. INSURED'S ADDRESS (No. Street)
	Self ☐ Spouse ☐ Child ☐ Other ☐	

CITY	STATE	8. PATIENT STATUS	CITY	STATE
		Single ☐ Married ☐ Other ☐		

ZIP CODE	TELEPHONE (Include Area Code) ( )		Employed ☐ Full-Time Student ☐ Part-Time Student ☐	ZIP CODE	TELEPHONE (INCLUDE AREA CODE) ( )

9. OTHER INSURED'S NAME (Last Name, First Name, Middle Initial)	10. IS PATIENT'S CONDITION RELATED TO:	11. INSURED'S POLICY GROUP OR FECA NUMBER

a. OTHER INSURED'S POLICY OR GROUP NUMBER	a. EMPLOYMENT? (CURRENT OR PREVIOUS) ☐ YES ☐ NO	a. INSURED'S DATE OF BIRTH MM ¦ DD ¦ YY SEX M ☐ F ☐

b. OTHER INSURED'S DATE OF BIRTH MM ¦ DD ¦ YY SEX M ☐ F ☐	b. AUTO ACCIDENT? PLACE (State) ☐ YES ☐ NO	b. EMPLOYER'S NAME OR SCHOOL NAME

c. EMPLOYER'S NAME OR SCHOOL NAME	c. OTHER ACCIDENT? ☐ YES ☐ NO	c. INSURANCE PLAN NAME OR PROGRAM NAME

d. INSURANCE PLAN NAME OR PROGRAM NAME	10d. RESERVED FOR LOCAL USE	d. IS THERE ANOTHER HEALTH BENEFIT PLAN? ☐ YES ☐ NO If yes, return to and complete item 9 a – d.

READ BACK OF FORM BEFORE COMPLETING & SIGNING THIS FORM.
12. PATIENT'S OR AUTHORIZED PERSON'S SIGNATURE I authorize the release of any medical or other information necessary to process this claim. I also request payment of government benefits either to myself or to the party who accepts assignment below.

SIGNED _____ DATE _____

13. INSURED'S OR AUTHORIZED PERSON'S SIGNATURE I authorize payment of medical benefits to the undersigned physician or supplier for services described below.

SIGNED _____

PATIENT AND INSURED INFORMATION

14. DATE OF CURRENT: ILLNESS (First symptom) OR INJURY (Accident) OR PREGNANCY (LMP) MM ¦ DD ¦ YY	15. IF PATIENT HAS HAD SAME OR SIMILAR ILLNESS, GIVE FIRST DATE MM ¦ DD ¦ YY	16. DATES PATIENT UNABLE TO WORK IN CURRENT OCCUPATION MM ¦ DD ¦ YY MM ¦ DD ¦ YY FROM TO

17. NAME OF REFERRING PHYSICIAN OR OTHER SOURCE	17a. I.D. NUMBER OF REFERRING PHYSICIAN	18. HOSPITALIZATION DATES RELATED TO CURRENT SERVICES MM ¦ DD ¦ YY MM ¦ DD ¦ YY FROM TO

19. RESERVED FOR LOCAL USE	20. OUTSIDE LAB? $ CHARGES ☐ YES ☐ NO

21. DIAGNOSIS OR NATURE OF ILLNESS OR INJURY. (RELATE ITEMS 1, 2, 3, OR 4 TO ITEM 24E BY LINE)

1. └── . ──   3. └── . ──

2. └── . ──   4. └── . ──

22. MEDICAID RESUBMISSION CODE   ORIGINAL REF. NO.
23. PRIOR AUTHORIZATION NUMBER

24. A. DATE(S) OF SERVICE From To MM DD YY MM DD YY	B. Place of Service	C. Type of Service	D. PROCEDURES, SERVICES, OR SUPPLIES (Explain Unusual Circumstances) CPT/HCPCS MODIFIER	E. DIAGNOSIS CODE	F. $ CHARGES	G. DAYS OR UNITS	H. EPSDT Family Plan	I. EMG	J. COB	K. RESERVED FOR LOCAL USE
1										
2										
3										
4										
5										
6										

25. FEDERAL TAX I.D. NUMBER SSN ☐ EIN ☐	26. PATIENT'S ACCOUNT NO.	27. ACCEPT ASSIGNMENT? (For govt. claims, see back) ☐ YES ☐ NO	28. TOTAL CHARGE $	29. AMOUNT PAID $	30. BALANCE DUE $

31. SIGNATURE OF PHYSICIAN OR SUPPLIER INCLUDING DEGREES OR CREDENTIALS (I certify that the statements on the reverse apply to this bill and are made a part thereof.) SIGNED DATE	32. NAME AND ADDRESS OF FACILITY WHERE SERVICES WERE RENDERED (If other than home or office)	33. PHYSICIAN'S, SUPPLIER'S BILLING NAME, ADDRESS, ZIP CODE & PHONE # PIN# GRP#

PHYSICIAN OR SUPPLIER INFORMATION

PLEASE PRINT OR TYPE

SAMPLE FORM 1500
SAMPLE FORM 1500 SAMPLE FORM 1500

45. Using Optical Scanning Guidelines, complete the blank claim for Thomas J. Meekes. Use the step-by-step instructions provided in the textbook to properly fill out the claim.

DONALD L. GIVINGS, M.D.

Encounter Form

11350 Medical Drive ■ Anywhere US 12345 ■ (101) 111-5555

EIN: 11-123456	SSN: 123-12-1234	MEDICARE: D1234
PIN: DG1234	GRP DG: 12345	MEDICAID: DLG1234
BCBS: 12345		

PATIENT INFORMATION:

Name:	Thomas J. Meekes
Address:	39567 Aliceville Rd.
City:	Anywhere
State:	US
Zip Code:	12345
Telephone:	(101) 333-4444
Gender:	Male
Date of Birth:	12-10-1949
Occupation:	
Employer:	Western Auto
Spouse's Employer:	

INSURANCE INFORMATION:

Patient Number:	411-44-1111
Place of Service:	Mercy Hospital
Primary Insurance Plan:	Atlantic Plus
Primary Insurance Plan ID #:	411-44-1111
Group #:	J276
Primary Policyholder:	Thomas J. Meekes
Policyholder Date of Birth:	12-10-1949
Relationship to Patient:	Self
Secondary Insurance Plan:	
Secondary Insurance Plan ID #:	
Secondary Policyholder:	

Patient Status   ☒ Married   ☐ Divorced   ☐ Single   ☐ Student   ☐ Other

DIAGNOSIS INFORMATION

Diagnosis	Code	Diagnosis	Code
1. Bronchial Pneumonia	485	5.	
2.		6.	
3.		7.	
4.		8.	

PROCEDURE INFORMATION

Description of Procedure or Service	Date	Code	Charge
1. Initial Hospital Care Level I	08-09-YYYY	99221	$75.00
2. Subsequent Hospital Care Level I	08-10-YYYY	99231	50.00
3. Subsequent Hospital Care Level I	08-11-YYYY	99231	50.00
4. Subsequent Hospital Care Level I	08-12-YYYY	99231	50.00
5. Discharge, 30 min.	08-13-YYYY	99238	75.00

SPECIAL NOTES:

Pt will call to set up appointment within one week

(SAMPLE ONLY - NOT APPROVED FOR USE)

CARRIER

| | PICA

HEALTH INSURANCE CLAIM FORM

PICA | | |

1. MEDICARE MEDICAID CHAMPUS CHAMPVA GROUP HEALTH PLAN FECA BLK LUNG OTHER	1a. INSURED'S I.D. NUMBER (FOR PROGRAM IN ITEM 1)
☐ (Medicare #) ☐ (Medicaid #) ☐ (Sponsor's SSN) ☐ (VA File #) ☐ (SSN or ID) ☐ (SSN) ☐ (ID)	

2. PATIENT'S NAME (Last Name, First Name, Middle Initial)	3. PATIENT'S BIRTH DATE SEX MM ǀ DD ǀ YY M ☐ F ☐	4. INSURED'S NAME (Last Name, First Name, Middle Initial)
5. PATIENT'S ADDRESS (No. Street)	6. PATIENT RELATIONSHIP TO INSURED Self ☐ Spouse ☐ Child ☐ Other ☐	7. INSURED'S ADDRESS (No. Street)
CITY STATE	8. PATIENT STATUS Single ☐ Married ☐ Other ☐	CITY STATE
ZIP CODE TELEPHONE (Include Area Code) ( )	Employed ☐ Full-Time Student ☐ Part-Time Student ☐	ZIP CODE TELEPHONE (INCLUDE AREA CODE) ( )

9. OTHER INSURED'S NAME (Last Name, First Name, Middle Initial)	10. IS PATIENT'S CONDITION RELATED TO:	11. INSURED'S POLICY GROUP OR FECA NUMBER
a. OTHER INSURED'S POLICY OR GROUP NUMBER	a. EMPLOYMENT? (CURRENT OR PREVIOUS) ☐ YES ☐ NO	a. INSURED'S DATE OF BIRTH SEX MM ǀ DD ǀ YY M ☐ F ☐
b. OTHER INSURED'S DATE OF BIRTH SEX MM ǀ DD ǀ YY M ☐ F ☐	b. AUTO ACCIDENT? PLACE (State) ☐ YES ☐ NO	b. EMPLOYER'S NAME OR SCHOOL NAME
c. EMPLOYER'S NAME OR SCHOOL NAME	c. OTHER ACCIDENT? ☐ YES ☐ NO	c. INSURANCE PLAN NAME OR PROGRAM NAME
d. INSURANCE PLAN NAME OR PROGRAM NAME	10d. RESERVED FOR LOCAL USE	d. IS THERE ANOTHER HEALTH BENEFIT PLAN? ☐ YES ☐ NO If yes, return to and complete item 9 a – d.

READ BACK OF FORM BEFORE COMPLETING & SIGNING THIS FORM. 12. PATIENT'S OR AUTHORIZED PERSON'S SIGNATURE I authorize the release of any medical or other information necessary to process this claim. I also request payment of government benefits either to myself or to the party who accepts assignment below. SIGNED _____ DATE _____	13. INSURED'S OR AUTHORIZED PERSON'S SIGNATURE I authorize payment of medical benefits to the undersigned physician or supplier for services described below. SIGNED _____

PATIENT AND INSURED INFORMATION

14. DATE OF CURRENT: ◀ ILLNESS (First symptom) OR MM ǀ DD ǀ YY INJURY (Accident) OR PREGNANCY (LMP)	15. IF PATIENT HAS HAD SAME OR SIMILAR ILLNESS, GIVE FIRST DATE MM ǀ DD ǀ YY	16. DATES PATIENT UNABLE TO WORK IN CURRENT OCCUPATION MM ǀ DD ǀ YY MM ǀ DD ǀ YY FROM TO
17. NAME OF REFERRING PHYSICIAN OR OTHER SOURCE	17a. I.D. NUMBER OF REFERRING PHYSICIAN	18. HOSPITALIZATION DATES RELATED TO CURRENT SERVICES MM ǀ DD ǀ YY MM ǀ DD ǀ YY FROM TO
19. RESERVED FOR LOCAL USE		20. OUTSIDE LAB? $ CHARGES ☐ YES ☐ NO
21. DIAGNOSIS OR NATURE OF ILLNESS OR INJURY. (RELATE ITEMS 1, 2, 3, OR 4 TO ITEM 24E BY LINE) 1. L__ . __ 3. L__ . __ 2. L__ . __ 4. L__ . __		22. MEDICAID RESUBMISSION CODE ORIGINAL REF. NO. 23. PRIOR AUTHORIZATION NUMBER

24. A DATE(S) OF SERVICE From To MM DD YY MM DD YY	B Place of Service	C Type of Service	D PROCEDURES, SERVICES, OR SUPPLIES (Explain Unusual Circumstances) CPT/HCPCS ǀ MODIFIER	E DIAGNOSIS CODE	F $ CHARGES	G DAYS OR UNITS	H EPSDT Family Plan	I EMG	J COB	K RESERVED FOR LOCAL USE
1										
2										
3										
4										
5										
6										

25. FEDERAL TAX I.D. NUMBER SSN EIN ☐ ☐	26. PATIENT'S ACCOUNT NO.	27. ACCEPT ASSIGNMENT? (For govt. claims, see back) ☐ YES ☐ NO	28. TOTAL CHARGE $	29. AMOUNT PAID $	30. BALANCE DUE $
31. SIGNATURE OF PHYSICIAN OR SUPPLIER INCLUDING DEGREES OR CREDENTIALS (I certify that the statements on the reverse apply to this bill and are made a part thereof.) SIGNED _____ DATE _____	32. NAME AND ADDRESS OF FACILITY WHERE SERVICES WERE RENDERED (If other than home or office)		33. PHYSICIAN'S, SUPPLIER'S BILLING NAME, ADDRESS, ZIP CODE & PHONE # PIN# GRP#		

PHYSICIAN OR SUPPLIER INFORMATION

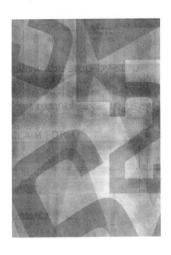

COMMERCIAL CLAIMS

1. Describe the *birthday rule.* _____

_____

STEP-BY-STEP CLAIM INSTRUCTIONS—BLOCKS 1–13— ENTERING PATIENT AND POLICY INFORMATION

2. For each item, enter **Y** for yes or **N** for no on the line provided. (For best results, answer the following questions while viewing the CMS-1500 claim.)

_____ a. Should the insurance identification number, as it appears on the patient's insurance card, be entered in Block 1A?

_____ b. If dashes appear on the insurance card, should they be entered in Block 1A?

_____ c. Should nicknames be entered in Block 2?

_____ d. Should the patient's birth date be entered in the MM DD YYYY (with spaces) format?

_____ e. Does an X in the appropriate box in Block 3 indicate the patient's race?

_____ f. If the patient is not the policyholder, should the policyholder's name be entered in Block 4?

_____ g. Should parentheses for the area code be entered in Block 5?

_____ h. Does entering an X in the appropriate box in Block 6 indicate the patient's relationship to the policyholder?

_____ i. Should the policyholder's address be entered in Block 7 if the patient is not the policyholder?

_____ j. If the patient does not have secondary insurance, should the word NONE be entered in Block 9?

_____ k. If the patient does not have secondary insurance, should Block 9 be left blank?

_____ l. If the patient's group policy number is provided on the patient's insurance card, should Block 11 be left blank?

_____ m. Should Block 11d be completed if the patient does not have secondary insurance?

3. What does an X in the appropriate boxes in Blocks 10a-10c indicate? _____

_____

4. When should Block 11a be left blank? _____

_____

5. What does entering SIGNATURE ON FILE in Block 12 indicate? _____

   _____

6. What does entering SIGNATURE ON FILE in Block 13 indicate? _____

   _____

STEP-BY-STEP CLAIM INSTRUCTIONS—BLOCKS 14-23—DATES OF SERVICE AND DIAGNOSIS CODES

7. The arrow in Block 14 indicates that the date refers to either ____. (Circle the correct answer.)
   a. illness
   b. injury
   c. pregnancy
   d. all of the above

8. In Block 14 enter the date of the first ___. (Circle the correct answer.)
   a. claim
   b. symptom
   c. visit
   d. any of the above

9. In Block 16 enter the dates the patient was ___. (Circle the correct answer.)
   a. able to work
   b. treated by physician
   c. unable to work
   d. all of the above

10. In Block 17 the full name of the ___ should be entered. (Circle the correct answer.)
    a. assistant surgeon
    b. referring physician
    c. testing facility
    d. none of the above

11. In Block 17A enter the payer assigned PIN for ___ providers. (Circle the correct answer.)
    a. nonPAR
    b. PAR

12. In Block 17A enter the Social Security Number for ___ providers. (Circle the correct answer.)
    a. nonPAR
    b. PAR

13. In Block 18 enter the admission and discharge date if any procedure/service is rendered to a patient with ___ status. (Circle the correct answer.)
    a. inpatient
    b. outpatient

14. In Block 21 enter the ___ code number. (Circle the correct answer.)
    a. CPT/HCPCS
    b. ICD-9-CM

15. In Block 23 enter the precertification or authorization number assigned by the ___. (Circle the correct answer.)
    a. payer
    b. provider

STEP-BY-STEP CLAIM INSTRUCTIONS—BLOCK 24— PROCEDURES, SERVICES, AND SUPPLIES

16. In Block 24 what date should be entered in the FROM column? _____

_____

17. What does the POS code in Block 24B identify? _____

_____

18. In Block 24D enter the ___ code number. (Circle the correct answer.)
    a. CPT/HCPCS
    b. ICD-9-CM

19. In Block 24E enter the ___. (Circle the correct answer.)
    a. ICD code number
    b. diagnosis reference number

20. In Block 24F enter the _____ charged to the patient's account.

21. In Block 24G enter the number of _____ / _____ of services or procedures reported in Block 24D.

22. Enter an X in Block 24I when the service was provided in a _____ _____
    _____.

STEP-BY-STEP CLAIM INSTRUCTIONS—BLOCKS 25–33—PROVIDER INFORMATION

23. Describe what an X in the NO box of Block 27 indicates. _____

_____

_____

24. When is it appropriate for a negative charge to appear in Block 28? _____

25. In which block would payment toward a patient's deductible for procedures appear? _____

26. When would it be appropriate to complete Block 32? _____

_____

_____

EXERCISES

27. Complete Case Studies 12-a through 12-j using the blank claims provided. Follow the step-by-step instructions in the textbook to properly complete each claim. If a patient has secondary insurance, complete an additional claim using secondary directions from the textbook. You may choose to use a pencil so corrections can be made.

DONALD L. GIVINGS, M.D.

11350 Medical Drive ■ Anywhere US 12345 ■ (101) 111-5555

EIN: 11-123456 SSN: 123-12-1234 MEDICARE: D1234
PIN: DG1234 GRP DG: 12345 MEDICAID: DLG1234
BCBS: 12345

Encounter Form

PATIENT INFORMATION:

Name:	Dawn L. Zapp
Address:	663 Hilltop Drive
City:	Anywhere
State:	US
Zip Code:	12345
Telephone:	(101) 333-4445
Gender:	Female
Date of Birth:	02-12-1967
Occupation:	
Employer:	Superfresh Foods
Spouse's Employer:	

INSURANCE INFORMATION:

Patient Number:	12-a
Place of Service:	Office
Primary Insurance Plan:	North West Health
Primary Insurance Plan ID #:	444-55-6666
Group #:	SF123
Primary Policyholder:	Dawn L. Zapp
Policyholder Date of Birth:	02-12-1967
Relationship to Patient:	Self
Secondary Insurance Plan:	
Secondary Insurance Plan ID #:	
Secondary Policyholder:	

Patient Status   ☐ Married   ☐ Divorced   ☒ Single   ☐ Student   ☐ Other

---

DIAGNOSIS INFORMATION

Diagnosis	Code	Diagnosis	Code
1. Headache, facial pain	784.0	5.	
2. Cough	786.2	6.	
3.		7.	
4.		8.	

PROCEDURE INFORMATION

Description of Procedure or Service	Date	Code	Charge
1. Est. patient OV level II	05-10-YYYY	99212	$65.00
2.			
3.			
4.			
5.			

SPECIAL NOTES:

Return visit: 2 weeks

PLEASE
DO NOT
STAPLE
IN THIS
AREA

CARRIER

| | PICA

HEALTH INSURANCE CLAIM FORM

PICA | |

1. MEDICARE ☐ (Medicare #) MEDICAID ☐ (Medicaid #) CHAMPUS ☐ (Sponsor's SSN) CHAMPVA ☐ (VA File #) GROUP HEALTH PLAN ☐ (SSN or ID) FECA BLK LUNG ☐ (SSN) OTHER ☐ (ID)

1a. INSURED'S I.D. NUMBER (FOR PROGRAM IN ITEM 1)

2. PATIENT'S NAME (Last Name, First Name, Middle Initial)

3. PATIENT'S BIRTH DATE MM | DD | YY   SEX M ☐ F ☐

4. INSURED'S NAME (Last Name, First Name, Middle Initial)

5. PATIENT'S ADDRESS (No. Street)

6. PATIENT RELATIONSHIP TO INSURED Self ☐ Spouse ☐ Child ☐ Other ☐

7. INSURED'S ADDRESS (No. Street)

CITY   STATE

8. PATIENT STATUS Single ☐ Married ☐ Other ☐   Employed ☐ Full-Time Student ☐ Part-Time Student ☐

CITY   STATE

ZIP CODE   TELEPHONE (Include Area Code) ( )

ZIP CODE   TELEPHONE (INCLUDE AREA CODE) ( )

9. OTHER INSURED'S NAME (Last Name, First Name, Middle Initial)

10. IS PATIENT'S CONDITION RELATED TO:

11. INSURED'S POLICY GROUP OR FECA NUMBER

a. OTHER INSURED'S POLICY OR GROUP NUMBER

a. EMPLOYMENT? (CURRENT OR PREVIOUS) ☐ YES ☐ NO

a. INSURED'S DATE OF BIRTH MM | DD | YY   SEX M ☐ F ☐

b. OTHER INSURED'S DATE OF BIRTH MM | DD | YY   SEX M ☐ F ☐

b. AUTO ACCIDENT? PLACE (State) ☐ YES ☐ NO

b. EMPLOYER'S NAME OR SCHOOL NAME

c. EMPLOYER'S NAME OR SCHOOL NAME

c. OTHER ACCIDENT? ☐ YES ☐ NO

c. INSURANCE PLAN NAME OR PROGRAM NAME

d. INSURANCE PLAN NAME OR PROGRAM NAME

10d. RESERVED FOR LOCAL USE

d. IS THERE ANOTHER HEALTH BENEFIT PLAN? ☐ YES ☐ NO If yes, return to and complete item 9 a – d.

READ BACK OF FORM BEFORE COMPLETING & SIGNING THIS FORM.
12. PATIENT'S OR AUTHORIZED PERSON'S SIGNATURE I authorize the release of any medical or other information necessary to process this claim. I also request payment of government benefits either to myself or to the party who accepts assignment below.

SIGNED _____   DATE _____

13. INSURED'S OR AUTHORIZED PERSON'S SIGNATURE I authorize payment of medical benefits to the undersigned physician or supplier for services described below.

SIGNED _____

14. DATE OF CURRENT: MM | DD | YY   ILLNESS (First symptom) OR INJURY (Accident) OR PREGNANCY (LMP)

15. IF PATIENT HAS HAD SAME OR SIMILAR ILLNESS. GIVE FIRST DATE MM | DD | YY

16. DATES PATIENT UNABLE TO WORK IN CURRENT OCCUPATION MM | DD | YY   FROM   TO   MM | DD | YY

17. NAME OF REFERRING PHYSICIAN OR OTHER SOURCE

17a. I.D. NUMBER OF REFERRING PHYSICIAN

18. HOSPITALIZATION DATES RELATED TO CURRENT SERVICES MM | DD | YY   FROM   TO   MM | DD | YY

19. RESERVED FOR LOCAL USE

20. OUTSIDE LAB? ☐ YES ☐ NO $ CHARGES

21. DIAGNOSIS OR NATURE OF ILLNESS OR INJURY. (RELATE ITEMS 1, 2, 3, OR 4 TO ITEM 24E BY LINE)
1. |___.__   3. |___.__
2. |___.__   4. |___.__

22. MEDICAID RESUBMISSION CODE   ORIGINAL REF. NO.

23. PRIOR AUTHORIZATION NUMBER

24. A DATE(S) OF SERVICE						B Place of Service	C Type of Service	D PROCEDURES, SERVICES, OR SUPPLIES (Explain Unusual Circumstances)		E DIAGNOSIS CODE	F $ CHARGES	G DAYS OR UNITS	H EPSDT Family Plan	I EMG	J COB	K RESERVED FOR LOCAL USE
From MM	DD	YY	To MM	DD	YY			CPT/HCPCS	MODIFIER							
1																
2																
3																
4																
5																
6																

25. FEDERAL TAX I.D. NUMBER SSN ☐ EIN ☐

26. PATIENT'S ACCOUNT NO.

27. ACCEPT ASSIGNMENT? (For govt. claims, see back) ☐ YES ☐ NO

28. TOTAL CHARGE $

29. AMOUNT PAID $

30. BALANCE DUE $

31. SIGNATURE OF PHYSICIAN OR SUPPLIER INCLUDING DEGREES OR CREDENTIALS (I certify that the statements on the reverse apply to this bill and are made a part thereof.)

SIGNED _____   DATE _____

32. NAME AND ADDRESS OF FACILITY WHERE SERVICES WERE RENDERED (If other than home or office)

33. PHYSICIAN'S, SUPPLIER'S BILLING NAME, ADDRESS, ZIP CODE & PHONE #

PIN#   GRP#

PATIENT AND INSURED INFORMATION

PHYSICIAN OR SUPPLIER INFORMATION

DONALD L. GIVINGS, M.D.

11350 Medical Drive ■ Anywhere US 12345 ■ (101) 111-5555

EIN: 11-123456   SSN: 123-12-1234   MEDICARE: D1234
PIN: DG1234   GRP DG: 12345   MEDICAID: DLG1234
BCBS: 12345

Encounter Form

PATIENT INFORMATION:

Name:	Bethany L. Branch
Address:	401 Cartvalley Court
City:	Anywhere
State:	US
Zip Code:	12345
Telephone:	(101) 333-4466
Gender:	Female
Date of Birth:	05-03-1986
Occupation:	
Employer:	Gateway Computers Inc.
Spouse's Employer:	

INSURANCE INFORMATION:

Patient Number:	12-b
Place of Service:	Office
Primary Insurance Plan:	Metropolitan
Primary Insurance Plan ID #:	212-22-4545
Group #:	GW292
Primary Policyholder:	John L. Branch
Policyholder Date of Birth:	10-10-54
Relationship to Patient:	Father
Secondary Insurance Plan:	
Secondary Insurance Plan ID #:	
Secondary Policyholder:	

Patient Status   ☐ Married   ☐ Divorced   ☒ Single   ☐ Student   ☐ Other

DIAGNOSIS INFORMATION

Diagnosis	Code	Diagnosis	Code
1. Bronchitis	466.0	5.	
2. Strep throat	034.0	6.	
3.		7.	
4.		8.	

PROCEDURE INFORMATION

Description of Procedure or Service	Date	Code	Charge
1. Office consult level II	12-04-YYYY	99242	$75.00
2. Quick strep test	12-04-YYYY	86403	12.00
3.			
4.			
5.			

SPECIAL NOTES:
    Return visit: PRN
    Referring physician: James R. Feltbetter, M.D.
    UPIN/SSN: 777-88-7878

PLEASE
DO NOT
STAPLE
IN THIS
AREA

CARRIER

HEALTH INSURANCE CLAIM FORM

PICA | | |

| | | PICA

1. MEDICARE (Medicare #) **MEDICAID** (Medicaid #) **CHAMPUS** (Sponsor's SSN) **CHAMPVA** (VA File #) **GROUP HEALTH PLAN** (SSN or ID) **FECA BLK LUNG** (SSN) **OTHER** (ID)

1a. INSURED'S I.D. NUMBER (FOR PROGRAM IN ITEM 1)

2. PATIENT'S NAME (Last Name, First Name, Middle Initial)

3. PATIENT'S BIRTH DATE MM | DD | YY **SEX** M □ F □

4. INSURED'S NAME (Last Name, First Name, Middle Initial)

5. PATIENT'S ADDRESS (No. Street)

6. PATIENT RELATIONSHIP TO INSURED Self □ Spouse □ Child □ Other □

7. INSURED'S ADDRESS (No. Street)

CITY | STATE

8. PATIENT STATUS Single □ Married □ Other □

Employed □ Full-Time Student □ Part-Time Student □

CITY | STATE

ZIP CODE | TELEPHONE (Include Area Code) ( )

ZIP CODE | TELEPHONE (INCLUDE AREA CODE) ( )

9. OTHER INSURED'S NAME (Last Name, First Name, Middle Initial)

10. IS PATIENT'S CONDITION RELATED TO:

11. INSURED'S POLICY GROUP OR FECA NUMBER

a. OTHER INSURED'S POLICY OR GROUP NUMBER

a. EMPLOYMENT? (CURRENT OR PREVIOUS) □ YES □ NO

a. INSURED'S DATE OF BIRTH MM | DD | YY **SEX** M □ F □

b. OTHER INSURED'S DATE OF BIRTH MM | DD | YY **SEX** M □ F □

b. AUTO ACCIDENT? **PLACE (State)** □ YES □ NO

b. EMPLOYER'S NAME OR SCHOOL NAME

c. EMPLOYER'S NAME OR SCHOOL NAME

c. OTHER ACCIDENT? □ YES □ NO

c. INSURANCE PLAN NAME OR PROGRAM NAME

d. INSURANCE PLAN NAME OR PROGRAM NAME

10d. RESERVED FOR LOCAL USE

d. IS THERE ANOTHER HEALTH BENEFIT PLAN? □ YES □ NO If yes, return to and complete item 9 a – d.

READ BACK OF FORM BEFORE COMPLETING & SIGNING THIS FORM.
12. PATIENT'S OR AUTHORIZED PERSON'S SIGNATURE I authorize the release of any medical or other information necessary to process this claim. I also request payment of government benefits either to myself or to the party who accepts assignment below.

SIGNED _____ DATE _____

13. INSURED'S OR AUTHORIZED PERSON'S SIGNATURE I authorize payment of medical benefits to the undersigned physician or supplier for services described below.

SIGNED _____

PATIENT AND INSURED INFORMATION

14. DATE OF CURRENT: MM | DD | YY ILLNESS (First symptom) OR INJURY (Accident) OR PREGNANCY (LMP)

15. IF PATIENT HAS HAD SAME OR SIMILAR ILLNESS, GIVE FIRST DATE MM | DD | YY

16. DATES PATIENT UNABLE TO WORK IN CURRENT OCCUPATION MM | DD | YY FROM TO MM | DD | YY

17. NAME OF REFERRING PHYSICIAN OR OTHER SOURCE

17a. I.D. NUMBER OF REFERRING PHYSICIAN

18. HOSPITALIZATION DATES RELATED TO CURRENT SERVICES MM | DD | YY FROM TO MM | DD | YY

19. RESERVED FOR LOCAL USE

20. OUTSIDE LAB? □ YES □ NO **$ CHARGES**

21. DIAGNOSIS OR NATURE OF ILLNESS OR INJURY. (RELATE ITEMS 1, 2, 3, OR 4 TO ITEM 24E BY LINE)

1. |___.___ 3. |___.___
2. |___.___ 4. |___.___

22. MEDICAID RESUBMISSION CODE ORIGINAL REF. NO.

23. PRIOR AUTHORIZATION NUMBER

24. A DATE(S) OF SERVICE						B Place of Service	C Type of Service	D PROCEDURES, SERVICES, OR SUPPLIES (Explain Unusual Circumstances)		E DIAGNOSIS CODE	F $ CHARGES	G DAYS OR UNITS	H EPSDT Family Plan	I EMG	J COB	K RESERVED FOR LOCAL USE
From MM	DD	YY	To MM	DD	YY			CPT/HCPCS	MODIFIER							
1																
2																
3																
4																
5																
6																

25. FEDERAL TAX I.D. NUMBER SSN □ EIN □

26. PATIENT'S ACCOUNT NO.

27. ACCEPT ASSIGNMENT? (For govt. claims, see back) □ YES □ NO

28. TOTAL CHARGE $

29. AMOUNT PAID $

30. BALANCE DUE $

31. SIGNATURE OF PHYSICIAN OR SUPPLIER INCLUDING DEGREES OR CREDENTIALS (I certify that the statements on the reverse apply to this bill and are made a part thereof.)

SIGNED _____ DATE _____

32. NAME AND ADDRESS OF FACILITY WHERE SERVICES WERE RENDERED (If other than home or office)

33. PHYSICIAN'S, SUPPLIER'S BILLING NAME, ADDRESS, ZIP CODE & PHONE #

PIN# | GRP#

PHYSICIAN OR SUPPLIER INFORMATION

PLEASE PRINT OR TYPE

SAMPLE FORM 1500
SAMPLE FORM 1500 SAMPLE FORM 1500

DONALD L. GIVINGS, M.D.

11350 Medical Drive ■ Anywhere US 12345 ■ (101) 111-5555

EIN: 11-123456　　SSN:　123-12-1234　　MEDICARE: D1234
PIN: DG1234　　GRP DG: 12345　　MEDICAID: DLG1234
BCBS: 12345

Encounter Form

PATIENT INFORMATION:

Name:	Laurie P. Reed
Address:	579 Vacation Drive
City:	Anywhere
State:	US
Zip Code:	12345
Telephone:	(101) 333-5555
Gender:	Female
Date of Birth:	06-05-1964
Occupation:	
Employer:	The Learning Center
Spouse's Employer:	

INSURANCE INFORMATION:

Patient Number:	12-c
Place of Service:	Office
Primary Insurance Plan:	US Health
Primary Insurance Plan ID #:	C748593
Group #:	TLC45
Primary Policyholder:	Laurie P. Reed
Policyholder Date of Birth:	06-05-1964
Relationship to Patient:	Self
Secondary Insurance Plan:	
Secondary Insurance Plan ID #:	
Secondary Policyholder:	

Patient Status　☐ Married　☐ Divorced　☒ Single　☐ Student　☐ Other

DIAGNOSIS INFORMATION

Diagnosis	Code	Diagnosis	Code
1. Allergic rhinitis	477.9	5.	
2.		6.	
3.		7.	
4.		8.	

PROCEDURE INFORMATION

Description of Procedure or Service	Date	Code	Charge
1. Est. patient OV level I	10/28/YYYY	99211	$55.00
2.			
3.			
4.			
5.			

SPECIAL NOTES:

　Return visit: PRN

PLEASE
DO NOT
STAPLE
IN THIS
AREA

CARRIER

□□ PICA

HEALTH INSURANCE CLAIM FORM PICA □□□

1. MEDICARE   MEDICAID   CHAMPUS   CHAMPVA   GROUP HEALTH PLAN   FECA BLK LUNG   OTHER
   □ (Medicare #)   □ (Medicaid #)   □ (Sponsor's SSN)   □ (VA File #)   □ (SSN or ID)   □ (SSN)   □ (ID)

1a. INSURED'S I.D. NUMBER   (FOR PROGRAM IN ITEM 1)

2. PATIENT'S NAME (Last Name, First Name, Middle Initial)

3. PATIENT'S BIRTH DATE   SEX
   MM   DD   YY   M □   F □

4. INSURED'S NAME (Last Name, First Name, Middle Initial)

5. PATIENT'S ADDRESS (No. Street)

6. PATIENT RELATIONSHIP TO INSURED
   Self □   Spouse □   Child □   Other □

7. INSURED'S ADDRESS (No. Street)

CITY   STATE

8. PATIENT STATUS
   Single □   Married □   Other □
   Employed □   Full-Time Student □   Part-Time Student □

CITY   STATE

ZIP CODE   TELEPHONE (Include Area Code)
(   )

ZIP CODE   TELEPHONE (INCLUDE AREA CODE)
(   )

9. OTHER INSURED'S NAME (Last Name, First Name, Middle Initial)

10. IS PATIENT'S CONDITION RELATED TO:

11. INSURED'S POLICY GROUP OR FECA NUMBER

a. OTHER INSURED'S POLICY OR GROUP NUMBER

a. EMPLOYMENT? (CURRENT OR PREVIOUS)
   □ YES   □ NO

a. INSURED'S DATE OF BIRTH   SEX
   MM   DD   YY   M □   F □

b. OTHER INSURED'S DATE OF BIRTH   SEX
   MM   DD   YY   M □   F □

b. AUTO ACCIDENT?   PLACE (State)
   □ YES   □ NO

b. EMPLOYER'S NAME OR SCHOOL NAME

c. EMPLOYER'S NAME OR SCHOOL NAME

c. OTHER ACCIDENT?
   □ YES   □ NO

c. INSURANCE PLAN NAME OR PROGRAM NAME

d. INSURANCE PLAN NAME OR PROGRAM NAME

10d. RESERVED FOR LOCAL USE

d. IS THERE ANOTHER HEALTH BENEFIT PLAN?
   □ YES   □ NO   If yes, return to and complete item 9 a – d.

READ BACK OF FORM BEFORE COMPLETING & SIGNING THIS FORM.
12. PATIENT'S OR AUTHORIZED PERSON'S SIGNATURE I authorize the release of any medical or other information necessary to process this claim. I also request payment of government benefits either to myself or to the party who accepts assignment below.

SIGNED _____   DATE _____

13. INSURED'S OR AUTHORIZED PERSON'S SIGNATURE I authorize payment of medical benefits to the undersigned physician or supplier for services described below.

SIGNED _____

PATIENT AND INSURED INFORMATION

14. DATE OF CURRENT: ILLNESS (First symptom) OR   INJURY (Accident) OR   PREGNANCY (LMP)
    MM   DD   YY

15. IF PATIENT HAS HAD SAME OR SIMILAR ILLNESS, GIVE FIRST DATE   MM   DD   YY

16. DATES PATIENT UNABLE TO WORK IN CURRENT OCCUPATION
    FROM   MM   DD   YY   TO   MM   DD   YY

17. NAME OF REFERRING PHYSICIAN OR OTHER SOURCE

17a. I.D. NUMBER OF REFERRING PHYSICIAN

18. HOSPITALIZATION DATES RELATED TO CURRENT SERVICES
    FROM   MM   DD   YY   TO   MM   DD   YY

19. RESERVED FOR LOCAL USE

20. OUTSIDE LAB? $ CHARGES
    □ YES   □ NO

21. DIAGNOSIS OR NATURE OF ILLNESS OR INJURY. (RELATE ITEMS 1, 2, 3, OR 4 TO ITEM 24E BY LINE)
   1. ⌊__ . __⌋   3. ⌊__ . __⌋
   2. ⌊__ . __⌋   4. ⌊__ . __⌋

22. MEDICAID RESUBMISSION CODE   ORIGINAL REF. NO.

23. PRIOR AUTHORIZATION NUMBER

24. A DATE(S) OF SERVICE						B Place of Service	C Type of Service	D PROCEDURES, SERVICES, OR SUPPLIES (Explain Unusual Circumstances) CPT/HCPCS MODIFIER	E DIAGNOSIS CODE	F $ CHARGES	G DAYS OR UNITS	H EPSDT Family Plan	I EMG	J COB	K RESERVED FOR LOCAL USE
From MM	DD	YY	To MM	DD	YY										
1															
2															
3															
4															
5															
6															

25. FEDERAL TAX I.D. NUMBER   SSN □ EIN □

26. PATIENT'S ACCOUNT NO.

27. ACCEPT ASSIGNMENT? (For govt. claims, see back)   □ YES   □ NO

28. TOTAL CHARGE $

29. AMOUNT PAID $

30. BALANCE DUE $

31. SIGNATURE OF PHYSICIAN OR SUPPLIER INCLUDING DEGREES OR CREDENTIALS (I certify that the statements on the reverse apply to this bill and are made a part thereof.)

SIGNED _____   DATE _____

32. NAME AND ADDRESS OF FACILITY WHERE SERVICES WERE RENDERED (If other than home or office)

33. PHYSICIAN'S, SUPPLIER'S BILLING NAME, ADDRESS, ZIP CODE & PHONE #

PIN# _____   GRP# _____

PHYSICIAN OR SUPPLIER INFORMATION

PLEASE PRINT OR TYPE

SAMPLE FORM 1500
SAMPLE FORM 1500 SAMPLE FORM 1500

DONALD L. GIVINGS, M.D.

11350 Medical Drive ■ Anywhere US 12345 ■ (101) 111-5555

EIN: 11-123456   SSN: 123-12-1234   MEDICARE: D1234
PIN: DG1234   GRP DG: 12345   MEDICAID: DLG1234
BCBS: 12345

Encounter Form

PATIENT INFORMATION:

Name:	Pamela Sharp
Address:	678 Heather Ave.
City:	Anywhere
State:	US
Zip Code:	12345
Telephone:	(101) 333-5559
Gender:	Female
Date of Birth:	05-09-1970
Occupation:	
Employer:	Design Consultants
Spouse's Employer:	

INSURANCE INFORMATION:

Patient Number:	12-d
Place of Service:	Office
Primary Insurance Plan:	Cigna
Primary Insurance Plan ID #:	123-66-6666
Group #:	DC22
Primary Policyholder:	Pamela Sharp
Policyholder Date of Birth:	05-09-1970
Relationship to Patient:	Self
Secondary Insurance Plan:	
Secondary Insurance Plan ID #:	
Secondary Policyholder:	

Patient Status   ☐ Married   ☐ Divorced   ☒ Single   ☐ Student   ☐ Other

DIAGNOSIS INFORMATION

Diagnosis	Code	Diagnosis	Code
1. Chronic obstructive asthma	493.20	5.	
2. Bronchial pneumonia	485	6.	
3.		7.	
4.		8.	

PROCEDURE INFORMATION

Description of Procedure or Service	Date	Code	Charge
1. Initial hospital level I	06-28-YYYY	99221	$75.00
2. Subsequent hospital level I	06-29-YYYY	99231	50.00
3. Subsequent hospital level I	06-30-YYYY	99231	50.00
4. Subsequent hospital level I	07-01-YYYY	99231	50.00
5. Subsequent hospital level I	07-02-YYYY	99231	50.00
6. Discharge, 30 min.	07-03-YYYY	99238	75.00

SPECIAL NOTES:

Referring physician: Ledger Masters, M.D.
UPIN/SSN: 595-33-4959

(SAMPLE ONLY - NOT APPROVED FOR USE)

HEALTH INSURANCE CLAIM FORM

PICA

PICA

1. MEDICARE ☐ (Medicare #) MEDICAID ☐ (Medicaid #) CHAMPUS ☐ (Sponsor's SSN) CHAMPVA ☐ (VA File #)	GROUP HEALTH PLAN ☐ (SSN or ID)	FECA BLK LUNG ☐ (SSN)	OTHER ☐ (ID)	1a. INSURED'S I.D. NUMBER (FOR PROGRAM IN ITEM 1)

2. PATIENT'S NAME (Last Name, First Name, Middle Initial)	3. PATIENT'S BIRTH DATE MM ┊ DD ┊ YY SEX M ☐ F ☐	4. INSURED'S NAME (Last Name, First Name, Middle Initial)

5. PATIENT'S ADDRESS (No. Street)	6. PATIENT RELATIONSHIP TO INSURED Self ☐ Spouse ☐ Child ☐ Other ☐	7. INSURED'S ADDRESS (No. Street)

| CITY | STATE | 8. PATIENT STATUS Single ☐ Married ☐ Other ☐ Employed ☐ Full-Time Student ☐ Part-Time Student ☐ | CITY | STATE |

| ZIP CODE | TELEPHONE (Include Area Code) ( ) | | ZIP CODE | TELEPHONE (INCLUDE AREA CODE) ( ) |

9. OTHER INSURED'S NAME (Last Name, First Name, Middle Initial)	10. IS PATIENT'S CONDITION RELATED TO:	11. INSURED'S POLICY GROUP OR FECA NUMBER

| a. OTHER INSURED'S POLICY OR GROUP NUMBER | a. EMPLOYMENT? (CURRENT OR PREVIOUS) ☐ YES ☐ NO | a. INSURED'S DATE OF BIRTH MM ┊ DD ┊ YY SEX M ☐ F ☐ |

| b. OTHER INSURED'S DATE OF BIRTH MM ┊ DD ┊ YY SEX M ☐ F ☐ | b. AUTO ACCIDENT? PLACE (State) ☐ YES ☐ NO | b. EMPLOYER'S NAME OR SCHOOL NAME |

| c. EMPLOYER'S NAME OR SCHOOL NAME | c. OTHER ACCIDENT? ☐ YES ☐ NO | c. INSURANCE PLAN NAME OR PROGRAM NAME |

| d. INSURANCE PLAN NAME OR PROGRAM NAME | 10d. RESERVED FOR LOCAL USE | d. IS THERE ANOTHER HEALTH BENEFIT PLAN? ☐ YES ☐ NO If yes, return to and complete item 9 a – d. |

READ BACK OF FORM BEFORE COMPLETING & SIGNING THIS FORM.
12. PATIENT'S OR AUTHORIZED PERSON'S SIGNATURE I authorize the release of any medical or other information necessary to process this claim. I also request payment of government benefits either to myself or to the party who accepts assignment below.

SIGNED _____ DATE _____

13. INSURED'S OR AUTHORIZED PERSON'S SIGNATURE I authorize payment of medical benefits to the undersigned physician or supplier for services described below.

SIGNED _____

| 14. DATE OF CURRENT: MM ┊ DD ┊ YY ILLNESS (First symptom) OR INJURY (Accident) OR PREGNANCY (LMP) | 15. IF PATIENT HAS HAD SAME OR SIMILAR ILLNESS, GIVE FIRST DATE MM ┊ DD ┊ YY | 16. DATES PATIENT UNABLE TO WORK IN CURRENT OCCUPATION MM ┊ DD ┊ YY MM ┊ DD ┊ YY FROM TO |

| 17. NAME OF REFERRING PHYSICIAN OR OTHER SOURCE | 17a. I.D. NUMBER OF REFERRING PHYSICIAN | 18. HOSPITALIZATION DATES RELATED TO CURRENT SERVICES MM ┊ DD ┊ YY MM ┊ DD ┊ YY FROM TO |

| 19. RESERVED FOR LOCAL USE | | 20. OUTSIDE LAB? ☐ YES ☐ NO $ CHARGES |

| 21. DIAGNOSIS OR NATURE OF ILLNESS OR INJURY. (RELATE ITEMS 1, 2, 3, OR 4 TO ITEM 24E BY LINE) 1. _____ 3. _____ 2. _____ 4. _____ | 22. MEDICAID RESUBMISSION CODE ORIGINAL REF. NO. 23. PRIOR AUTHORIZATION NUMBER |

24. A DATE(S) OF SERVICE From MM DD YY	To MM DD YY	B Place of Service	C Type of Service	D PROCEDURES, SERVICES, OR SUPPLIES (Explain Unusual Circumstances) CPT/HCPCS	MODIFIER	E DIAGNOSIS CODE	F $ CHARGES	G DAYS OR UNITS	H EPSDT Family Plan	I EMG	J COB	K RESERVED FOR LOCAL USE
1												
2												
3												
4												
5												
6												

| 25. FEDERAL TAX I.D. NUMBER SSN ☐ EIN ☐ | 26. PATIENT'S ACCOUNT NO. | 27. ACCEPT ASSIGNMENT? (For govt. claims, see back) ☐ YES ☐ NO | 28. TOTAL CHARGE $ | 29. AMOUNT PAID $ | 30. BALANCE DUE $ |

| 31. SIGNATURE OF PHYSICIAN OR SUPPLIER INCLUDING DEGREES OR CREDENTIALS (I certify that the statements on the reverse apply to this bill and are made a part thereof.) SIGNED _____ DATE _____ | 32. NAME AND ADDRESS OF FACILITY WHERE SERVICES WERE RENDERED (If other than home or office) | 33. PHYSICIAN'S, SUPPLIER'S BILLING NAME, ADDRESS, ZIP CODE & PHONE # PIN# GRP# |

(SAMPLE ONLY - NOT APPROVED FOR USE)

PLEASE PRINT OR TYPE

SAMPLE FORM 1500
SAMPLE FORM 1500 SAMPLE FORM 1500

DONALD L. GIVINGS, M.D.

11350 Medical Drive ■ Anywhere US 12345 ■ (101) 111-5555

EIN: 11-123456	SSN: 123-12-1234	MEDICARE: D1234
PIN: DG1234	GRP DG: 12345	MEDICAID: DLG1234
BCBS: 12345		

Encounter Form

PATIENT INFORMATION:

Name:	James R. Brandt
Address:	95 Commission Circle
City:	Anywhere
State:	US
Zip Code:	12345
Telephone:	(101) 223-5555
Gender:	Male
Date of Birth:	12-05-1948
Occupation:	
Employer:	The Yard Guard
Spouse's Employer:	

INSURANCE INFORMATION:

Patient Number:	12-e
Place of Service:	Office
Primary Insurance Plan:	Prudential
Primary Insurance Plan ID #:	555-66-7777
Group #:	YG4
Primary Policyholder:	James R. Brandt
Policyholder Date of Birth:	12-05-1948
Relationship to Patient:	Self
Secondary Insurance Plan:	
Secondary Insurance Plan ID #:	
Secondary Policyholder:	

Patient Status ☐ Married ☒ Divorced ☐ Single ☐ Student ☐ Other

DIAGNOSIS INFORMATION

Diagnosis	Code	Diagnosis	Code
1. Diabetes, type II	250.00	5.	
2. Hypertension, benign	401.1	6.	
3. Gout	274.0	7.	
4.		8.	

PROCEDURE INFORMATION

Description of Procedure or Service	Date	Code	Charge
1. New patient OV level IV	02-02-YYYY	99204	$100.00
2. EKG	02-02-YYYY	93000	50.00
3. Glucose	02-02-YYYY	82947	10.00
4. Est. patient OV level III	02-03-YYYY	99213	75.00
5. Glucose	02-03-YYYY	82947	10.00

SPECIAL NOTES:

Referring physician: Rita M. Michaels, M.D., UPIN/SSN: 343-54-7979
Onset 02/02/YYYY
Return visit: 2 weeks

PLEASE
DO NOT
STAPLE
IN THIS
AREA

CARRIER

HEALTH INSURANCE CLAIM FORM

PICA | | | PICA

1. MEDICARE ☐ (Medicare #) MEDICAID ☐ (Medicaid #) CHAMPUS ☐ (Sponsor's SSN) CHAMPVA ☐ (VA File #) GROUP HEALTH PLAN ☐ (SSN or ID) FECA BLK LUNG ☐ (SSN) OTHER ☐ (ID)	1a. INSURED'S I.D. NUMBER (FOR PROGRAM IN ITEM 1)
2. PATIENT'S NAME (Last Name, First Name, Middle Initial)	3. PATIENT'S BIRTH DATE MM ┆ DD ┆ YY SEX M ☐ F ☐	4. INSURED'S NAME (Last Name, First Name, Middle Initial)

PATIENT AND INSURED INFORMATION

5. PATIENT'S ADDRESS (No. Street)

6. PATIENT RELATIONSHIP TO INSURED
Self ☐ Spouse ☐ Child ☐ Other ☐

7. INSURED'S ADDRESS (No. Street)

CITY STATE

8. PATIENT STATUS
Single ☐ Married ☐ Other ☐
Employed ☐ Full-Time Student ☐ Part-Time Student ☐

CITY STATE

ZIP CODE TELEPHONE (Include Area Code) ( )

ZIP CODE TELEPHONE (INCLUDE AREA CODE) ( )

9. OTHER INSURED'S NAME (Last Name, First Name, Middle Initial)

10. IS PATIENT'S CONDITION RELATED TO:

11. INSURED'S POLICY GROUP OR FECA NUMBER

a. OTHER INSURED'S POLICY OR GROUP NUMBER

a. EMPLOYMENT? (CURRENT OR PREVIOUS) ☐ YES ☐ NO

a. INSURED'S DATE OF BIRTH MM ┆ DD ┆ YY SEX M ☐ F ☐

b. OTHER INSURED'S DATE OF BIRTH MM ┆ DD ┆ YY SEX M ☐ F ☐

b. AUTO ACCIDENT? PLACE (State) ☐ YES ☐ NO

b. EMPLOYER'S NAME OR SCHOOL NAME

c. EMPLOYER'S NAME OR SCHOOL NAME

c. OTHER ACCIDENT? ☐ YES ☐ NO

c. INSURANCE PLAN NAME OR PROGRAM NAME

d. INSURANCE PLAN NAME OR PROGRAM NAME

10d. RESERVED FOR LOCAL USE

d. IS THERE ANOTHER HEALTH BENEFIT PLAN? ☐ YES ☐ NO If yes, return to and complete item 9 a – d.

READ BACK OF FORM BEFORE COMPLETING & SIGNING THIS FORM.
12. PATIENT'S OR AUTHORIZED PERSON'S SIGNATURE I authorize the release of any medical or other information necessary to process this claim. I also request payment of government benefits either to myself or to the party who accepts assignment below.

SIGNED _____ DATE _____

13. INSURED'S OR AUTHORIZED PERSON'S SIGNATURE I authorize payment of medical benefits to the undersigned physician or supplier for services described below.

SIGNED _____

14. DATE OF CURRENT: MM ┆ DD ┆ YY ILLNESS (First symptom) OR INJURY (Accident) OR PREGNANCY (LMP)

15. IF PATIENT HAS HAD SAME OR SIMILAR ILLNESS, GIVE FIRST DATE MM ┆ DD ┆ YY

16. DATES PATIENT UNABLE TO WORK IN CURRENT OCCUPATION MM ┆ DD ┆ YY TO MM ┆ DD ┆ YY FROM

17. NAME OF REFERRING PHYSICIAN OR OTHER SOURCE

17a. I.D. NUMBER OF REFERRING PHYSICIAN

18. HOSPITALIZATION DATES RELATED TO CURRENT SERVICES MM ┆ DD ┆ YY TO MM ┆ DD ┆ YY FROM

19. RESERVED FOR LOCAL USE

20. OUTSIDE LAB? ☐ YES ☐ NO $ CHARGES

21. DIAGNOSIS OR NATURE OF ILLNESS OR INJURY. (RELATE ITEMS 1, 2, 3, OR 4 TO ITEM 24E BY LINE)
1. └──┘ ┆ ──
2. └──┘ ┆ ──
3. └──┘ ┆ ──
4. └──┘ ┆ ──

22. MEDICAID RESUBMISSION CODE ORIGINAL REF. NO.

23. PRIOR AUTHORIZATION NUMBER

PHYSICIAN OR SUPPLIER INFORMATION

24. A DATE(S) OF SERVICE From MM DD YY To MM DD YY	B Place of Service	C Type of Service	D PROCEDURES, SERVICES, OR SUPPLIES (Explain Unusual Circumstances) CPT/HCPCS ┆ MODIFIER	E DIAGNOSIS CODE	F $ CHARGES	G DAYS OR UNITS	H EPSDT Family Plan	I EMG	J COB	K RESERVED FOR LOCAL USE
1										
2										
3										
4										
5										
6										

25. FEDERAL TAX I.D. NUMBER SSN ☐ EIN ☐

26. PATIENT'S ACCOUNT NO.

27. ACCEPT ASSIGNMENT? (For govt. claims, see back) YES ☐ NO ☐

28. TOTAL CHARGE $

29. AMOUNT PAID $

30. BALANCE DUE $

31. SIGNATURE OF PHYSICIAN OR SUPPLIER INCLUDING DEGREES OR CREDENTIALS (I certify that the statements on the reverse apply to this bill and are made a part thereof.)

SIGNED _____ DATE _____

32. NAME AND ADDRESS OF FACILITY WHERE SERVICES WERE RENDERED (If other than home or office)

33. PHYSICIAN'S, SUPPLIER'S BILLING NAME, ADDRESS, ZIP CODE & PHONE #

PIN# GRP#

PLEASE PRINT OR TYPE

SAMPLE FORM 1500
SAMPLE FORM 1500 SAMPLE FORM 1500

DONALD L. GIVINGS, M.D.

11350 Medical Drive ■ Anywhere US 12345 ■ (101) 111-5555

EIN: 11-123456   SSN: 123-12-1234   MEDICARE: D1234
PIN: DG1234   GRP DG: 12345   MEDICAID: DLG1234
BCBS: 12345

Encounter Form

PATIENT INFORMATION:

Name:	Judy R. Hudnet
Address:	548 Dayton Terr.
City:	Anywhere
State:	US
Zip Code:	12345
Telephone:	(101) 333-5555
Gender:	Female
Date of Birth:	03-28-1950
Occupation:	
Employer:	Printers "R" Us
Spouse's Employer:	

INSURANCE INFORMATION:

Patient Number:	12-f
Place of Service:	Office
Primary Insurance Plan:	Great West
Primary Insurance Plan ID #:	21785
Group #:	
Primary Policyholder:	Judy R. Hudnet
Policyholder Date of Birth:	03-28-1950
Relationship to Patient:	Self
Secondary Insurance Plan:	
Secondary Insurance Plan ID #:	
Secondary Policyholder:	

Patient Status   ☐ Married   ☐ Divorced   ☒ Single   ☐ Student   ☐ Other

---

DIAGNOSIS INFORMATION

Diagnosis	Code	Diagnosis	Code
1. Incontinence of urine	788.30	5.	
2. Polyuria	788.42	6.	
3.		7.	
4.		8.	

PROCEDURE INFORMATION

Description of Procedure or Service	Date	Code	Charge
1. Est. patient OV level II	04-23-YYYY	99212	$65.00
2. Urinalysis	04-23-YYYY	81000	10.00
3.			
4.			
5.			

SPECIAL NOTES:

Patient referred to Dr. Stream.

Patient paid $10.00 toward today's bill.

(SAMPLE ONLY - NOT APPROVED FOR USE)

CARRIER

HEALTH INSURANCE CLAIM FORM

PICA ☐☐☐

PICA ☐☐

1. MEDICARE ☐ (Medicare #) MEDICAID ☐ (Medicaid #) CHAMPUS ☐ (Sponsor's SSN) CHAMPVA ☐ (VA File #) GROUP HEALTH PLAN ☐ (SSN or ID) FECA BLK LUNG ☐ (SSN) OTHER ☐ (ID)

1a. INSURED'S I.D. NUMBER   (FOR PROGRAM IN ITEM 1)

2. PATIENT'S NAME (Last Name, First Name, Middle Initial)

3. PATIENT'S BIRTH DATE MM | DD | YY   SEX M ☐ F ☐

4. INSURED'S NAME (Last Name, First Name, Middle Initial)

5. PATIENT'S ADDRESS (No. Street)

6. PATIENT RELATIONSHIP TO INSURED Self ☐ Spouse ☐ Child ☐ Other ☐

7. INSURED'S ADDRESS (No. Street)

CITY   STATE

8. PATIENT STATUS Single ☐ Married ☐ Other ☐

Employed ☐ Full-Time Student ☐ Part-Time Student ☐

CITY   STATE

ZIP CODE   TELEPHONE (Include Area Code) (   )

ZIP CODE   TELEPHONE (INCLUDE AREA CODE) (   )

9. OTHER INSURED'S NAME (Last Name, First Name, Middle Initial)

10. IS PATIENT'S CONDITION RELATED TO:

11. INSURED'S POLICY GROUP OR FECA NUMBER

a. OTHER INSURED'S POLICY OR GROUP NUMBER

a. EMPLOYMENT? (CURRENT OR PREVIOUS) ☐ YES ☐ NO

a. INSURED'S DATE OF BIRTH MM | DD | YY   SEX M ☐ F ☐

b. OTHER INSURED'S DATE OF BIRTH MM | DD | YY SEX M ☐ F ☐

b. AUTO ACCIDENT?   PLACE (State) ☐ YES ☐ NO

b. EMPLOYER'S NAME OR SCHOOL NAME

c. EMPLOYER'S NAME OR SCHOOL NAME

c. OTHER ACCIDENT? ☐ YES ☐ NO

c. INSURANCE PLAN NAME OR PROGRAM NAME

d. INSURANCE PLAN NAME OR PROGRAM NAME

10d. RESERVED FOR LOCAL USE

d. IS THERE ANOTHER HEALTH BENEFIT PLAN? ☐ YES ☐ NO If yes, return to and complete item 9 a – d.

READ BACK OF FORM BEFORE COMPLETING & SIGNING THIS FORM.
12. PATIENT'S OR AUTHORIZED PERSON'S SIGNATURE I authorize the release of any medical or other information necessary to process this claim. I also request payment of government benefits either to myself or to the party who accepts assignment below.

SIGNED _____ DATE _____

13. INSURED'S OR AUTHORIZED PERSON'S SIGNATURE I authorize payment of medical benefits to the undersigned physician or supplier for services described below.

SIGNED _____

PATIENT AND INSURED INFORMATION

14. DATE OF CURRENT: ILLNESS (First symptom) OR INJURY (Accident) OR PREGNANCY (LMP) MM | DD | YY

15. IF PATIENT HAS HAD SAME OR SIMILAR ILLNESS, GIVE FIRST DATE MM | DD | YY

16. DATES PATIENT UNABLE TO WORK IN CURRENT OCCUPATION FROM MM | DD | YY TO MM | DD | YY

17. NAME OF REFERRING PHYSICIAN OR OTHER SOURCE

17a. I.D. NUMBER OF REFERRING PHYSICIAN

18. HOSPITALIZATION DATES RELATED TO CURRENT SERVICES FROM MM | DD | YY TO MM | DD | YY

19. RESERVED FOR LOCAL USE

20. OUTSIDE LAB? ☐ YES ☐ NO $ CHARGES

21. DIAGNOSIS OR NATURE OF ILLNESS OR INJURY. (RELATE ITEMS 1, 2, 3, OR 4 TO ITEM 24E BY LINE)

1. ___.___   3. ___.___
2. ___.___   4. ___.___

22. MEDICAID RESUBMISSION CODE   ORIGINAL REF. NO.

23. PRIOR AUTHORIZATION NUMBER

24. A DATE(S) OF SERVICE						B Place of Service	C Type of Service	D PROCEDURES, SERVICES, OR SUPPLIES (Explain Unusual Circumstances)		E DIAGNOSIS CODE	F $ CHARGES	G DAYS OR UNITS	H EPSDT Family Plan	I EMG	J COB	K RESERVED FOR LOCAL USE
From MM	DD	YY	To MM	DD	YY			CPT/HCPCS	MODIFIER							
1																
2																
3																
4																
5																
6																

25. FEDERAL TAX I.D. NUMBER   SSN ☐ EIN ☐

26. PATIENT'S ACCOUNT NO.

27. ACCEPT ASSIGNMENT? (For govt. claims, see back) ☐ YES ☐ NO

28. TOTAL CHARGE $

29. AMOUNT PAID $

30. BALANCE DUE $

31. SIGNATURE OF PHYSICIAN OR SUPPLIER INCLUDING DEGREES OR CREDENTIALS (I certify that the statements on the reverse apply to this bill and are made a part thereof.)

SIGNED _____ DATE _____

32. NAME AND ADDRESS OF FACILITY WHERE SERVICES WERE RENDERED (If other than home or office)

33. PHYSICIAN'S, SUPPLIER'S BILLING NAME, ADDRESS, ZIP CODE & PHONE #

PIN#   GRP#

PHYSICIAN OR SUPPLIER INFORMATION

PLEASE PRINT OR TYPE

SAMPLE FORM 1500
SAMPLE FORM 1500 SAMPLE FORM 1500

107

PAUL R. STREAM, M.D., UROLOGY

456 Hospital Drive ■ Anywhere US 12345 ■ (101) 111-5555

EIN: 11-223344	SSN: 555-12-1234	MEDICARE: P1234
PIN: PS1234	GRP: PS12345	MEDICAID: PRS1234
BCBS: 12345		

Encounter Form

PATIENT INFORMATION:

Name:	Judy R. Hudnet
Address:	548 Dayton Terr.
City:	Anywhere
State:	US
Zip Code:	12345
Telephone:	(101) 333-5555
Gender:	Female
Date of Birth:	03-28-1950
Occupation:	
Employer:	Printers "R" US
Spouse's Employer:	

INSURANCE INFORMATION:

Patient Number:	12-g
Place of Service:	Office
Primary Insurance Plan:	Great West
Primary Insurance Plan ID #:	21785
Group #:	
Primary Policyholder:	Judy R. Hudnet
Policyholder Date of Birth:	03-28-1950
Relationship to Patient:	Self
Secondary Insurance Plan:	
Secondary Insurance Plan ID #:	
Secondary Policyholder:	

Patient Status   ☐ Married   ☐ Divorced   ☒ Single   ☐ Student   ☐ Other

DIAGNOSIS INFORMATION

Diagnosis	Code	Diagnosis	Code
1. Incontinence of urine	788.30	5.	
2. Polyuria	788.42	6.	
3.		7.	
4.		8.	

PROCEDURE INFORMATION

Description of Procedure or Service	Date	Code	Charge
1. Office consultation level III	05-12-YYYY	99243	$85.00
2. Urinalysis, with microscopy	05-12-YYYY	81001	10.00
3.			
4.			
5.			

SPECIAL NOTES:

Referring physician: Donald L. Givings, M.D., UPIN/SSN: 123-12-1234
Patient to be scheduled at St. John's Hospital for surgery.
Prior authorization #29704 / Onset of symptoms 4/23/YYYY

PLEASE
DO NOT
STAPLE
IN THIS
AREA

CARRIER

| | PICA | | | |

HEALTH INSURANCE CLAIM FORM

PICA

| | | |

1.
MEDICARE ☐ (Medicare #) MEDICAID ☐ (Medicaid #) CHAMPUS ☐ (Sponsor's SSN) CHAMPVA ☐ (VA File #) GROUP HEALTH PLAN ☐ (SSN or ID) FECA BLK LUNG ☐ (SSN) OTHER ☐ (ID)

1a. INSURED'S I.D. NUMBER   (FOR PROGRAM IN ITEM 1)

2. PATIENT'S NAME (Last Name, First Name, Middle Initial)

3. PATIENT'S BIRTH DATE MM │ DD │ YY   SEX   M ☐   F ☐

4. INSURED'S NAME (Last Name, First Name, Middle Initial)

5. PATIENT'S ADDRESS (No. Street)

6. PATIENT RELATIONSHIP TO INSURED   Self ☐   Spouse ☐   Child ☐   Other ☐

7. INSURED'S ADDRESS (No. Street)

CITY   STATE

8. PATIENT STATUS   Single ☐   Married ☐   Other ☐

CITY   STATE

ZIP CODE   TELEPHONE (Include Area Code) (   )

Employed ☐   Full-Time Student ☐   Part-Time Student ☐

ZIP CODE   TELEPHONE (INCLUDE AREA CODE) (   )

9. OTHER INSURED'S NAME (Last Name, First Name, Middle Initial)

10. IS PATIENT'S CONDITION RELATED TO:

11. INSURED'S POLICY GROUP OR FECA NUMBER

a. OTHER INSURED'S POLICY OR GROUP NUMBER

a. EMPLOYMENT? (CURRENT OR PREVIOUS)   YES ☐   NO ☐

a. INSURED'S DATE OF BIRTH MM │ DD │ YY   SEX   M ☐   F ☐

b. OTHER INSURED'S DATE OF BIRTH MM │ DD │ YY   SEX M ☐ F ☐

b. AUTO ACCIDENT?   PLACE (State)   YES ☐   NO ☐

b. EMPLOYER'S NAME OR SCHOOL NAME

c. EMPLOYER'S NAME OR SCHOOL NAME

c. OTHER ACCIDENT?   YES ☐   NO ☐

c. INSURANCE PLAN NAME OR PROGRAM NAME

d. INSURANCE PLAN NAME OR PROGRAM NAME

10d. RESERVED FOR LOCAL USE

d. IS THERE ANOTHER HEALTH BENEFIT PLAN?   YES ☐   NO ☐   If yes, return to and complete item 9 a – d.

READ BACK OF FORM BEFORE COMPLETING & SIGNING THIS FORM.
12. PATIENT'S OR AUTHORIZED PERSON'S SIGNATURE I authorize the release of any medical or other information necessary to process this claim. I also request payment of government benefits either to myself or to the party who accepts assignment below.

SIGNED _____   DATE _____

13. INSURED'S OR AUTHORIZED PERSON'S SIGNATURE I authorize payment of medical benefits to the undersigned physician or supplier for services described below.

SIGNED _____

PATIENT AND INSURED INFORMATION

14. DATE OF CURRENT: MM │ DD │ YY   ◀ ILLNESS (First symptom) OR INJURY (Accident) OR PREGNANCY (LMP)

15. IF PATIENT HAS HAD SAME OR SIMILAR ILLNESS, GIVE FIRST DATE MM │ DD │ YY

16. DATES PATIENT UNABLE TO WORK IN CURRENT OCCUPATION MM │ DD │ YY   FROM   TO   MM │ DD │ YY

17. NAME OF REFERRING PHYSICIAN OR OTHER SOURCE

17a. I.D. NUMBER OF REFERRING PHYSICIAN

18. HOSPITALIZATION DATES RELATED TO CURRENT SERVICES MM │ DD │ YY   FROM   TO   MM │ DD │ YY

19. RESERVED FOR LOCAL USE

20. OUTSIDE LAB?   YES ☐   NO ☐ $ CHARGES

21. DIAGNOSIS OR NATURE OF ILLNESS OR INJURY. (RELATE ITEMS 1, 2, 3, OR 4 TO ITEM 24E BY LINE)

1. └___ . __   3. └___ . __

2. └___ . __   4. └___ . __

22. MEDICAID RESUBMISSION CODE   ORIGINAL REF. NO.

23. PRIOR AUTHORIZATION NUMBER

24. A DATE(S) OF SERVICE						B Place of Service	C Type of Service	D PROCEDURES, SERVICES, OR SUPPLIES (Explain Unusual Circumstances) CPT/HCPCS │ MODIFIER	E DIAGNOSIS CODE	F $ CHARGES	G DAYS OR UNITS	H EPSDT Family Plan	I EMG	J COB	K RESERVED FOR LOCAL USE
From MM │ DD │ YY			To MM │ DD │ YY												
1															
2															
3															
4															
5															
6															

25. FEDERAL TAX I.D. NUMBER   SSN ☐ EIN ☐

26. PATIENT'S ACCOUNT NO.

27. ACCEPT ASSIGNMENT? (For govt. claims, see back)   YES ☐   NO ☐

28. TOTAL CHARGE $

29. AMOUNT PAID $

30. BALANCE DUE $

31. SIGNATURE OF PHYSICIAN OR SUPPLIER INCLUDING DEGREES OR CREDENTIALS (I certify that the statements on the reverse apply to this bill and are made a part thereof.)

SIGNED _____   DATE _____

32. NAME AND ADDRESS OF FACILITY WHERE SERVICES WERE RENDERED (If other than home or office)

33. PHYSICIAN'S, SUPPLIER'S BILLING NAME, ADDRESS, ZIP CODE & PHONE #

PIN#   GRP#

PHYSICIAN OR SUPPLIER INFORMATION

PLEASE PRINT OR TYPE

SAMPLE FORM 1500
SAMPLE FORM 1500 SAMPLE FORM 1500

PAUL R. STREAM, M.D., UROLOGY

456 Hospital Drive ■ Anywhere US 12345 ■ (101) 111-5555

EIN: 11-223344	SSN: 555-12-1234	MEDICARE: P1234
PIN: PS1234	GRP: PS12345	MEDICAID: PRS1234
BCBS: 12345		

Encounter Form

PATIENT INFORMATION:

Name:	Judy R. Hudnet
Address:	548 Dayton Terr.
City:	Anywhere
State:	US
Zip Code:	12345
Telephone:	(101) 333-5555
Gender:	Female
Date of Birth:	03-28-1950
Occupation:	
Employer:	Printers "R" US
Spouse's Employer:	

INSURANCE INFORMATION:

Patient Number:	12-h
Place of Service:	St. John's Hospital (Outpatient)
Primary Insurance Plan:	Great West
Primary Insurance Plan ID #:	21785
Group #:	
Primary Policyholder:	Judy R. Hudnet
Policyholder Date of Birth:	03-28-1950
Relationship to Patient:	Self
Secondary Insurance Plan:	
Secondary Insurance Plan ID #:	
Secondary Policyholder:	

Patient Status ☐ Married ☐ Divorced ☒ Single ☐ Student ☐ Other

DIAGNOSIS INFORMATION

Diagnosis	Code	Diagnosis	Code
1. Bladder tumor, anterior wall	239.4	5.	
2.		6.	
3.		7.	
4.		8.	

PROCEDURE INFORMATION

Description of Procedure or Service	Date	Code	Charge
1. Cystourethroscopy w/ fulgration of bladder tumor	05-19-YYYY	52235	$1200.00
2.			
3.			
4.			
5.			

SPECIAL NOTES:

Referring physician: Donald L. Givings, M.D., UPIN/SSN: 123-12-1234
Prior Authorization Number: 29948

PLEASE
DO NOT
STAPLE
IN THIS
AREA

CARRIER

[ ][ ] PICA

HEALTH INSURANCE CLAIM FORM   PICA [ ][ ][ ]

1. MEDICARE   MEDICAID   CHAMPUS   CHAMPVA   GROUP HEALTH PLAN   FECA BLK LUNG   OTHER
    [ ] (Medicare #)   [ ] (Medicaid #)   [ ] (Sponsor's SSN)   [ ] (VA File #)   [ ] (SSN or ID)   [ ] (SSN)   [ ] (ID)

1a. INSURED'S I.D. NUMBER   (FOR PROGRAM IN ITEM 1)

2. PATIENT'S NAME (Last Name, First Name, Middle Initial)

3. PATIENT'S BIRTH DATE   MM   DD   YY   SEX   M [ ]   F [ ]

4. INSURED'S NAME (Last Name, First Name, Middle Initial)

5. PATIENT'S ADDRESS (No. Street)

6. PATIENT RELATIONSHIP TO INSURED
    Self [ ]   Spouse [ ]   Child [ ]   Other [ ]

7. INSURED'S ADDRESS (No. Street)

CITY   STATE

8. PATIENT STATUS
    Single [ ]   Married [ ]   Other [ ]
    Employed [ ]   Full-Time Student [ ]   Part-Time Student [ ]

CITY   STATE

ZIP CODE   TELEPHONE (Include Area Code)
              (   )

ZIP CODE   TELEPHONE (INCLUDE AREA CODE)
              (   )

9. OTHER INSURED'S NAME (Last Name, First Name, Middle Initial)

10. IS PATIENT'S CONDITION RELATED TO:

11. INSURED'S POLICY GROUP OR FECA NUMBER

a. OTHER INSURED'S POLICY OR GROUP NUMBER

a. EMPLOYMENT? (CURRENT OR PREVIOUS)
    [ ] YES   [ ] NO

a. INSURED'S DATE OF BIRTH   MM   DD   YY   SEX   M [ ]   F [ ]

b. OTHER INSURED'S DATE OF BIRTH   MM   DD   YY   SEX   M [ ]   F [ ]

b. AUTO ACCIDENT?   PLACE (State)
    [ ] YES   [ ] NO

b. EMPLOYER'S NAME OR SCHOOL NAME

c. EMPLOYER'S NAME OR SCHOOL NAME

c. OTHER ACCIDENT?
    [ ] YES   [ ] NO

c. INSURANCE PLAN NAME OR PROGRAM NAME

d. INSURANCE PLAN NAME OR PROGRAM NAME

10d. RESERVED FOR LOCAL USE

d. IS THERE ANOTHER HEALTH BENEFIT PLAN?
    [ ] YES   [ ] NO   If yes, return to and complete item 9 a – d.

READ BACK OF FORM BEFORE COMPLETING & SIGNING THIS FORM.
12. PATIENT'S OR AUTHORIZED PERSON'S SIGNATURE I authorize the release of any medical or other information necessary to process this claim. I also request payment of government benefits either to myself or to the party who accepts assignment below.

SIGNED _____   DATE _____

13. INSURED'S OR AUTHORIZED PERSON'S SIGNATURE I authorize payment of medical benefits to the undersigned physician or supplier for services described below.

SIGNED _____

PATIENT AND INSURED INFORMATION

14. DATE OF CURRENT: ILLNESS (First symptom) OR   MM   DD   YY
     INJURY (Accident) OR
     PREGNANCY (LMP)

15. IF PATIENT HAS HAD SAME OR SIMILAR ILLNESS.
     GIVE FIRST DATE   MM   DD   YY

16. DATES PATIENT UNABLE TO WORK IN CURRENT OCCUPATION
     MM   DD   YY   MM   DD   YY
     FROM   TO

17. NAME OF REFERRING PHYSICIAN OR OTHER SOURCE

17a. I.D. NUMBER OF REFERRING PHYSICIAN

18. HOSPITALIZATION DATES RELATED TO CURRENT SERVICES
     MM   DD   YY   MM   DD   YY
     FROM   TO

19. RESERVED FOR LOCAL USE

20. OUTSIDE LAB? $ CHARGES
     [ ] YES   [ ] NO

21. DIAGNOSIS OR NATURE OF ILLNESS OR INJURY. (RELATE ITEMS 1, 2, 3, OR 4 TO ITEM 24E BY LINE)

1. |___.___| 3. |___.___|

2. |___.___| 4. |___.___|

22. MEDICAID RESUBMISSION CODE   ORIGINAL REF. NO.

23. PRIOR AUTHORIZATION NUMBER

24. A DATE(S) OF SERVICE					B Place of Service	C Type of Service	D PROCEDURES, SERVICES, OR SUPPLIES (Explain Unusual Circumstances) CPT/HCPCS	MODIFIER	E DIAGNOSIS CODE	F $ CHARGES	G DAYS OR UNITS	H EPSDT Family Plan	I EMG	J COB	K RESERVED FOR LOCAL USE
From			To													
MM	DD	YY	MM	DD	YY											
1																
2																
3																
4																
5																
6																

25. FEDERAL TAX I.D. NUMBER   SSN [ ]   EIN [ ]

26. PATIENT'S ACCOUNT NO.

27. ACCEPT ASSIGNMENT? (For govt. claims, see back)   [ ] YES   [ ] NO

28. TOTAL CHARGE $

29. AMOUNT PAID $

30. BALANCE DUE $

31. SIGNATURE OF PHYSICIAN OR SUPPLIER INCLUDING DEGREES OR CREDENTIALS
     (I certify that the statements on the reverse apply to this bill and are made a part thereof.)

SIGNED _____   DATE _____

32. NAME AND ADDRESS OF FACILITY WHERE SERVICES WERE RENDERED (If other than home or office)

33. PHYSICIAN'S, SUPPLIER'S BILLING NAME, ADDRESS, ZIP CODE & PHONE #

PIN#   GRP#

PHYSICIAN OR SUPPLIER INFORMATION

(SAMPLE ONLY - NOT APPROVED FOR USE)

PLEASE PRINT OR TYPE

SAMPLE FORM 1500
SAMPLE FORM 1500   SAMPLE FORM 1500

111

DONALD L. GIVINGS, M.D.

11350 Medical Drive ■ Anywhere US 12345 ■ (101) 111-5555

EIN: 11-123456   SSN: 123-12-1234   MEDICARE: D1234
PIN: DG1234   GRP DG: 12345   MEDICAID: DLG1234
BCBS: 12345

Encounter Form

PATIENT INFORMATION:

Name:	Ben A. Hanson
Address:	632 Greenvalley Ct.
City:	Anywhere
State:	US
Zip Code:	12345
Telephone:	(101) 223-5555
Gender:	Male
Date of Birth:	08-09-1975
Occupation:	
Employer:	Ace Plumbing Service
Spouse's Employer:	Dew Drop Inn

INSURANCE INFORMATION:

Patient Number:	12-i
Place of Service:	Office
Primary Insurance Plan:	Guardian
Primary Insurance Plan ID #:	334-55-8686
Group #:	4596
Primary Policyholder:	Ben A. Hanson
Policyholder Date of Birth:	08-09-1975
Relationship to Patient:	Self
Secondary Insurance Plan:	Liberty Mutual
Secondary Insurance Plan ID #:	334-88-7788 GR# DD12
Secondary Policyholder:	Joy M. Hanson
Secondary Policyholder DOB:	10-10-1977

Patient Status   ☒ Married   ☐ Divorced   ☐ Single   ☐ Student   ☐ Other

DIAGNOSIS INFORMATION

Diagnosis	Code	Diagnosis	Code
1. Painful respiration	786.52	5.	
2. Chest tightness	786.59	6.	
3.		7.	
4.		8.	

PROCEDURE INFORMATION

Description of Procedure or Service	Date	Code	Charge
1. Est. patient OV level III	09-03-YYYY	99213	$75.00
2. EKG	09-03-YYYY	93000	50.00
3.			
4.			
5.			

SPECIAL NOTES:

Return visit: 2 weeks after seeing Dr. Hart

Case Study 12-i Primary

PLEASE
DO NOT
STAPLE
IN THIS
AREA

CARRIER

| | PICA | | **HEALTH INSURANCE CLAIM FORM** | PICA | | | |

HEALTH INSURANCE CLAIM FORM

1.	MEDICARE	MEDICAID	CHAMPUS	CHAMPVA	GROUP HEALTH PLAN	FECA BLK LUNG	OTHER	1a. INSURED'S I.D. NUMBER (FOR PROGRAM IN ITEM 1)
	(Medicare #)	(Medicaid #)	(Sponsor's SSN)	(VA File #)	(SSN or ID)	(SSN)	(ID)	

2. PATIENT'S NAME (Last Name, First Name, Middle Initial)

3. PATIENT'S BIRTH DATE MM DD YY   SEX M F

4. INSURED'S NAME (Last Name, First Name, Middle Initial)

5. PATIENT'S ADDRESS (No. Street)

6. PATIENT RELATIONSHIP TO INSURED   Self Spouse Child Other

7. INSURED'S ADDRESS (No. Street)

CITY   STATE

8. PATIENT STATUS   Single Married Other

CITY   STATE

ZIP CODE   TELEPHONE (Include Area Code) (   )

Employed   Full-Time Student   Part-Time Student

ZIP CODE   TELEPHONE (INCLUDE AREA CODE) (   )

9. OTHER INSURED'S NAME (Last Name, First Name, Middle Initial)

10. IS PATIENT'S CONDITION RELATED TO:

11. INSURED'S POLICY GROUP OR FECA NUMBER

a. OTHER INSURED'S POLICY OR GROUP NUMBER

a. EMPLOYMENT? (CURRENT OR PREVIOUS)   YES NO

a. INSURED'S DATE OF BIRTH MM DD YY   SEX M F

b. OTHER INSURED'S DATE OF BIRTH MM DD YY   SEX M F

b. AUTO ACCIDENT?   PLACE (State)   YES NO

b. EMPLOYER'S NAME OR SCHOOL NAME

c. EMPLOYER'S NAME OR SCHOOL NAME

c. OTHER ACCIDENT?   YES NO

c. INSURANCE PLAN NAME OR PROGRAM NAME

d. INSURANCE PLAN NAME OR PROGRAM NAME

10d. RESERVED FOR LOCAL USE

d. IS THERE ANOTHER HEALTH BENEFIT PLAN?   YES NO   If yes, return to and complete item 9 a – d.

READ BACK OF FORM BEFORE COMPLETING & SIGNING THIS FORM.
12. PATIENT'S OR AUTHORIZED PERSON'S SIGNATURE I authorize the release of any medical or other information necessary to process this claim. I also request payment of government benefits either to myself or to the party who accepts assignment below.

SIGNED _____ DATE _____

13. INSURED'S OR AUTHORIZED PERSON'S SIGNATURE I authorize payment of medical benefits to the undersigned physician or supplier for services described below.

SIGNED _____

PATIENT AND INSURED INFORMATION

14. DATE OF CURRENT: ILLNESS (First symptom) OR INJURY (Accident) OR PREGNANCY (LMP) MM DD YY

15. IF PATIENT HAS HAD SAME OR SIMILAR ILLNESS, GIVE FIRST DATE MM DD YY

16. DATES PATIENT UNABLE TO WORK IN CURRENT OCCUPATION MM DD YY FROM TO MM DD YY

17. NAME OF REFERRING PHYSICIAN OR OTHER SOURCE

17a. I.D. NUMBER OF REFERRING PHYSICIAN

18. HOSPITALIZATION DATES RELATED TO CURRENT SERVICES MM DD YY FROM TO MM DD YY

19. RESERVED FOR LOCAL USE

20. OUTSIDE LAB?   YES NO $ CHARGES

21. DIAGNOSIS OR NATURE OF ILLNESS OR INJURY. (RELATE ITEMS 1, 2, 3, OR 4 TO ITEM 24E BY LINE)
1. ___ . ___   3. ___ . ___
2. ___ . ___   4. ___ . ___

22. MEDICAID RESUBMISSION CODE   ORIGINAL REF. NO.

23. PRIOR AUTHORIZATION NUMBER

24. A DATE(S) OF SERVICE						B Place of Service	C Type of Service	D PROCEDURES, SERVICES, OR SUPPLIES (Explain Unusual Circumstances) CPT/HCPCS MODIFIER	E DIAGNOSIS CODE	F $ CHARGES	G DAYS OR UNITS	H EPSDT Family Plan	I EMG	J COB	K RESERVED FOR LOCAL USE
From MM DD YY			To MM DD YY												
1															
2															
3															
4															
5															
6															

25. FEDERAL TAX I.D. NUMBER   SSN EIN

26. PATIENT'S ACCOUNT NO.

27. ACCEPT ASSIGNMENT? (For govt. claims, see back)   YES NO

28. TOTAL CHARGE $

29. AMOUNT PAID $

30. BALANCE DUE $

31. SIGNATURE OF PHYSICIAN OR SUPPLIER INCLUDING DEGREES OR CREDENTIALS (I certify that the statements on the reverse apply to this bill and are made a part thereof.)

SIGNED _____ DATE _____

32. NAME AND ADDRESS OF FACILITY WHERE SERVICES WERE RENDERED (If other than home or office)

33. PHYSICIAN'S, SUPPLIER'S BILLING NAME, ADDRESS, ZIP CODE & PHONE #

PIN#   GRP#

PHYSICIAN OR SUPPLIER INFORMATION

PLEASE PRINT OR TYPE

SAMPLE FORM 1500
SAMPLE FORM 1500 SAMPLE FORM 1500

Case Study 12-i Secondary

(SAMPLE ONLY - NOT APPROVED FOR USE)

CARRIER

| | | PICA | | | | | **HEALTH INSURANCE CLAIM FORM** | PICA | | |

HEALTH INSURANCE CLAIM FORM

1. MEDICARE	MEDICAID	CHAMPUS	CHAMPVA	GROUP HEALTH PLAN	FECA BLK LUNG	OTHER	1a. INSURED'S I.D. NUMBER	(FOR PROGRAM IN ITEM 1)
(Medicare #)	(Medicaid #)	(Sponsor's SSN)	(VA File #)	(SSN or ID)	(SSN)	(ID)		

2. PATIENT'S NAME (Last Name, First Name, Middle Initial)

3. PATIENT'S BIRTH DATE MM DD YY   SEX M F

4. INSURED'S NAME (Last Name, First Name, Middle Initial)

5. PATIENT'S ADDRESS (No. Street)

6. PATIENT RELATIONSHIP TO INSURED
Self Spouse Child Other

7. INSURED'S ADDRESS (No. Street)

CITY   STATE

8. PATIENT STATUS
Single Married Other

CITY   STATE

ZIP CODE   TELEPHONE (Include Area Code) ( )

Employed Full-Time Student Part-Time Student

ZIP CODE   TELEPHONE (INCLUDE AREA CODE) ( )

9. OTHER INSURED'S NAME (Last Name, First Name, Middle Initial)

10. IS PATIENT'S CONDITION RELATED TO:

11. INSURED'S POLICY GROUP OR FECA NUMBER

a. OTHER INSURED'S POLICY OR GROUP NUMBER

a. EMPLOYMENT? (CURRENT OR PREVIOUS)
YES NO

a. INSURED'S DATE OF BIRTH MM DD YY   SEX M F

b. OTHER INSURED'S DATE OF BIRTH MM DD YY   SEX M F

b. AUTO ACCIDENT?   PLACE (State)
YES NO

b. EMPLOYER'S NAME OR SCHOOL NAME

c. EMPLOYER'S NAME OR SCHOOL NAME

c. OTHER ACCIDENT?
YES NO

c. INSURANCE PLAN NAME OR PROGRAM NAME

d. INSURANCE PLAN NAME OR PROGRAM NAME

10d. RESERVED FOR LOCAL USE

d. IS THERE ANOTHER HEALTH BENEFIT PLAN?
YES NO   If yes, return to and complete item 9 a – d.

READ BACK OF FORM BEFORE COMPLETING & SIGNING THIS FORM.
12. PATIENT'S OR AUTHORIZED PERSON'S SIGNATURE I authorize the release of any medical or other information necessary to process this claim. I also request payment of government benefits either to myself or to the party who accepts assignment below.

SIGNED _____ DATE _____

13. INSURED'S OR AUTHORIZED PERSON'S SIGNATURE I authorize payment of medical benefits to the undersigned physician or supplier for services described below.

SIGNED _____

PATIENT AND INSURED INFORMATION

14. DATE OF CURRENT: ILLNESS (First symptom) OR MM DD YY INJURY (Accident) OR PREGNANCY (LMP)

15. IF PATIENT HAS HAD SAME OR SIMILAR ILLNESS, GIVE FIRST DATE MM DD YY

16. DATES PATIENT UNABLE TO WORK IN CURRENT OCCUPATION MM DD YY FROM TO MM DD YY

17. NAME OF REFERRING PHYSICIAN OR OTHER SOURCE

17a. I.D. NUMBER OF REFERRING PHYSICIAN

18. HOSPITALIZATION DATES RELATED TO CURRENT SERVICES MM DD YY FROM TO MM DD YY

19. RESERVED FOR LOCAL USE

20. OUTSIDE LAB? YES NO $ CHARGES

21. DIAGNOSIS OR NATURE OF ILLNESS OR INJURY. (RELATE ITEMS 1, 2, 3, OR 4 TO ITEM 24E BY LINE)
1. ___ . ___
2. ___ . ___
3. ___ . ___
4. ___ . ___

22. MEDICAID RESUBMISSION CODE   ORIGINAL REF. NO.

23. PRIOR AUTHORIZATION NUMBER

24. A DATE(S) OF SERVICE						B Place of Service	C Type of Service	D PROCEDURES, SERVICES, OR SUPPLIES (Explain Unusual Circumstances) CPT/HCPCS MODIFIER	E DIAGNOSIS CODE	F $ CHARGES	G DAYS OR UNITS	H EPSDT Family Plan	I EMG	J COB	K RESERVED FOR LOCAL USE
From MM	DD	YY	To MM	DD	YY										
1															
2															
3															
4															
5															
6															

25. FEDERAL TAX I.D. NUMBER   SSN EIN

26. PATIENT'S ACCOUNT NO.

27. ACCEPT ASSIGNMENT? (For govt. claims, see back) YES NO

28. TOTAL CHARGE $

29. AMOUNT PAID $

30. BALANCE DUE $

31. SIGNATURE OF PHYSICIAN OR SUPPLIER INCLUDING DEGREES OR CREDENTIALS (I certify that the statements on the reverse apply to this bill and are made a part thereof.)

SIGNED _____ DATE _____

32. NAME AND ADDRESS OF FACILITY WHERE SERVICES WERE RENDERED (If other than home or office)

33. PHYSICIAN'S, SUPPLIER'S BILLING NAME, ADDRESS, ZIP CODE & PHONE #

PIN# _____ GRP# _____

PHYSICIAN OR SUPPLIER INFORMATION

(SAMPLE ONLY - NOT APPROVED FOR USE)

PLEASE PRINT OR TYPE

SAMPLE FORM 1500
SAMPLE FORM 1500 SAMPLE FORM 1500

STANLEY M. HART, M.D. CARDIOLOGY

316 Grace Way, Suite 102 ■ Anywhere US 12345 ■ (101) 111-5555

Encounter Form

EIN: 11-785678	SSN: 133-12-1254	MEDICARE: S1234
PIN: SH1234	GRP: SH12345	MEDICAID: SMH1234
BCBS: 12388		

PATIENT INFORMATION:

Name:	Ben A. Hanson
Address:	632 Greenvalley Ct.
City:	Anywhere
State:	US
Zip Code:	12345
Telephone:	(101) 223-5555
Gender:	Male
Date of Birth:	08-09-1975
Occupation:	
Employer:	Ace Plumbing Service
Spouse's Employer:	Dew Drop Inn

INSURANCE INFORMATION:

Patient Number:	12-j
Place of Service:	Office
Primary Insurance Plan:	Guardian
Primary Insurance Plan ID #:	334-55-8686
Group #:	4596
Primary Policyholder:	Ben A. Hanson
Policyholder Date of Birth:	08-09-1975
Relationship to Patient:	Self
Secondary Insurance Plan:	Liberty Mutual
Secondary Insurance Plan ID #:	334-88-7788 GR# DD12
Secondary Policyholder:	Joy M. Hanson
Secondary Policyholder DOB:	10-10-1977

Patient Status ☒ Married ☐ Divorced ☐ Single ☐ Student ☐ Other

DIAGNOSIS INFORMATION

Diagnosis	Code	Diagnosis	Code
1. Painful respiration	786.52	5.	
2. Chest tightness	786.59	6.	
3. Abnormal chest sounds	786.7	7.	
4.		8.	

PROCEDURE INFORMATION

Description of Procedure or Service	Date	Code	Charge
1. Office consult level II	09-04-YYYY	99242	$ 75.00
2. Cardiovascular stress test, with interpretation and report	09-04-YYYY	93015	150.00
3.			
4.			
5.			

SPECIAL NOTES:
Referring physician: Donald L. Givings, M.D.
Return visit: PRN
Prior authorization #659427

Case Study 12-j Primary

CARRIER

| | PICA | | **HEALTH INSURANCE CLAIM FORM** | PICA | | |

1. MEDICARE	MEDICAID	CHAMPUS	CHAMPVA	GROUP HEALTH PLAN	FECA BLK LUNG	OTHER	1a. INSURED'S I.D. NUMBER	(FOR PROGRAM IN ITEM 1)
(Medicare #)	(Medicaid #)	(Sponsor's SSN)	(VA File #)	(SSN or ID)	(SSN)	(ID)		

2. PATIENT'S NAME (Last Name, First Name, Middle Initial)

3. PATIENT'S BIRTH DATE MM | DD | YY   SEX   M □ F □

4. INSURED'S NAME (Last Name, First Name, Middle Initial)

5. PATIENT'S ADDRESS (No. Street)

6. PATIENT RELATIONSHIP TO INSURED
Self □ Spouse □ Child □ Other □

7. INSURED'S ADDRESS (No. Street)

CITY   STATE

8. PATIENT STATUS
Single □ Married □ Other □

CITY   STATE

ZIP CODE   TELEPHONE (Include Area Code) (   )

Employed □ Full-Time Student □ Part-Time Student □

ZIP CODE   TELEPHONE (INCLUDE AREA CODE) (   )

9. OTHER INSURED'S NAME (Last Name, First Name, Middle Initial)

10. IS PATIENT'S CONDITION RELATED TO:

11. INSURED'S POLICY GROUP OR FECA NUMBER

a. OTHER INSURED'S POLICY OR GROUP NUMBER

a. EMPLOYMENT? (CURRENT OR PREVIOUS)
□ YES □ NO

a. INSURED'S DATE OF BIRTH MM | DD | YY   SEX   M □ F □

b. OTHER INSURED'S DATE OF BIRTH MM | DD | YY   SEX   M □ F □

b. AUTO ACCIDENT?   PLACE (State)
□ YES □ NO

b. EMPLOYER'S NAME OR SCHOOL NAME

c. EMPLOYER'S NAME OR SCHOOL NAME

c. OTHER ACCIDENT?
□ YES □ NO

c. INSURANCE PLAN NAME OR PROGRAM NAME

d. INSURANCE PLAN NAME OR PROGRAM NAME

10d. RESERVED FOR LOCAL USE

d. IS THERE ANOTHER HEALTH BENEFIT PLAN?
□ YES □ NO If yes, return to and complete item 9 a – d.

READ BACK OF FORM BEFORE COMPLETING & SIGNING THIS FORM.
12. PATIENT'S OR AUTHORIZED PERSON'S SIGNATURE I authorize the release of any medical or other information necessary to process this claim. I also request payment of government benefits either to myself or to the party who accepts assignment below.

SIGNED _____   DATE _____

13. INSURED'S OR AUTHORIZED PERSON'S SIGNATURE I authorize payment of medical benefits to the undersigned physician or supplier for services described below.

SIGNED _____

PATIENT AND INSURED INFORMATION

14. DATE OF CURRENT: MM | DD | YY   ILLNESS (First symptom) OR INJURY (Accident) OR PREGNANCY (LMP)

15. IF PATIENT HAS HAD SAME OR SIMILAR ILLNESS, GIVE FIRST DATE MM | DD | YY

16. DATES PATIENT UNABLE TO WORK IN CURRENT OCCUPATION MM | DD | YY FROM   TO   MM | DD | YY

17. NAME OF REFERRING PHYSICIAN OR OTHER SOURCE

17a. I.D. NUMBER OF REFERRING PHYSICIAN

18. HOSPITALIZATION DATES RELATED TO CURRENT SERVICES MM | DD | YY FROM   TO   MM | DD | YY

19. RESERVED FOR LOCAL USE

20. OUTSIDE LAB? $ CHARGES
□ YES □ NO

21. DIAGNOSIS OR NATURE OF ILLNESS OR INJURY. (RELATE ITEMS 1, 2, 3, OR 4 TO ITEM 24E BY LINE)
1. _____ . _____   3. _____ . _____
2. _____ . _____   4. _____ . _____

22. MEDICAID RESUBMISSION CODE   ORIGINAL REF. NO.

23. PRIOR AUTHORIZATION NUMBER

24. A DATE(S) OF SERVICE From MM DD YY To MM DD YY	B Place of Service	C Type of Service	D PROCEDURES, SERVICES, OR SUPPLIES (Explain Unusual Circumstances) CPT/HCPCS	MODIFIER	E DIAGNOSIS CODE	F $ CHARGES	G DAYS OR UNITS	H EPSDT Family Plan	I EMG	J COB	K RESERVED FOR LOCAL USE
1											
2											
3											
4											
5											
6											

25. FEDERAL TAX I.D. NUMBER   SSN □ EIN □

26. PATIENT'S ACCOUNT NO.

27. ACCEPT ASSIGNMENT? (For govt. claims, see back) □ YES □ NO

28. TOTAL CHARGE $

29. AMOUNT PAID $

30. BALANCE DUE $

31. SIGNATURE OF PHYSICIAN OR SUPPLIER INCLUDING DEGREES OR CREDENTIALS (I certify that the statements on the reverse apply to this bill and are made a part thereof.)

SIGNED   DATE

32. NAME AND ADDRESS OF FACILITY WHERE SERVICES WERE RENDERED (If other than home or office)

33. PHYSICIAN'S, SUPPLIER'S BILLING NAME, ADDRESS, ZIP CODE & PHONE #

PIN#   GRP#

PHYSICIAN OR SUPPLIER INFORMATION

PLEASE PRINT OR TYPE   SAMPLE FORM 1500
SAMPLE FORM 1500 SAMPLE FORM 1500

PLEASE
DO NOT
STAPLE
IN THIS
AREA

(SAMPLE ONLY - NOT APPROVED FOR USE)

CARRIER

| | PICA

HEALTH INSURANCE CLAIM FORM PICA | |

1. MEDICARE MEDICAID CHAMPUS CHAMPVA GROUP HEALTH PLAN FECA BLK LUNG OTHER	1a. INSURED'S I.D. NUMBER (FOR PROGRAM IN ITEM 1)

[ ] (Medicare #) [ ] (Medicaid #) [ ] (Sponsor's SSN) [ ] (VA File #) [ ] (SSN or ID) [ ] (SSN) [ ] (ID)

2. PATIENT'S NAME (Last Name, First Name, Middle Initial)

3. PATIENT'S BIRTH DATE MM DD YY   SEX   M [ ]   F [ ]

4. INSURED'S NAME (Last Name, First Name, Middle Initial)

5. PATIENT'S ADDRESS (No. Street)

6. PATIENT RELATIONSHIP TO INSURED   Self [ ]   Spouse [ ]   Child [ ]   Other [ ]

7. INSURED'S ADDRESS (No. Street)

CITY   STATE

8. PATIENT STATUS   Single [ ]   Married [ ]   Other [ ]   Employed [ ]   Full-Time Student [ ]   Part-Time Student [ ]

CITY   STATE

ZIP CODE   TELEPHONE (Include Area Code) (   )

ZIP CODE   TELEPHONE (INCLUDE AREA CODE) (   )

9. OTHER INSURED'S NAME (Last Name, First Name, Middle Initial)

10. IS PATIENT'S CONDITION RELATED TO:

11. INSURED'S POLICY GROUP OR FECA NUMBER

a. OTHER INSURED'S POLICY OR GROUP NUMBER

a. EMPLOYMENT? (CURRENT OR PREVIOUS) [ ] YES [ ] NO

a. INSURED'S DATE OF BIRTH MM DD YY   SEX M [ ] F [ ]

b. OTHER INSURED'S DATE OF BIRTH MM DD YY   SEX M [ ] F [ ]

b. AUTO ACCIDENT?   PLACE (State) [ ] YES [ ] NO

b. EMPLOYER'S NAME OR SCHOOL NAME

c. EMPLOYER'S NAME OR SCHOOL NAME

c. OTHER ACCIDENT? [ ] YES [ ] NO

c. INSURANCE PLAN NAME OR PROGRAM NAME

d. INSURANCE PLAN NAME OR PROGRAM NAME

10d. RESERVED FOR LOCAL USE

d. IS THERE ANOTHER HEALTH BENEFIT PLAN? [ ] YES [ ] NO   If yes, return to and complete item 9 a – d.

READ BACK OF FORM BEFORE COMPLETING & SIGNING THIS FORM.
12. PATIENT'S OR AUTHORIZED PERSON'S SIGNATURE I authorize the release of any medical or other information necessary to process this claim. I also request payment of government benefits either to myself or to the party who accepts assignment below.

SIGNED _____   DATE _____

13. INSURED'S OR AUTHORIZED PERSON'S SIGNATURE I authorize payment of medical benefits to the undersigned physician or supplier for services described below.

SIGNED _____

PATIENT AND INSURED INFORMATION

14. DATE OF CURRENT: MM DD YY ILLNESS (First symptom) OR INJURY (Accident) OR PREGNANCY (LMP)

15. IF PATIENT HAS HAD SAME OR SIMILAR ILLNESS, GIVE FIRST DATE MM DD YY

16. DATES PATIENT UNABLE TO WORK IN CURRENT OCCUPATION MM DD YY   FROM   TO MM DD YY

17. NAME OF REFERRING PHYSICIAN OR OTHER SOURCE

17a. I.D. NUMBER OF REFERRING PHYSICIAN

18. HOSPITALIZATION DATES RELATED TO CURRENT SERVICES MM DD YY   FROM   TO MM DD YY

19. RESERVED FOR LOCAL USE

20. OUTSIDE LAB? [ ] YES [ ] NO $ CHARGES

21. DIAGNOSIS OR NATURE OF ILLNESS OR INJURY. (RELATE ITEMS 1, 2, 3, OR 4 TO ITEM 24E BY LINE)

1. |___.___| 3. |___.___|

2. |___.___| 4. |___.___|

22. MEDICAID RESUBMISSION CODE   ORIGINAL REF. NO.

23. PRIOR AUTHORIZATION NUMBER

24. A. DATE(S) OF SERVICE From MM DD YY To MM DD YY	B. Place of Service	C. Type of Service	D. PROCEDURES, SERVICES, OR SUPPLIES (Explain Unusual Circumstances) CPT/HCPCS MODIFIER	E. DIAGNOSIS CODE	F. $ CHARGES	G. DAYS OR UNITS	H. EPSDT Family Plan	I. EMG	J. COB	K. RESERVED FOR LOCAL USE
1										
2										
3										
4										
5										
6										

25. FEDERAL TAX I.D. NUMBER   SSN [ ] EIN [ ]

26. PATIENT'S ACCOUNT NO.

27. ACCEPT ASSIGNMENT? (For govt. claims, see back) [ ] YES [ ] NO

28. TOTAL CHARGE $

29. AMOUNT PAID $

30. BALANCE DUE $

31. SIGNATURE OF PHYSICIAN OR SUPPLIER INCLUDING DEGREES OR CREDENTIALS (I certify that the statements on the reverse apply to this bill and are made a part thereof.)

SIGNED _____   DATE _____

32. NAME AND ADDRESS OF FACILITY WHERE SERVICES WERE RENDERED (If other than home or office)

33. PHYSICIAN'S, SUPPLIER'S BILLING NAME, ADDRESS, ZIP CODE & PHONE #

PIN#   GRP#

PHYSICIAN OR SUPPLIER INFORMATION

(SAMPLE ONLY - NOT APPROVED FOR USE)

PLEASE PRINT OR TYPE

SAMPLE FORM 1500
SAMPLE FORM 1500 SAMPLE FORM 1500

Chapter 13
Blue Cross and Blue Shield Plans

HISTORY OF BLUE CROSS AND BLUE SHIELD

1. The forerunner of what is known today as the Blue Cross plan began when Baylor University Hospital approached ___. (Circle the correct answer.)
    a. doctors
    b. teachers
    c. hospital employees
    d. none of the above

2. The Blue Cross Association grew out of what need? (Circle the correct answer.)
    a. additional national coordination among plans
    b. additional member hospitals
    c. additional participating physicians
    d. all of the above

3. The Blue Shield plans began as a resolution passed by the House of Delegates at a meeting of the ___. (Circle the correct answer.)
    a. Blue Cross Association
    b. American Hospital Association
    c. American Medical Association
    d. none of the above

4. The first Blue Shield plan was formed in 1939 and was called ___. (Circle the correct answer.)
    a. California Physicians' Service
    b. Blue Shield of California
    c. Blue Cross Association
    d. none of the above

5. The Blue Shield design was first used as a trademark by the ___. (Circle the correct answer.)
    a. California Physicians' Service
    b. Buffalo, New York plan
    c. American Medical Association
    d. none of the above

6. Blue Cross plans originally covered only _____ bills.

7. Blue Shield plans were set up to cover fees for _____ services.

8. List four functions of the Blue Cross and Blue Shield Association (BCBSA).

   a. _____

   b. _____

   c. _____

   d. _____

9. BCBSA is the registered owner of the BC and BS _____ .

10. The "Blues" were pioneers in ____ prepaid health care. (Circle the correct answer.)

    a. profit

    b. nonprofit

    c. premium

    d. all of the above

11. The "Blues" agreed to perform which of the following service(s)? (Circle the correct answer.)

    a. make prompt, direct payments of claims

    b. maintain regional professional representatives to assist participating providers with claim problems

    c. provide educational seminars, workshops, billing manuals, and newsletters

    d. all of the above

12. Define *nonprofit corporation.* _____

    _____

13. Define *for-profit corporation.* _____

    _____

14. BCBS plans are forbidden by state law from _____ _____
    for an individual because he or she is in poor health or if BCBS payments to providers have far exceed-
    ed the average.

15. Describe when a BCBS policy can be canceled or an individual disenrolled. _____

    _____

    _____

16. BCBS plans must obtain approval for any rate increase or benefit change from the ____. (Circle the
    correct answer.)

    a. state insurance commissioner

    b. American Hospital Association

    c. American Medical Association

    d. all of the above

17. When a health care provider elects to become a participating provider (PAR), that provider enters into
    a contract with a BCBS corporation and agrees to ____. (Circle the correct answer.)

    a. submit insurance claims for all BCBS subscribers

    b. write off the difference between the amount charged and the approved fee

    c. bill patients for only the deductible and copay/coinsurance amounts and the full fee for any
       uncovered service

    d. all of the above

18. List five services BCBS agrees to provide to PAR providers.

a. _____

b. _____

c. _____

d. _____

e. _____

19. Nonparticipating providers ___. (Circle the correct answer.)

a. have not signed participating provider contracts

b. expect to be paid the full fee charged for services rendered

c. understand the insurance company will send payment for claims directly to the patient

d. all of the above

Critical Thinking

20. Write a paragraph describing the basic differences between a participating provider and a nonparticipating provider.

_____

_____

_____

_____

_____

BLUE CROSS BLUE SHIELD PLANS

21. Name two types of coverage into which BCBS fee-for-service contracts are divided.

a. _____

b. _____

22. List seven benefits routinely included under BCBS basic coverage.

a. _____

b. _____

c. _____

d. _____

e. _____

f. _____

g. _____

23. List seven benefits routinely included under the BCBS major medical coverage.

a. _____

b. _____

c. _____

d. _____

e. _____

f. _____

g. _____

24. Major Medical services are usually subject to patient _____ and _____
requirements.

Critical Thinking

25. Write a paragraph describing riders; include special accidental injury riders and medical emergency care riders.

_____

_____

_____

_____

_____

_____

_____

26. For each item, enter **T** for a true statement or **F** for a false statement on the line provided.

_____ a. BCBS indemnity coverage offers choice and flexibility to subscribers.

_____ b. Managed care is a health care delivery system that provides health care through a network of physicians, veterinarians, and other health care providers.

_____ c. Members who have an EPO are required to select a PCP.

_____ d. All BCBS corporations now offer at least one HMO.

_____ e. POS subscribers are not required to choose a PCP.

_____ f. The PCP assumes responsibility for coordinating subscriber and dependent medical care.

_____ g. The PCP is often referred to as the gatekeeper of the patient's medical care.

_____ h. When POS subscribers go outside the network for health care, costs are usually lower.

_____ i. After providing care to the BlueCard® subscriber, the provider submits the claim to the local Blue plan for reimbursement.

27. BlueCard® subscribers have identification numbers that begin with a(n) _____. (Circle the correct answer.)
    a. alpha prefix
    b. asterisk as a prefix
    c. numerical prefix
    d. none of the above

28. BlueCard® PPO provides subscribers with access to a large national health care network of participating _____. (Circle the correct answer.)
    a. hospitals
    b. physicians
    c. specialists
    d. all of the above

29. Which program allows subscribers who travel or live abroad to receive covered services from a network of hospitals and doctors around the world? (Circle the correct answer.)

    a. BlueCard® Program

    b. BlueCard® Worldwide

    c. BlueCard® PPO

    d. all of the above

30. FEP provides benefits to over nine million _____ enrollees and dependents. (Circle the correct answer.)

    a. civil

    b. federal

    c. state

    d. all of the above

31. FEP cards contain the phrase _____-_____ _____ _____ _____.

32. FEP enrollees have identification numbers that begin with the letter _____ followed by eight numeric digits.

33. The three-digit enrollment code located on the front of the FEP card should be entered as the _____ ID number on BCBS claims.

34. BCBS corporations offer several federally-designed and regulated Medicare Supplemental plans which augment the Medicare program by paying for Medicare _____ and _____.

BILLING INFORMATION SUMMARY

35. The deadline for filing claims is customarily ___ from the date of service, unless otherwise specified in the subscriber's or provider's contracts. (Circle the correct answer.)

    a. five years

    b. 90 days

    c. one year

    d. none of the above

36. Most payers currently accept the ___. (Circle the correct answer.)

    a. BCBS claim

    b. CMS-1500 claim

    c. CMS-1450 claim

    d. none of the above

37. The transmittal notice sent to PAR and PPN providers clearly states the patient's ___.
(Circle the correct answer.)

    a. coinsurance

    b. deductible

    c. copayment

    d. all of the above

38. Participating providers must accept the allowable rate on all _____ _____.

39. NonPARs may collect the _____ _____ from the patient. BCBS payments are then sent directly to the _____ .

40. All claims filed by participating providers qualify for an assignment of benefits to the _____ .

41. For each item, enter **T** for a true statement or **F** for a false statement on the line provided.

_____ a. You need to retain a current photocopy of only the front of all patient ID cards.

_____ b. Claims for BlueCard® patients with more than one insurance policy must be billed directly to the plan from which the program originated.

_____ c. NonPARs must bill the patient's plan for all non-national account patients with BlueCards®.

_____ d. Rebill claims not paid within 60 days.

_____ e. Some mental health claims are forwarded to a third-party administrator specializing in mental health case management.

Know Your Acronyms

42. Define the following acronyms:

a. AHA _____

b. BC _____

c. BCBS _____

d. BS _____

e. BCBSA _____

f. DME _____

g. EOB _____

h. EPO _____

i. FEHBP _____

j. FEP _____

k. HMO _____

l. OPAP _____

m. PAR _____

n. PCP _____

o. POS _____

p. PPN _____

q. SSO _____

r. TPA _____

s. UCR _____

EXERCISES

43. Complete Case Studies 13-a through 13-h using the blank claims provided. Follow the step-by-step instructions in the textbook to properly complete each claim. If a patient has secondary coverage, complete an additional claim using secondary directions from the textbook. You may choose to use a pencil so corrections can be made.

DONALD L. GIVINGS, M.D.

11350 Medical Drive ■ Anywhere US 12345 ■ (101) 111-5555

EIN: 11-123456	SSN: 123-12-1234	MEDICARE: D1234
PIN: DG1234	GRP: DG12345	MEDICAID: DLG1234
BCBS: 12345		

Encounter Form

PATIENT INFORMATION:

Name:	Monty L. Booker
Address:	47 Snowflake Road
City:	Anywhere
State:	US
Zip Code:	12345
Telephone:	(101) 333-5555
Gender:	Male
Date of Birth:	12-25-1966
Occupation:	
Employer:	Atlanta Publisher
Spouse's Employer:	

INSURANCE INFORMATION:

Patient Number:	13-a
Place of Service:	Office
Primary Insurance Plan:	BCBS US
Primary Insurance Plan ID #:	NXY 678-22-3434
Group #:	678
Primary Policyholder:	Monty L. Booker
Policyholder Date of Birth:	12-25-1966
Relationship to Patient:	Self
Secondary Insurance Plan:	
Secondary Insurance Plan ID #:	
Secondary Policyholder:	

Patient Status [X] Married ☐ Divorced ☐ Single ☐ Student ☐ Other

DIAGNOSIS INFORMATION

Diagnosis	Code	Diagnosis	Code
1. Abnormal loss of weight	783.21	5.	
2. Polydipsia	783.5	6.	
3. Polyphagia	783.6	7.	
4.		8.	

PROCEDURE INFORMATION

Description of Procedure or Service	Date	Code	Charge
1. New patient OV level IV	01-19-YYYY	99204	$100.00
2. Urinalysis, with microscopy	01-19-YYYY	81001	10.00
3.			
4.			
5.			

SPECIAL NOTES:

Return visit: 3 weeks

PLEASE
DO NOT
STAPLE
IN THIS
AREA

□□ PICA

HEALTH INSURANCE CLAIM FORM   PICA □□□

1. MEDICARE	MEDICAID	CHAMPUS	CHAMPVA	GROUP HEALTH PLAN	FECA BLK LUNG	OTHER	1a. INSURED'S I.D. NUMBER	(FOR PROGRAM IN ITEM 1)
□ (Medicare #)	□ (Medicaid #)	□ (Sponsor's SSN)	□ (VA File #)	□ (SSN or ID)	□ (SSN)	□ (ID)		

2. PATIENT'S NAME (Last Name, First Name, Middle Initial)

3. PATIENT'S BIRTH DATE MM | DD | YY   SEX M □ F □

4. INSURED'S NAME (Last Name, First Name, Middle Initial)

5. PATIENT'S ADDRESS (No. Street)

6. PATIENT RELATIONSHIP TO INSURED Self □ Spouse □ Child □ Other □

7. INSURED'S ADDRESS (No. Street)

CITY   STATE

8. PATIENT STATUS Single □ Married □ Other □

CITY   STATE

ZIP CODE   TELEPHONE (Include Area Code) ( )

Employed □   Full-Time Student □   Part-Time Student □

ZIP CODE   TELEPHONE (INCLUDE AREA CODE) ( )

9. OTHER INSURED'S NAME (Last Name, First Name, Middle Initial)

10. IS PATIENT'S CONDITION RELATED TO:

11. INSURED'S POLICY GROUP OR FECA NUMBER

a. OTHER INSURED'S POLICY OR GROUP NUMBER

a. EMPLOYMENT? (CURRENT OR PREVIOUS) □ YES □ NO

a. INSURED'S DATE OF BIRTH MM | DD | YY   SEX M □ F □

b. OTHER INSURED'S DATE OF BIRTH MM | DD | YY SEX M □ F □

b. AUTO ACCIDENT?   PLACE (State) □ YES □ NO

b. EMPLOYER'S NAME OR SCHOOL NAME

c. EMPLOYER'S NAME OR SCHOOL NAME

c. OTHER ACCIDENT? □ YES □ NO

c. INSURANCE PLAN NAME OR PROGRAM NAME

d. INSURANCE PLAN NAME OR PROGRAM NAME

10d. RESERVED FOR LOCAL USE

d. IS THERE ANOTHER HEALTH BENEFIT PLAN? □ YES □ NO If yes, return to and complete item 9 a – d.

READ BACK OF FORM BEFORE COMPLETING & SIGNING THIS FORM.
12. PATIENT'S OR AUTHORIZED PERSON'S SIGNATURE I authorize the release of any medical or other information necessary to process this claim. I also request payment of government benefits either to myself or to the party who accepts assignment below.

SIGNED _____   DATE _____

13. INSURED'S OR AUTHORIZED PERSON'S SIGNATURE I authorize payment of medical benefits to the undersigned physician or supplier for services described below.

SIGNED _____

14. DATE OF CURRENT: ILLNESS (First symptom) OR INJURY (Accident) OR PREGNANCY (LMP) MM | DD | YY

15. IF PATIENT HAS HAD SAME OR SIMILAR ILLNESS, GIVE FIRST DATE MM | DD | YY

16. DATES PATIENT UNABLE TO WORK IN CURRENT OCCUPATION MM | DD | YY FROM   TO   MM | DD | YY

17. NAME OF REFERRING PHYSICIAN OR OTHER SOURCE

17a. I.D. NUMBER OF REFERRING PHYSICIAN

18. HOSPITALIZATION DATES RELATED TO CURRENT SERVICES MM | DD | YY FROM   TO   MM | DD | YY

19. RESERVED FOR LOCAL USE

20. OUTSIDE LAB? □ YES □ NO $ CHARGES

21. DIAGNOSIS OR NATURE OF ILLNESS OR INJURY. (RELATE ITEMS 1, 2, 3, OR 4 TO ITEM 24E BY LINE)
1. |___.__   3. |___.__
2. |___.__   4. |___.__

22. MEDICAID RESUBMISSION CODE   ORIGINAL REF. NO.

23. PRIOR AUTHORIZATION NUMBER

24. A. DATE(S) OF SERVICE						B. Place of Service	C. Type of Service	D. PROCEDURES, SERVICES, OR SUPPLIES (Explain Unusual Circumstances)		E. DIAGNOSIS CODE	F. $ CHARGES	G. DAYS OR UNITS	H. EPSDT Family Plan	I. EMG	J. COB	K. RESERVED FOR LOCAL USE
From MM	DD	YY	To MM	DD	YY			CPT/HCPCS	MODIFIER							
1																
2																
3																
4																
5																
6																

25. FEDERAL TAX I.D. NUMBER SSN □ EIN □

26. PATIENT'S ACCOUNT NO.

27. ACCEPT ASSIGNMENT? (For govt. claims, see back) □ YES □ NO

28. TOTAL CHARGE $

29. AMOUNT PAID $

30. BALANCE DUE $

31. SIGNATURE OF PHYSICIAN OR SUPPLIER INCLUDING DEGREES OR CREDENTIALS (I certify that the statements on the reverse apply to this bill and are made a part thereof.)

SIGNED _____ DATE _____

32. NAME AND ADDRESS OF FACILITY WHERE SERVICES WERE RENDERED (If other than home or office)

33. PHYSICIAN'S, SUPPLIER'S BILLING NAME, ADDRESS, ZIP CODE & PHONE #

PIN#   GRP#

PLEASE PRINT OR TYPE

SAMPLE FORM 1500
SAMPLE FORM 1500 SAMPLE FORM 1500

CARRIER

PATIENT AND INSURED INFORMATION

PHYSICIAN OR SUPPLIER INFORMATION

127

DONALD L. GIVINGS, M.D.

11350 Medical Drive ■ Anywhere US 12345 ■ (101) 111-5555

EIN: 11-123456	SSN: 123-12-1234	MEDICARE: D1234
PIN: DG1234	GRP: DG12345	MEDICAID: DLG1234
BCBS: 12345		

Encounter Form

PATIENT INFORMATION:

Name:	Anita B. Strong
Address:	124 Prosper Way
City:	Anywhere
State:	US
Zip Code:	12345
Telephone:	(101) 333-5555
Gender:	Female
Date of Birth:	04-25-1959
Occupation:	
Employer:	Self
Spouse's Employer:	

INSURANCE INFORMATION:

Patient Number:	13-b
Place of Service:	Office
Primary Insurance Plan:	BCBS US
Primary Insurance Plan ID #:	XWG 214-55-6666
Group #:	1357
Primary Policyholder:	Anita B. Strong
Policyholder Date of Birth:	04-25-1959
Relationship to Patient:	Self
Secondary Insurance Plan:	
Secondary Insurance Plan ID #:	
Secondary Policyholder:	

Patient Status   ☒ Married   ☐ Divorced   ☐ Single   ☐ Student   ☐ Other

DIAGNOSIS INFORMATION

Diagnosis	Code	Diagnosis	Code
1. Migraine, classical	346.01	5.	
2.		6.	
3.		7.	
4.		8.	

PROCEDURE INFORMATION

Description of Procedure or Service	Date	Code	Charge
1. Est. patient OV level I	11-07-YYYY	99211	$55.00
2.			
3.			
4.			
5.			

SPECIAL NOTES:

Return visit: PRN
Patient paid $20.00 toward today's bill.

(SAMPLE ONLY - NOT APPROVED FOR USE)

CARRIER

| | PICA | | | **HEALTH INSURANCE CLAIM FORM** | PICA | | |

HEALTH INSURANCE CLAIM FORM

1. MEDICARE ☐ (Medicare #) MEDICAID ☐ (Medicaid #) CHAMPUS ☐ (Sponsor's SSN) CHAMPVA ☐ (VA File #) GROUP HEALTH PLAN ☐ (SSN or ID) FECA BLK LUNG ☐ (SSN) OTHER ☐ (ID)   1a. INSURED'S I.D. NUMBER   (FOR PROGRAM IN ITEM 1)

2. PATIENT'S NAME (Last Name, First Name, Middle Initial)

3. PATIENT'S BIRTH DATE MM ┆ DD ┆ YY   SEX   M ☐ F ☐

4. INSURED'S NAME (Last Name, First Name, Middle Initial)

5. PATIENT'S ADDRESS (No. Street)

6. PATIENT RELATIONSHIP TO INSURED Self ☐ Spouse ☐ Child ☐ Other ☐

7. INSURED'S ADDRESS (No. Street)

CITY | STATE

8. PATIENT STATUS Single ☐ Married ☐ Other ☐   Employed ☐ Full-Time Student ☐ Part-Time Student ☐

CITY | STATE

ZIP CODE   TELEPHONE (Include Area Code) (   )

ZIP CODE   TELEPHONE (INCLUDE AREA CODE) (   )

9. OTHER INSURED'S NAME (Last Name, First Name, Middle Initial)

10. IS PATIENT'S CONDITION RELATED TO:

11. INSURED'S POLICY GROUP OR FECA NUMBER

a. OTHER INSURED'S POLICY OR GROUP NUMBER

a. EMPLOYMENT? (CURRENT OR PREVIOUS) ☐ YES ☐ NO

a. INSURED'S DATE OF BIRTH MM ┆ DD ┆ YY   SEX   M ☐ F ☐

b. OTHER INSURED'S DATE OF BIRTH MM ┆ DD ┆ YY   SEX   M ☐ F ☐

b. AUTO ACCIDENT?   PLACE (State) ☐ YES ☐ NO

b. EMPLOYER'S NAME OR SCHOOL NAME

c. EMPLOYER'S NAME OR SCHOOL NAME

c. OTHER ACCIDENT? ☐ YES ☐ NO

c. INSURANCE PLAN NAME OR PROGRAM NAME

d. INSURANCE PLAN NAME OR PROGRAM NAME

10d. RESERVED FOR LOCAL USE

d. IS THERE ANOTHER HEALTH BENEFIT PLAN? ☐ YES ☐ NO If yes, return to and complete item 9 a – d.

READ BACK OF FORM BEFORE COMPLETING & SIGNING THIS FORM.
12. PATIENT'S OR AUTHORIZED PERSON'S SIGNATURE I authorize the release of any medical or other information necessary to process this claim. I also request payment of government benefits either to myself or to the party who accepts assignment below.

SIGNED _____ DATE _____

13. INSURED'S OR AUTHORIZED PERSON'S SIGNATURE I authorize payment of medical benefits to the undersigned physician or supplier for services described below.

SIGNED _____

PATIENT AND INSURED INFORMATION

14. DATE OF CURRENT: MM ┆ DD ┆ YY ◄ ILLNESS (First symptom) OR INJURY (Accident) OR PREGNANCY (LMP)

15. IF PATIENT HAS HAD SAME OR SIMILAR ILLNESS, GIVE FIRST DATE MM ┆ DD ┆ YY

16. DATES PATIENT UNABLE TO WORK IN CURRENT OCCUPATION MM ┆ DD ┆ YY   MM ┆ DD ┆ YY FROM   TO

17. NAME OF REFERRING PHYSICIAN OR OTHER SOURCE

17a. I.D. NUMBER OF REFERRING PHYSICIAN

18. HOSPITALIZATION DATES RELATED TO CURRENT SERVICES MM ┆ DD ┆ YY   MM ┆ DD ┆ YY FROM   TO

19. RESERVED FOR LOCAL USE

20. OUTSIDE LAB? ☐ YES ☐ NO $ CHARGES

21. DIAGNOSIS OR NATURE OF ILLNESS OR INJURY. (RELATE ITEMS 1, 2, 3, OR 4 TO ITEM 24E BY LINE)

1. L___ . __
2. L___ . __
3. L___ . __
4. L___ . __

22. MEDICAID RESUBMISSION CODE   ORIGINAL REF. NO.

23. PRIOR AUTHORIZATION NUMBER

24. A					B	C	D		E	F	G	H	I	J	K
DATE(S) OF SERVICE					Place of Service	Type of Service	PROCEDURES, SERVICES, OR SUPPLIES (Explain Unusual Circumstances)		DIAGNOSIS CODE	$ CHARGES	DAYS OR UNITS	EPSDT Family Plan	EMG	COB	RESERVED FOR LOCAL USE
From			To				CPT/HCPCS	MODIFIER							
MM	DD	YY	MM	DD	YY											
1															
2															
3															
4															
5															
6															

25. FEDERAL TAX I.D. NUMBER   SSN ☐ EIN ☐

26. PATIENT'S ACCOUNT NO.

27. ACCEPT ASSIGNMENT? (For govt. claims, see back) ☐ YES ☐ NO

28. TOTAL CHARGE $

29. AMOUNT PAID $

30. BALANCE DUE $

31. SIGNATURE OF PHYSICIAN OR SUPPLIER INCLUDING DEGREES OR CREDENTIALS (I certify that the statements on the reverse apply to this bill and are made a part thereof.)

SIGNED _____ DATE _____

32. NAME AND ADDRESS OF FACILITY WHERE SERVICES WERE RENDERED (If other than home or office)

33. PHYSICIAN'S, SUPPLIER'S BILLING NAME, ADDRESS, ZIP CODE & PHONE #

PIN#   GRP#

PHYSICIAN OR SUPPLIER INFORMATION

(SAMPLE ONLY - NOT APPROVED FOR USE)   *PLEASE PRINT OR TYPE*   SAMPLE FORM 1500 SAMPLE FORM 1500 SAMPLE FORM 1500

DONALD L. GIVINGS, M.D.

11350 Medical Drive ■ Anywhere US 12345 ■ (101) 111-5555

EIN: 11-123456   SSN: 123-12-1234   MEDICARE: D1234
PIN: DG1234   GRP: DG12345   MEDICAID: DLG1234
BCBS: 12345

Encounter Form

PATIENT INFORMATION:

Name:	Virginia A. Love
Address:	61 Isaiah Circle
City:	Anywhere
State:	US
Zip Code:	12345
Telephone:	(101) 333-5555
Gender:	Female
Date of Birth:	07-04-1962
Occupation:	
Employer:	None
Spouse's Employer:	Imperial Bayliners

INSURANCE INFORMATION:

Patient Number:	13-c
Place of Service:	Office
Primary Insurance Plan:	BCBS POS
Primary Insurance Plan ID #:	XWN 212-56-7972
Group #:	123
Primary Policyholder:	Charles L. Love
Policyholder Date of Birth:	10-06-60
Relationship to Patient:	Spouse
Secondary Insurance Plan:	
Secondary Insurance Plan ID #:	
Secondary Policyholder:	

Patient Status   ☒ Married   ☐ Divorced   ☐ Single   ☐ Student   ☐ Other

DIAGNOSIS INFORMATION

Diagnosis	Code	Diagnosis	Code
1. Chronic conjunctivitis	372.10	5.	
2. Contact dermatitis	692.9	6.	
3.		7.	
4.		8.	

PROCEDURE INFORMATION

Description of Procedure or Service	Date	Code	Charge
1. Est. patient OV level I	07-03-YYYY	99211	$55.00
2.			
3.			
4.			
5.			

SPECIAL NOTES:

If conjunctivitis does not clear within one week refer to Dr. Glance.

Return visit: PRN

(SAMPLE ONLY - NOT APPROVED FOR USE)

CARRIER

☐☐ PICA

HEALTH INSURANCE CLAIM FORM

PICA ☐☐☐

1. MEDICARE   MEDICAID   CHAMPUS   CHAMPVA   GROUP   FECA   OTHER   1a. INSURED'S I.D. NUMBER   (FOR PROGRAM IN ITEM 1)
   ☐ (Medicare #) ☐ (Medicaid #) ☐ (Sponsor's SSN) ☐ (VA File #)   HEALTH PLAN BLK LUNG
                                                                        ☐ (SSN or ID) ☐ (SSN) ☐ (ID)

2. PATIENT'S NAME (Last Name, First Name, Middle Initial)   3. PATIENT'S BIRTH DATE   SEX   4. INSURED'S NAME (Last Name, First Name, Middle Initial)
                                                                MM ┆ DD ┆ YY   M ☐ F ☐

5. PATIENT'S ADDRESS (No. Street)   6. PATIENT RELATIONSHIP TO INSURED   7. INSURED'S ADDRESS (No. Street)
                                        Self ☐ Spouse ☐ Child ☐ Other ☐

CITY   STATE   8. PATIENT STATUS   CITY   STATE
                    Single ☐ Married ☐ Other ☐

ZIP CODE   TELEPHONE (Include Area Code)   Employed ☐ Full-Time Student ☐ Part-Time Student ☐   ZIP CODE   TELEPHONE (INCLUDE AREA CODE)
            (   )   (   )

9. OTHER INSURED'S NAME (Last Name, First Name, Middle Initial)   10. IS PATIENT'S CONDITION RELATED TO: 11. INSURED'S POLICY GROUP OR FECA NUMBER

a. OTHER INSURED'S POLICY OR GROUP NUMBER   a. EMPLOYMENT? (CURRENT OR PREVIOUS)   a. INSURED'S DATE OF BIRTH   SEX
                                                ☐ YES ☐ NO   MM ┆ DD ┆ YY   M ☐ F ☐

b. OTHER INSURED'S DATE OF BIRTH   SEX   b. AUTO ACCIDENT?   PLACE (State)   b. EMPLOYER'S NAME OR SCHOOL NAME
   MM ┆ DD ┆ YY   M ☐ F ☐   ☐ YES ☐ NO

c. EMPLOYER'S NAME OR SCHOOL NAME   c. OTHER ACCIDENT?   c. INSURANCE PLAN NAME OR PROGRAM NAME
                                        ☐ YES ☐ NO

d. INSURANCE PLAN NAME OR PROGRAM NAME   10d. RESERVED FOR LOCAL USE   d. IS THERE ANOTHER HEALTH BENEFIT PLAN?
                                                                            ☐ YES ☐ NO   If yes, return to and complete item 9 a – d.

READ BACK OF FORM BEFORE COMPLETING & SIGNING THIS FORM.
12. PATIENT'S OR AUTHORIZED PERSON'S SIGNATURE I authorize the release of any medical or other information necessary to process this claim. I also request payment of government benefits either to myself or to the party who accepts assignment below.

SIGNED _____   DATE _____

13. INSURED'S OR AUTHORIZED PERSON'S SIGNATURE I authorize payment of medical benefits to the undersigned physician or supplier for services described below.

SIGNED _____

PATIENT AND INSURED INFORMATION

14. DATE OF CURRENT: ILLNESS (First symptom) OR   15. IF PATIENT HAS HAD SAME OR SIMILAR ILLNESS,   16. DATES PATIENT UNABLE TO WORK IN CURRENT OCCUPATION
    MM ┆ DD ┆ YY   INJURY (Accident) OR   GIVE FIRST DATE MM ┆ DD ┆ YY   MM ┆ DD ┆ YY   MM ┆ DD ┆ YY
                    PREGNANCY (LMP)   FROM   TO

17. NAME OF REFERRING PHYSICIAN OR OTHER SOURCE   17a. I.D. NUMBER OF REFERRING PHYSICIAN   18. HOSPITALIZATION DATES RELATED TO CURRENT SERVICES
                                                                                                MM ┆ DD ┆ YY   MM ┆ DD ┆ YY
                                                                                            FROM   TO

19. RESERVED FOR LOCAL USE   20. OUTSIDE LAB? $ CHARGES
                                ☐ YES ☐ NO

21. DIAGNOSIS OR NATURE OF ILLNESS OR INJURY. (RELATE ITEMS 1, 2, 3, OR 4 TO ITEM 24E BY LINE)   22. MEDICAID RESUBMISSION
                                                                                                    CODE   ORIGINAL REF. NO.
1. └___ . __   3. └___ . __
                                                                                                23. PRIOR AUTHORIZATION NUMBER
2. └___ . __   4. └___ . __

24. A DATE(S) OF SERVICE						B	C	D		E	F	G	H	I	J	K
From			To			Place of Service	Type of Service	PROCEDURES, SERVICES, OR SUPPLIES (Explain Unusual Circumstances)		DIAGNOSIS CODE	$ CHARGES	DAYS OR UNITS	EPSDT Family Plan	EMG	COB	RESERVED FOR LOCAL USE
MM	DD	YY	MM	DD	YY			CPT/HCPCS	MODIFIER							
1																
2																
3																
4																
5																
6																

25. FEDERAL TAX I.D. NUMBER   SSN EIN ☐☐   26. PATIENT'S ACCOUNT NO.   27. ACCEPT ASSIGNMENT? (For govt. claims, see back) ☐ YES ☐ NO   28. TOTAL CHARGE $ 29. AMOUNT PAID $ 30. BALANCE DUE $

31. SIGNATURE OF PHYSICIAN OR SUPPLIER INCLUDING DEGREES OR CREDENTIALS (I certify that the statements on the reverse apply to this bill and are made a part thereof.)

SIGNED _____   DATE _____

32. NAME AND ADDRESS OF FACILITY WHERE SERVICES WERE RENDERED (If other than home or office)

33. PHYSICIAN'S, SUPPLIER'S BILLING NAME, ADDRESS, ZIP CODE & PHONE #

PIN# _____   GRP# _____

PHYSICIAN OR SUPPLIER INFORMATION

(SAMPLE ONLY - NOT APPROVED FOR USE)   PLEASE PRINT OR TYPE   SAMPLE FORM 1500
SAMPLE FORM 1500 SAMPLE FORM 1500

IRIS A. GLANCE, M.D. OPHTHALMOLOGIST

66 Granite Drive ■ Anywhere US 12345 ■ (101) 111-5555

EIN: 11-616161	SSN: 166-12-1234	MEDICARE: I1234
PIN: IG1234	GRP: IG12345	MEDICAID: IG1234
BCBS: 45678		

Encounter Form

PATIENT INFORMATION:

Name:	Virginia A. Love
Address:	61 Isaiah Circle
City:	Anywhere
State:	US
Zip Code:	12345
Telephone:	(101) 333-5555
Gender:	Female
Date of Birth:	07-04-1962
Occupation:	
Employer:	None
Spouse's Employer:	Imperial Bayliners

INSURANCE INFORMATION:

Patient Number:	13-d
Place of Service:	Office
Primary Insurance Plan:	BCBS POS
Primary Insurance Plan ID #:	XWN 212-56-7972
Group #:	123
Primary Policyholder:	Charles L. Love
Policyholder Date of Birth:	10-06-60
Relationship to Patient:	Spouse
Secondary Insurance Plan:	
Secondary Insurance Plan ID #:	
Secondary Policyholder:	

Patient Status   ☒ Married   ☐ Divorced   ☐ Single   ☐ Student   ☐ Other

DIAGNOSIS INFORMATION

Diagnosis	Code	Diagnosis	Code
1. Chronic conjunctivitis	372.10	5.	
2. Conjunctival degeneration	372.50	6.	
3.		7.	
4.		8.	

PROCEDURE INFORMATION

Description of Procedure or Service	Date	Code	Charge
1. Office consult level I	07-03-YYYY	99241	$65.00
2.			
3.			
4.			
5.			

SPECIAL NOTES:

Referring physician: Donald L. Givings, M.D. UPIN/SSN: 12345

PLEASE
DO NOT
STAPLE
IN THIS
AREA

CARRIER

| | | PICA | | |

HEALTH INSURANCE CLAIM FORM

PICA | | |

| 1. MEDICARE ☐ (Medicare #) | MEDICAID ☐ (Medicaid #) | CHAMPUS ☐ (Sponsor's SSN) | CHAMPVA ☐ (VA File #) | GROUP HEALTH PLAN ☐ (SSN or ID) | FECA BLK LUNG ☐ (SSN) | OTHER ☐ (ID) | 1a. INSURED'S I.D. NUMBER (FOR PROGRAM IN ITEM 1) |

| 2. PATIENT'S NAME (Last Name, First Name, Middle Initial) | 3. PATIENT'S BIRTH DATE MM | DD | YY   SEX M ☐ F ☐ | 4. INSURED'S NAME (Last Name, First Name, Middle Initial) |

| 5. PATIENT'S ADDRESS (No. Street) | 6. PATIENT RELATIONSHIP TO INSURED Self ☐ Spouse ☐ Child ☐ Other ☐ | 7. INSURED'S ADDRESS (No. Street) |

| CITY | STATE | 8. PATIENT STATUS Single ☐ Married ☐ Other ☐ | CITY | STATE |

| ZIP CODE | TELEPHONE (Include Area Code) ( ) | Employed ☐ Full-Time Student ☐ Part-Time Student ☐ | ZIP CODE | TELEPHONE (INCLUDE AREA CODE) ( ) |

| 9. OTHER INSURED'S NAME (Last Name, First Name, Middle Initial) | 10. IS PATIENT'S CONDITION RELATED TO: | 11. INSURED'S POLICY GROUP OR FECA NUMBER |

| a. OTHER INSURED'S POLICY OR GROUP NUMBER | a. EMPLOYMENT? (CURRENT OR PREVIOUS) ☐ YES ☐ NO | a. INSURED'S DATE OF BIRTH MM | DD | YY   SEX M ☐ F ☐ |

| b. OTHER INSURED'S DATE OF BIRTH MM | DD | YY   SEX M ☐ F ☐ | b. AUTO ACCIDENT? PLACE (State) ☐ YES ☐ NO | b. EMPLOYER'S NAME OR SCHOOL NAME |

| c. EMPLOYER'S NAME OR SCHOOL NAME | c. OTHER ACCIDENT? ☐ YES ☐ NO | c. INSURANCE PLAN NAME OR PROGRAM NAME |

| d. INSURANCE PLAN NAME OR PROGRAM NAME | 10d. RESERVED FOR LOCAL USE | d. IS THERE ANOTHER HEALTH BENEFIT PLAN? ☐ YES ☐ NO If yes, return to and complete item 9 a – d. |

READ BACK OF FORM BEFORE COMPLETING & SIGNING THIS FORM.
12. PATIENT'S OR AUTHORIZED PERSON'S SIGNATURE. I authorize the release of any medical or other information necessary to process this claim. I also request payment of government benefits either to myself or to the party who accepts assignment below.

SIGNED _____ DATE _____

13. INSURED'S OR AUTHORIZED PERSON'S SIGNATURE. I authorize payment of medical benefits to the undersigned physician or supplier for services described below.

SIGNED _____

PATIENT AND INSURED INFORMATION

| 14. DATE OF CURRENT: ILLNESS (First symptom) OR MM | DD | YY   INJURY (Accident) OR PREGNANCY (LMP) | 15. IF PATIENT HAS HAD SAME OR SIMILAR ILLNESS, GIVE FIRST DATE MM | DD | YY | 16. DATES PATIENT UNABLE TO WORK IN CURRENT OCCUPATION MM | DD | YY   MM | DD | YY FROM   TO |

| 17. NAME OF REFERRING PHYSICIAN OR OTHER SOURCE | 17a. I.D. NUMBER OF REFERRING PHYSICIAN | 18. HOSPITALIZATION DATES RELATED TO CURRENT SERVICES MM | DD | YY   MM | DD | YY FROM   TO |

| 19. RESERVED FOR LOCAL USE | 20. OUTSIDE LAB? ☐ YES ☐ NO $ CHARGES |

| 21. DIAGNOSIS OR NATURE OF ILLNESS OR INJURY. (RELATE ITEMS 1, 2, 3, OR 4 TO ITEM 24E BY LINE) 1. |___|.|___| 3. |___|.|___| 2. |___|.|___| 4. |___|.|___| | 22. MEDICAID RESUBMISSION CODE   ORIGINAL REF. NO. |
| | 23. PRIOR AUTHORIZATION NUMBER |

24. A DATE(S) OF SERVICE						B Place of Service	C Type of Service	D PROCEDURES, SERVICES, OR SUPPLIES (Explain Unusual Circumstances) CPT/HCPCS MODIFIER	E DIAGNOSIS CODE	F $ CHARGES	G DAYS OR UNITS	H EPSDT Family Plan	I EMG	J COB	K RESERVED FOR LOCAL USE
From MM	DD	YY	To MM	DD	YY										
1															
2															
3															
4															
5															
6															

| 25. FEDERAL TAX I.D. NUMBER SSN ☐ EIN ☐ | 26. PATIENT'S ACCOUNT NO. | 27. ACCEPT ASSIGNMENT? (For govt. claims, see back) ☐ YES ☐ NO | 28. TOTAL CHARGE $ | 29. AMOUNT PAID $ | 30. BALANCE DUE $ |

| 31. SIGNATURE OF PHYSICIAN OR SUPPLIER INCLUDING DEGREES OR CREDENTIALS (I certify that the statements on the reverse apply to this bill and are made a part thereof.) SIGNED _____ DATE _____ | 32. NAME AND ADDRESS OF FACILITY WHERE SERVICES WERE RENDERED (If other than home or office) | 33. PHYSICIAN'S, SUPPLIER'S BILLING NAME, ADDRESS, ZIP CODE & PHONE # PIN#   GRP# |

PHYSICIAN OR SUPPLIER INFORMATION

PLEASE PRINT OR TYPE

SAMPLE FORM 1500
SAMPLE FORM 1500 SAMPLE FORM 1500

DONALD L. GIVINGS, M.D.

Encounter Form

11350 Medical Drive ■ Anywhere US 12345 ■ (101) 111-5555

EIN: 11-123456   SSN: 123-12-1234   MEDICARE: D1234
PIN: DG1234   GRP: DG12345   MEDICAID: DLG1234
BCBS: 12345

PATIENT INFORMATION:

Name:	Keith S. Kutter
Address:	22 Pinewood Avenue
City:	Anywhere
State:	US
Zip Code:	12345
Telephone:	(101) 333-5555
Gender:	Male
Date of Birth:	12-01-1955
Occupation:	
Employer:	First League
Spouse's Employer:	Anderson Music & Sound

INSURANCE INFORMATION:

Patient Number:	13-e
Place of Service:	Office
Primary Insurance Plan:	BCBS US
Primary Insurance Plan ID #:	FLX 313-99-7777
Group #:	567
Primary Policyholder:	Keith S. Kutter
Policyholder Date of Birth:	12-01-1955
Relationship to Patient:	Self
Secondary Insurance Plan:	Aetna
Secondary Insurance Plan ID #:	212-44-6868
Secondary Policyholder:	Linda Kutter
Secondary Policyholder DOB:	05-22-1956

Patient Status   ☒ Married   ☐ Divorced   ☐ Single   ☐ Student   ☐ Other

DIAGNOSIS INFORMATION

Diagnosis	Code	Diagnosis	Code
1. Muscle spasms	728.85	5.	
2.		6.	
3.		7.	
4.		8.	

PROCEDURE INFORMATION

Description of Procedure or Service	Date	Code	Charge
1. Est. patient OV level II	09-03-YYYY	99212	$65.00
2.			
3.			
4.			
5.			

SPECIAL NOTES:

Refer to a chiropractor

Case Study 13-e Primary

(SAMPLE ONLY - NOT APPROVED FOR USE)

CARRIER

| | PICA | | | **HEALTH INSURANCE CLAIM FORM** | PICA | | |

1. MEDICARE MEDICAID CHAMPUS CHAMPVA GROUP HEALTH PLAN FECA BLK LUNG OTHER	1a. INSURED'S I.D. NUMBER (FOR PROGRAM IN ITEM 1)
(Medicare #) (Medicaid #) (Sponsor's SSN) (VA File #) (SSN or ID) (SSN) (ID)	

2. PATIENT'S NAME (Last Name, First Name, Middle Initial)	3. PATIENT'S BIRTH DATE MM DD YY SEX M F	4. INSURED'S NAME (Last Name, First Name, Middle Initial)

5. PATIENT'S ADDRESS (No. Street)	6. PATIENT RELATIONSHIP TO INSURED Self Spouse Child Other	7. INSURED'S ADDRESS (No. Street)

CITY	STATE	8. PATIENT STATUS Single Married Other	CITY	STATE

ZIP CODE	TELEPHONE (Include Area Code) ( )	Employed Full-Time Student Part-Time Student	ZIP CODE	TELEPHONE (INCLUDE AREA CODE) ( )

9. OTHER INSURED'S NAME (Last Name, First Name, Middle Initial)	10. IS PATIENT'S CONDITION RELATED TO:	11. INSURED'S POLICY GROUP OR FECA NUMBER

a. OTHER INSURED'S POLICY OR GROUP NUMBER	a. EMPLOYMENT? (CURRENT OR PREVIOUS) YES NO	a. INSURED'S DATE OF BIRTH MM DD YY SEX M F

b. OTHER INSURED'S DATE OF BIRTH MM DD YY SEX M F	b. AUTO ACCIDENT? PLACE (State) YES NO	b. EMPLOYER'S NAME OR SCHOOL NAME

c. EMPLOYER'S NAME OR SCHOOL NAME	c. OTHER ACCIDENT? YES NO	c. INSURANCE PLAN NAME OR PROGRAM NAME

d. INSURANCE PLAN NAME OR PROGRAM NAME	10d. RESERVED FOR LOCAL USE	d. IS THERE ANOTHER HEALTH BENEFIT PLAN? YES NO If yes, return to and complete item 9 a – d.

READ BACK OF FORM BEFORE COMPLETING & SIGNING THIS FORM.

12. PATIENT'S OR AUTHORIZED PERSON'S SIGNATURE I authorize the release of any medical or other information necessary to process this claim. I also request payment of government benefits either to myself or to the party who accepts assignment below.

SIGNED _____ DATE _____

13. INSURED'S OR AUTHORIZED PERSON'S SIGNATURE I authorize payment of medical benefits to the undersigned physician or supplier for services described below.

SIGNED _____

PATIENT AND INSURED INFORMATION

14. DATE OF CURRENT: MM DD YY ILLNESS (First symptom) OR INJURY (Accident) OR PREGNANCY (LMP)	15. IF PATIENT HAS HAD SAME OR SIMILAR ILLNESS, GIVE FIRST DATE MM DD YY	16. DATES PATIENT UNABLE TO WORK IN CURRENT OCCUPATION MM DD YY MM DD YY FROM TO

17. NAME OF REFERRING PHYSICIAN OR OTHER SOURCE	17a. I.D. NUMBER OF REFERRING PHYSICIAN	18. HOSPITALIZATION DATES RELATED TO CURRENT SERVICES MM DD YY MM DD YY FROM TO

19. RESERVED FOR LOCAL USE	20. OUTSIDE LAB? YES NO $ CHARGES

21. DIAGNOSIS OR NATURE OF ILLNESS OR INJURY. (RELATE ITEMS 1, 2, 3, OR 4 TO ITEM 24E BY LINE) 1. ___.___ 3. ___.___ 2. ___.___ 4. ___.___	22. MEDICAID RESUBMISSION CODE ORIGINAL REF. NO. 23. PRIOR AUTHORIZATION NUMBER

24. A DATE(S) OF SERVICE From MM DD YY To MM DD YY	B Place of Service	C Type of Service	D PROCEDURES, SERVICES, OR SUPPLIES (Explain Unusual Circumstances) CPT/HCPCS MODIFIER	E DIAGNOSIS CODE	F $ CHARGES	G DAYS OR UNITS	H EPSDT Family Plan	I EMG	J COB	K RESERVED FOR LOCAL USE
1										
2										
3										
4										
5										
6										

25. FEDERAL TAX I.D. NUMBER SSN EIN	26. PATIENT'S ACCOUNT NO.	27. ACCEPT ASSIGNMENT? (For govt. claims, see back) YES NO	28. TOTAL CHARGE $	29. AMOUNT PAID $	30. BALANCE DUE $

31. SIGNATURE OF PHYSICIAN OR SUPPLIER INCLUDING DEGREES OR CREDENTIALS (I certify that the statements on the reverse apply to this bill and are made a part thereof.) SIGNED _____ DATE _____	32. NAME AND ADDRESS OF FACILITY WHERE SERVICES WERE RENDERED (If other than home or office)	33. PHYSICIAN'S, SUPPLIER'S BILLING NAME, ADDRESS, ZIP CODE & PHONE # PIN# GRP#

PHYSICIAN OR SUPPLIER INFORMATION

(SAMPLE ONLY - NOT APPROVED FOR USE)   *PLEASE PRINT OR TYPE*

SAMPLE FORM 1500
SAMPLE FORM 1500 SAMPLE FORM 1500

Case Study 13-e Secondary

(SAMPLE ONLY - NOT APPROVED FOR USE)

CARRIER

| | PICA | | **HEALTH INSURANCE CLAIM FORM** | PICA | | |

1. MEDICARE	MEDICAID	CHAMPUS	CHAMPVA	GROUP HEALTH PLAN	FECA BLK LUNG	OTHER	1a. INSURED'S I.D. NUMBER	(FOR PROGRAM IN ITEM 1)
(Medicare #)	(Medicaid #)	(Sponsor's SSN)	(VA File #)	(SSN or ID)	(SSN)	(ID)		

2. PATIENT'S NAME (Last Name, First Name, Middle Initial)

3. PATIENT'S BIRTH DATE MM | DD | YY SEX M | F

4. INSURED'S NAME (Last Name, First Name, Middle Initial)

5. PATIENT'S ADDRESS (No. Street)

6. PATIENT RELATIONSHIP TO INSURED Self | Spouse | Child | Other

7. INSURED'S ADDRESS (No. Street)

CITY | STATE

8. PATIENT STATUS Single | Married | Other

Employed | Full-Time Student | Part-Time Student

CITY | STATE

ZIP CODE | TELEPHONE (Include Area Code) ( )

ZIP CODE | TELEPHONE (INCLUDE AREA CODE) ( )

9. OTHER INSURED'S NAME (Last Name, First Name, Middle Initial)

10. IS PATIENT'S CONDITION RELATED TO:

11. INSURED'S POLICY GROUP OR FECA NUMBER

a. OTHER INSURED'S POLICY OR GROUP NUMBER

a. EMPLOYMENT? (CURRENT OR PREVIOUS) YES | NO

a. INSURED'S DATE OF BIRTH MM | DD | YY SEX M | F

b. OTHER INSURED'S DATE OF BIRTH MM | DD | YY SEX M | F

b. AUTO ACCIDENT? PLACE (State) YES | NO

b. EMPLOYER'S NAME OR SCHOOL NAME

c. EMPLOYER'S NAME OR SCHOOL NAME

c. OTHER ACCIDENT? YES | NO

c. INSURANCE PLAN NAME OR PROGRAM NAME

d. INSURANCE PLAN NAME OR PROGRAM NAME

10d. RESERVED FOR LOCAL USE

d. IS THERE ANOTHER HEALTH BENEFIT PLAN? YES | NO If yes, return to and complete item 9 a – d.

READ BACK OF FORM BEFORE COMPLETING & SIGNING THIS FORM.
12. PATIENT'S OR AUTHORIZED PERSON'S SIGNATURE I authorize the release of any medical or other information necessary to process this claim. I also request payment of government benefits either to myself or to the party who accepts assignment below.

SIGNED _____ DATE _____

13. INSURED'S OR AUTHORIZED PERSON'S SIGNATURE I authorize payment of medical benefits to the undersigned physician or supplier for services described below.

SIGNED _____

PATIENT AND INSURED INFORMATION

14. DATE OF CURRENT: ILLNESS (First symptom) OR INJURY (Accident) OR PREGNANCY (LMP) MM | DD | YY

15. IF PATIENT HAS HAD SAME OR SIMILAR ILLNESS, GIVE FIRST DATE MM | DD | YY

16. DATES PATIENT UNABLE TO WORK IN CURRENT OCCUPATION FROM MM | DD | YY TO MM | DD | YY

17. NAME OF REFERRING PHYSICIAN OR OTHER SOURCE

17a. I.D. NUMBER OF REFERRING PHYSICIAN

18. HOSPITALIZATION DATES RELATED TO CURRENT SERVICES FROM MM | DD | YY TO MM | DD | YY

19. RESERVED FOR LOCAL USE

20. OUTSIDE LAB? YES | NO $ CHARGES

21. DIAGNOSIS OR NATURE OF ILLNESS OR INJURY. (RELATE ITEMS 1, 2, 3, OR 4 TO ITEM 24E BY LINE)

1. |___.___| 3. |___.___|

2. |___.___| 4. |___.___|

22. MEDICAID RESUBMISSION CODE | ORIGINAL REF. NO.

23. PRIOR AUTHORIZATION NUMBER

24. A DATE(S) OF SERVICE						B Place of Service	C Type of Service	D PROCEDURES, SERVICES, OR SUPPLIES (Explain Unusual Circumstances) CPT/HCPCS	MODIFIER	E DIAGNOSIS CODE	F $ CHARGES	G DAYS OR UNITS	H EPSDT Family Plan	I EMG	J COB	K RESERVED FOR LOCAL USE
From MM	DD	YY	To MM	DD	YY												
1																
2																
3																
4																
5																
6																

25. FEDERAL TAX I.D. NUMBER SSN | EIN

26. PATIENT'S ACCOUNT NO.

27. ACCEPT ASSIGNMENT? (For govt. claims, see back) YES | NO

28. TOTAL CHARGE $

29. AMOUNT PAID $

30. BALANCE DUE $

31. SIGNATURE OF PHYSICIAN OR SUPPLIER INCLUDING DEGREES OR CREDENTIALS (I certify that the statements on the reverse apply to this bill and are made a part thereof.)

SIGNED _____ DATE _____

32. NAME AND ADDRESS OF FACILITY WHERE SERVICES WERE RENDERED (If other than home or office)

33. PHYSICIAN'S, SUPPLIER'S BILLING NAME, ADDRESS, ZIP CODE & PHONE #

PIN# | GRP#

PHYSICIAN OR SUPPLIER INFORMATION

(SAMPLE ONLY - NOT APPROVED FOR USE)

PLEASE PRINT OR TYPE

SAMPLE FORM 1500
SAMPLE FORM 1500 SAMPLE FORM 1500

ROBERT STRAIN, D.C. CHIROPRACTOR

234 Winding Bend Road ■ Anywhere US 12345 ■ (101) 111-5555

EIN: 11-446688	SSN: 222-12-1234	MEDICARE: R1234
PIN: RS1234	GRP: RS12345	MEDICAID: RSD1234
BCBS: 98765		

Encounter Form

PATIENT INFORMATION:

Name:	Keith S. Kutter
Address:	22 Pinewood Avenue
City:	Anywhere
State:	US
Zip Code:	12345
Telephone:	(101) 333-5555
Gender:	Male
Date of Birth:	12-01-1955
Occupation:	
Employer:	First League
Spouse's Employer:	Anderson Music & Sound

INSURANCE INFORMATION:

Patient Number:	13-f
Place of Service:	Office
Primary Insurance Plan:	BCBS US
Primary Insurance Plan ID #:	FLX 313-99-7777
Group #:	567
Primary Policyholder:	Keith S. Kutter
Policyholder Date of Birth:	12-01-1955
Relationship to Patient:	Self
Secondary Insurance Plan:	Aetna
Secondary Insurance Plan ID #:	212-44-6868
Secondary Policyholder:	Linda Kutter
Secondary Policyholder DOB:	05-22-1956

Patient Status ☒ Married ☐ Divorced ☐ Single ☐ Student ☐ Other

DIAGNOSIS INFORMATION

Diagnosis	Code	Diagnosis	Code
1. Cervical lesion	739.1	5.	
2. Rib cage lesion	739.8	6.	
3. Disorder of soft tissue	729.1	7.	
4. Muscle spasms	728.85	8.	

PROCEDURE INFORMATION

Description of Procedure or Service	Date	Code	Charge
1. Manipulation, 3-4 regions	09-10-YYYY	98941	$55.00
2. Manipulation, extraspinal	09-10-YYYY	98943-51	35.00
3. Massage	09-10-YYYY	97124-51	30.00
4. Mechanical traction	09-10-YYYY	97012-51	27.00
5. Electrical stimulation	09-10-YYYY	97014-51	25.00

SPECIAL NOTES:

Referring physician: Donald L. Givings, M.D. UPIN/SSN: 12345

Return visit: PRN

Case Study 13-f Primary

(SAMPLE ONLY - NOT APPROVED FOR USE)

CARRIER

| | PICA | | | **HEALTH INSURANCE CLAIM FORM** | PICA | | |

HEALTH INSURANCE CLAIM FORM

1. MEDICARE	MEDICAID	CHAMPUS	CHAMPVA	GROUP HEALTH PLAN	FECA BLK LUNG	OTHER
(Medicare #)	(Medicaid #)	(Sponsor's SSN)	(VA File #)	(SSN or ID)	(SSN)	(ID)

1a. INSURED'S I.D. NUMBER   (FOR PROGRAM IN ITEM 1)

2. PATIENT'S NAME (Last Name, First Name, Middle Initial)

3. PATIENT'S BIRTH DATE MM | DD | YY   SEX M   F

4. INSURED'S NAME (Last Name, First Name, Middle Initial)

5. PATIENT'S ADDRESS (No. Street)

6. PATIENT RELATIONSHIP TO INSURED   Self   Spouse   Child   Other

7. INSURED'S ADDRESS (No. Street)

CITY   STATE

8. PATIENT STATUS   Single   Married   Other

CITY   STATE

ZIP CODE   TELEPHONE (Include Area Code) (   )

Employed   Full-Time Student   Part-Time Student

ZIP CODE   TELEPHONE (INCLUDE AREA CODE) (   )

9. OTHER INSURED'S NAME (Last Name, First Name, Middle Initial)

10. IS PATIENT'S CONDITION RELATED TO:

11. INSURED'S POLICY GROUP OR FECA NUMBER

a. OTHER INSURED'S POLICY OR GROUP NUMBER

a. EMPLOYMENT? (CURRENT OR PREVIOUS)   YES   NO

a. INSURED'S DATE OF BIRTH MM | DD | YY   SEX M   F

b. OTHER INSURED'S DATE OF BIRTH MM | DD | YY   SEX M   F

b. AUTO ACCIDENT?   PLACE (State)   YES   NO

b. EMPLOYER'S NAME OR SCHOOL NAME

c. EMPLOYER'S NAME OR SCHOOL NAME

c. OTHER ACCIDENT?   YES   NO

c. INSURANCE PLAN NAME OR PROGRAM NAME

d. INSURANCE PLAN NAME OR PROGRAM NAME

10d. RESERVED FOR LOCAL USE

d. IS THERE ANOTHER HEALTH BENEFIT PLAN?   YES   NO   If yes, return to and complete item 9 a – d.

READ BACK OF FORM BEFORE COMPLETING & SIGNING THIS FORM.

12. PATIENT'S OR AUTHORIZED PERSON'S SIGNATURE I authorize the release of any medical or other information necessary to process this claim. I also request payment of government benefits either to myself or to the party who accepts assignment below.

SIGNED _____   DATE _____

13. INSURED'S OR AUTHORIZED PERSON'S SIGNATURE I authorize payment of medical benefits to the undersigned physician or supplier for services described below.

SIGNED _____

14. DATE OF CURRENT: MM | DD | YY   ILLNESS (First symptom) OR INJURY (Accident) OR PREGNANCY (LMP)

15. IF PATIENT HAS HAD SAME OR SIMILAR ILLNESS, GIVE FIRST DATE MM | DD | YY

16. DATES PATIENT UNABLE TO WORK IN CURRENT OCCUPATION MM | DD | YY   FROM   TO   MM | DD | YY

17. NAME OF REFERRING PHYSICIAN OR OTHER SOURCE

17a. I.D. NUMBER OF REFERRING PHYSICIAN

18. HOSPITALIZATION DATES RELATED TO CURRENT SERVICES MM | DD | YY   FROM   TO   MM | DD | YY

19. RESERVED FOR LOCAL USE

20. OUTSIDE LAB?   YES   NO $ CHARGES

21. DIAGNOSIS OR NATURE OF ILLNESS OR INJURY. (RELATE ITEMS 1, 2, 3, OR 4 TO ITEM 24E BY LINE)

1. ____ . __   3. ____ . __

2. ____ . __   4. ____ . __

22. MEDICAID RESUBMISSION CODE   ORIGINAL REF. NO.

23. PRIOR AUTHORIZATION NUMBER

24. A DATE(S) OF SERVICE						B Place of Service	C Type of Service	D PROCEDURES, SERVICES, OR SUPPLIES (Explain Unusual Circumstances) CPT/HCPCS MODIFIER	E DIAGNOSIS CODE	F $ CHARGES	G DAYS OR UNITS	H EPSDT Family Plan	I EMG	J COB	K RESERVED FOR LOCAL USE
From MM	DD	YY	To MM	DD	YY										
1															
2															
3															
4															
5															
6															

25. FEDERAL TAX I.D. NUMBER   SSN   EIN

26. PATIENT'S ACCOUNT NO.

27. ACCEPT ASSIGNMENT? (For govt. claims, see back)   YES   NO

28. TOTAL CHARGE $

29. AMOUNT PAID $

30. BALANCE DUE $

31. SIGNATURE OF PHYSICIAN OR SUPPLIER INCLUDING DEGREES OR CREDENTIALS (I certify that the statements on the reverse apply to this bill and are made a part thereof.)

SIGNED _____   DATE _____

32. NAME AND ADDRESS OF FACILITY WHERE SERVICES WERE RENDERED (If other than home or office)

33. PHYSICIAN'S, SUPPLIER'S BILLING NAME, ADDRESS, ZIP CODE & PHONE #

PIN#   GRP#

(SAMPLE ONLY - NOT APPROVED FOR USE)   *PLEASE PRINT OR TYPE*   SAMPLE FORM 1500 SAMPLE FORM 1500 SAMPLE FORM 1500

Case Study 13-f Secondary

PLEASE
DO NOT
STAPLE
IN THIS
AREA

CARRIER

HEALTH INSURANCE CLAIM FORM   PICA

PICA

1. MEDICARE MEDICAID CHAMPUS CHAMPVA GROUP HEALTH PLAN FECA BLK LUNG OTHER	1a. INSURED'S I.D. NUMBER (FOR PROGRAM IN ITEM 1)
(Medicare #) (Medicaid #) (Sponsor's SSN) (VA File #) (SSN or ID) (SSN) (ID)	

2. PATIENT'S NAME (Last Name, First Name, Middle Initial)

3. PATIENT'S BIRTH DATE   MM   DD   YY   SEX   M   F

4. INSURED'S NAME (Last Name, First Name, Middle Initial)

5. PATIENT'S ADDRESS (No. Street)

6. PATIENT RELATIONSHIP TO INSURED   Self   Spouse   Child   Other

7. INSURED'S ADDRESS (No. Street)

CITY   STATE

8. PATIENT STATUS   Single   Married   Other   Employed   Full-Time Student   Part-Time Student

CITY   STATE

ZIP CODE   TELEPHONE (Include Area Code)   (   )

ZIP CODE   TELEPHONE (INCLUDE AREA CODE)   (   )

9. OTHER INSURED'S NAME (Last Name, First Name, Middle Initial)

10. IS PATIENT'S CONDITION RELATED TO:

11. INSURED'S POLICY GROUP OR FECA NUMBER

a. OTHER INSURED'S POLICY OR GROUP NUMBER

a. EMPLOYMENT? (CURRENT OR PREVIOUS)   YES   NO

a. INSURED'S DATE OF BIRTH   MM   DD   YY   SEX   M   F

b. OTHER INSURED'S DATE OF BIRTH   MM   DD   YY   SEX   M   F

b. AUTO ACCIDENT?   PLACE (State)   YES   NO

b. EMPLOYER'S NAME OR SCHOOL NAME

c. EMPLOYER'S NAME OR SCHOOL NAME

c. OTHER ACCIDENT?   YES   NO

c. INSURANCE PLAN NAME OR PROGRAM NAME

d. INSURANCE PLAN NAME OR PROGRAM NAME

10d. RESERVED FOR LOCAL USE

d. IS THERE ANOTHER HEALTH BENEFIT PLAN?   YES   NO   If yes, return to and complete item 9 a – d.

READ BACK OF FORM BEFORE COMPLETING & SIGNING THIS FORM.
12. PATIENT'S OR AUTHORIZED PERSON'S SIGNATURE I authorize the release of any medical or other information necessary to process this claim. I also request payment of government benefits either to myself or to the party who accepts assignment below.

SIGNED _____   DATE _____

13. INSURED'S OR AUTHORIZED PERSON'S SIGNATURE I authorize payment of medical benefits to the undersigned physician or supplier for services described below.

SIGNED _____

PATIENT AND INSURED INFORMATION

14. DATE OF CURRENT: ILLNESS (First symptom) OR   MM   DD   YY   INJURY (Accident) OR   PREGNANCY (LMP)

15. IF PATIENT HAS HAD SAME OR SIMILAR ILLNESS, GIVE FIRST DATE   MM   DD   YY

16. DATES PATIENT UNABLE TO WORK IN CURRENT OCCUPATION   MM   DD   YY   FROM   TO   MM   DD   YY

17. NAME OF REFERRING PHYSICIAN OR OTHER SOURCE

17a. I.D. NUMBER OF REFERRING PHYSICIAN

18. HOSPITALIZATION DATES RELATED TO CURRENT SERVICES   MM   DD   YY   FROM   TO   MM   DD   YY

19. RESERVED FOR LOCAL USE

20. OUTSIDE LAB? $ CHARGES   YES   NO

21. DIAGNOSIS OR NATURE OF ILLNESS OR INJURY. (RELATE ITEMS 1, 2, 3, OR 4 TO ITEM 24E BY LINE)

1. |___.___| 3. |___.___|

2. |___.___| 4. |___.___|

22. MEDICAID RESUBMISSION   CODE   ORIGINAL REF. NO.

23. PRIOR AUTHORIZATION NUMBER

24. A DATE(S) OF SERVICE						B	C	D PROCEDURES, SERVICES, OR SUPPLIES		E	F	G	H	I	J	K
From			To			Place of Service	Type of Service	(Explain Unusual Circumstances)		DIAGNOSIS CODE	$ CHARGES	DAYS OR UNITS	EPSDT Family Plan	EMG	COB	RESERVED FOR LOCAL USE
MM	DD	YY	MM	DD	YY			CPT/HCPCS	MODIFIER							
1																
2																
3																
4																
5																
6																

25. FEDERAL TAX I.D. NUMBER   SSN   EIN

26. PATIENT'S ACCOUNT NO.

27. ACCEPT ASSIGNMENT?   (For govt. claims, see back)   YES   NO

28. TOTAL CHARGE $

29. AMOUNT PAID $

30. BALANCE DUE $

31. SIGNATURE OF PHYSICIAN OR SUPPLIER INCLUDING DEGREES OR CREDENTIALS   (I certify that the statements on the reverse apply to this bill and are made a part thereof.)

SIGNED _____   DATE _____

32. NAME AND ADDRESS OF FACILITY WHERE SERVICES WERE RENDERED (If other than home or office)

33. PHYSICIAN'S, SUPPLIER'S BILLING NAME, ADDRESS, ZIP CODE & PHONE #

PIN#   GRP#

PHYSICIAN OR SUPPLIER INFORMATION

PLEASE PRINT OR TYPE

SAMPLE FORM 1500
SAMPLE FORM 1500 SAMPLE FORM 1500

DONALD L. GIVINGS, M.D.

11350 Medical Drive ■ Anywhere US 12345 ■ (101) 111-5555

EIN: 11-123456	SSN: 123-12-1234	MEDICARE: D1234
PIN: DG1234	GRP: DG12345	MEDICAID: DLG1234
BCBS: 12345		

Encounter Form

PATIENT INFORMATION:

Name:	Kristen A. Wonder
Address:	1654 Willow Tree Dr.
City:	Anywhere
State:	US
Zip Code:	12345
Telephone:	(101) 333-5555
Gender:	Female
Date of Birth:	04-16-1999
Occupation:	
Employer:	None
Spouse's Employer:	

INSURANCE INFORMATION:

Patient Number:	13-g
Place of Service:	Office
Primary Insurance Plan:	BCBS US
Primary Insurance Plan ID #:	NYV 415-55-6767
Group #:	678
Primary Policyholder:	John F. Wonder
Policyholder Date of Birth:	05-22-1975
Relationship to Patient:	Father
Secondary Insurance Plan:	
Secondary Insurance Plan ID #:	
Secondary Policyholder:	

Patient Status ☐ Married ☐ Divorced ☒ Single ☐ Student ☐ Other

DIAGNOSIS INFORMATION

Diagnosis	Code	Diagnosis	Code
1. Impacted wax	380.4	5.	
2.		6.	
3.		7.	
4.		8.	

PROCEDURE INFORMATION

Description of Procedure or Service	Date	Code	Charge
1. Est. patient OV level II	10-23-YYYY	99212	$65.00
2. Removal, impacted cerumen	10-23-YYYY	69210	25.00
3.			
4.			
5.			

SPECIAL NOTES:

Return visit: PRN

PLEASE
DO NOT
STAPLE
IN THIS
AREA

HEALTH INSURANCE CLAIM FORM

PICA | | | PICA | | |

1. MEDICARE MEDICAID CHAMPUS CHAMPVA GROUP HEALTH PLAN FECA BLK LUNG OTHER	1a. INSURED'S I.D. NUMBER (FOR PROGRAM IN ITEM 1)

(Medicare #) (Medicaid #) (Sponsor's SSN) (VA File #) (SSN or ID) (SSN) (ID)

2. PATIENT'S NAME (Last Name, First Name, Middle Initial)

3. PATIENT'S BIRTH DATE MM DD YY SEX M F

4. INSURED'S NAME (Last Name, First Name, Middle Initial)

5. PATIENT'S ADDRESS (No. Street)

6. PATIENT RELATIONSHIP TO INSURED Self Spouse Child Other

7. INSURED'S ADDRESS (No. Street)

CITY STATE

8. PATIENT STATUS Single Married Other

Employed Full-Time Student Part-Time Student

CITY STATE

ZIP CODE TELEPHONE (Include Area Code) ( )

ZIP CODE TELEPHONE (INCLUDE AREA CODE) ( )

9. OTHER INSURED'S NAME (Last Name, First Name, Middle Initial)

10. IS PATIENT'S CONDITION RELATED TO:

11. INSURED'S POLICY GROUP OR FECA NUMBER

a. OTHER INSURED'S POLICY OR GROUP NUMBER

a. EMPLOYMENT? (CURRENT OR PREVIOUS) YES NO

a. INSURED'S DATE OF BIRTH MM DD YY SEX M F

b. OTHER INSURED'S DATE OF BIRTH MM DD YY SEX M F

b. AUTO ACCIDENT? PLACE (State) YES NO

b. EMPLOYER'S NAME OR SCHOOL NAME

c. EMPLOYER'S NAME OR SCHOOL NAME

c. OTHER ACCIDENT? YES NO

c. INSURANCE PLAN NAME OR PROGRAM NAME

d. INSURANCE PLAN NAME OR PROGRAM NAME

10d. RESERVED FOR LOCAL USE

d. IS THERE ANOTHER HEALTH BENEFIT PLAN? YES NO If yes, return to and complete item 9 a – d.

READ BACK OF FORM BEFORE COMPLETING & SIGNING THIS FORM.
12. PATIENT'S OR AUTHORIZED PERSON'S SIGNATURE I authorize the release of any medical or other information necessary to process this claim. I also request payment of government benefits either to myself or to the party who accepts assignment below.

SIGNED _____ DATE _____

13. INSURED'S OR AUTHORIZED PERSON'S SIGNATURE I authorize payment of medical benefits to the undersigned physician or supplier for services described below.

SIGNED _____

14. DATE OF CURRENT: MM DD YY ILLNESS (First symptom) OR INJURY (Accident) OR PREGNANCY (LMP)

15. IF PATIENT HAS HAD SAME OR SIMILAR ILLNESS. GIVE FIRST DATE MM DD YY

16. DATES PATIENT UNABLE TO WORK IN CURRENT OCCUPATION MM DD YY MM DD YY FROM TO

17. NAME OF REFERRING PHYSICIAN OR OTHER SOURCE

17a. I.D. NUMBER OF REFERRING PHYSICIAN

18. HOSPITALIZATION DATES RELATED TO CURRENT SERVICES MM DD YY MM DD YY FROM TO

19. RESERVED FOR LOCAL USE

20. OUTSIDE LAB? YES NO $ CHARGES

21. DIAGNOSIS OR NATURE OF ILLNESS OR INJURY. (RELATE ITEMS 1, 2, 3, OR 4 TO ITEM 24E BY LINE)

1. ____.____   3. ____.____

2. ____.____   4. ____.____

22. MEDICAID RESUBMISSION CODE ORIGINAL REF. NO.

23. PRIOR AUTHORIZATION NUMBER

24. A DATE(S) OF SERVICE		B Place of Service	C Type of Service	D PROCEDURES, SERVICES, OR SUPPLIES (Explain Unusual Circumstances)		E DIAGNOSIS CODE	F $ CHARGES	G DAYS OR UNITS	H EPSDT Family Plan	I EMG	J COB	K RESERVED FOR LOCAL USE
From MM DD YY	To MM DD YY			CPT/HCPCS	MODIFIER							
1												
2												
3												
4												
5												
6												

25. FEDERAL TAX I.D. NUMBER SSN EIN

26. PATIENT'S ACCOUNT NO.

27. ACCEPT ASSIGNMENT? (For govt. claims, see back) YES NO

28. TOTAL CHARGE $

29. AMOUNT PAID $

30. BALANCE DUE $

31. SIGNATURE OF PHYSICIAN OR SUPPLIER INCLUDING DEGREES OR CREDENTIALS (I certify that the statements on the reverse apply to this bill and are made a part thereof.)

SIGNED _____ DATE _____

32. NAME AND ADDRESS OF FACILITY WHERE SERVICES WERE RENDERED (If other than home or office)

33. PHYSICIAN'S, SUPPLIER'S BILLING NAME, ADDRESS, ZIP CODE & PHONE #

PIN# GRP#

PLEASE PRINT OR TYPE

SAMPLE FORM 1500
SAMPLE FORM 1500 SAMPLE FORM 1500

PATIENT AND INSURED INFORMATION

PHYSICIAN OR SUPPLIER INFORMATION

DONALD L. GIVINGS, M.D.

11350 Medical Drive ■ Anywhere US 12345 ■ (101) 111-5555

EIN: 11-123456　　SSN: 123-12-1234　　MEDICARE: D1234
PIN: DG1234　　　GRP: DG12345　　　MEDICAID: DLG1234
BCBS: 12345

Encounter Form

PATIENT INFORMATION:

Name:	Edward R. Turtle
Address:	68 North Street
City:	Anywhere
State:	US
Zip Code:	12345
Telephone:	(101) 333-5555
Gender:	Male
Date of Birth:	09-15-1949
Occupation:	
Employer:	Carpet Pro
Spouse's Employer:	

INSURANCE INFORMATION:

Patient Number:	13-h
Place of Service:	Mercy Hospital
Primary Insurance Plan:	BCBS Federal
Primary Insurance Plan ID #:	R12345678
Group #:	105
Primary Policyholder:	Edward R. Turtle
Policyholder Date of Birth:	09-15-1949
Relationship to Patient:	Self
Secondary Insurance Plan:	
Secondary Insurance Plan ID #:	
Secondary Policyholder:	

Patient Status　　☒ Married　　☐ Divorced　　☐ Single　　☐ Student　　☐ Other

DIAGNOSIS INFORMATION

Diagnosis	Code	Diagnosis	Code
1. Rectal bleeding	569.3	5.	
2. Irritable bowel	564.1	6.	
3. Abdominal pain	789.00	7.	
4.		8.	

PROCEDURE INFORMATION

Description of Procedure or Service	Date	Code	Charge
1. Init. hospital level IV	4-14-YYYY	99224	$175.00
2. Subsq. hospital level III	4-15-YYYY	99233	85.00
3. Hospital discharge 30 min.	4-16-YYYY	99238	75.00
4.			
5.			

SPECIAL NOTES:

Return visit: 4 weeks

PLEASE
DO NOT
STAPLE
IN THIS
AREA

CARRIER

| PICA | | |

HEALTH INSURANCE CLAIM FORM

PICA | | |

| 1. MEDICARE   MEDICAID   CHAMPUS   CHAMPVA   GROUP HEALTH PLAN   FECA BLK LUNG   OTHER | 1a. INSURED'S I.D. NUMBER   (FOR PROGRAM IN ITEM 1) |

☐ (Medicare #) ☐ (Medicaid #) ☐ (Sponsor's SSN) ☐ (VA File #) ☐ (SSN or ID) ☐ (SSN) ☐ (ID)

2. PATIENT'S NAME (Last Name, First Name, Middle Initial)

3. PATIENT'S BIRTH DATE   SEX
MM | DD | YY   M ☐   F ☐

4. INSURED'S NAME (Last Name, First Name, Middle Initial)

5. PATIENT'S ADDRESS (No. Street)

6. PATIENT RELATIONSHIP TO INSURED
Self ☐   Spouse ☐   Child ☐   Other ☐

7. INSURED'S ADDRESS (No. Street)

CITY   STATE

8. PATIENT STATUS
Single ☐   Married ☐   Other ☐
Employed ☐   Full-Time Student ☐   Part-Time Student ☐

CITY   STATE

ZIP CODE   TELEPHONE (Include Area Code)
(   )

ZIP CODE   TELEPHONE (INCLUDE AREA CODE)
(   )

9. OTHER INSURED'S NAME (Last Name, First Name, Middle Initial)

10. IS PATIENT'S CONDITION RELATED TO:

11. INSURED'S POLICY GROUP OR FECA NUMBER

a. OTHER INSURED'S POLICY OR GROUP NUMBER

a. EMPLOYMENT? (CURRENT OR PREVIOUS)
☐ YES   ☐ NO

a. INSURED'S DATE OF BIRTH   SEX
MM | DD | YY   M ☐   F ☐

b. OTHER INSURED'S DATE OF BIRTH   SEX
MM | DD | YY   M ☐   F ☐

b. AUTO ACCIDENT?   PLACE (State)
☐ YES   ☐ NO

b. EMPLOYER'S NAME OR SCHOOL NAME

c. EMPLOYER'S NAME OR SCHOOL NAME

c. OTHER ACCIDENT?
☐ YES   ☐ NO

c. INSURANCE PLAN NAME OR PROGRAM NAME

d. INSURANCE PLAN NAME OR PROGRAM NAME

10d. RESERVED FOR LOCAL USE

d. IS THERE ANOTHER HEALTH BENEFIT PLAN?
☐ YES   ☐ NO   If yes, return to and complete item 9 a – d.

READ BACK OF FORM BEFORE COMPLETING & SIGNING THIS FORM.
12. PATIENT'S OR AUTHORIZED PERSON'S SIGNATURE. I authorize the release of any medical or other information necessary to process this claim. I also request payment of government benefits either to myself or to the party who accepts assignment below.

SIGNED _____   DATE _____

13. INSURED'S OR AUTHORIZED PERSON'S SIGNATURE. I authorize payment of medical benefits to the undersigned physician or supplier for services described below.

SIGNED _____

PATIENT AND INSURED INFORMATION

14. DATE OF CURRENT: ILLNESS (First symptom) OR INJURY (Accident) OR PREGNANCY (LMP)
MM | DD | YY

15. IF PATIENT HAS HAD SAME OR SIMILAR ILLNESS, GIVE FIRST DATE   MM | DD | YY

16. DATES PATIENT UNABLE TO WORK IN CURRENT OCCUPATION
MM | DD | YY   MM | DD | YY
FROM   TO

17. NAME OF REFERRING PHYSICIAN OR OTHER SOURCE

17a. I.D. NUMBER OF REFERRING PHYSICIAN

18. HOSPITALIZATION DATES RELATED TO CURRENT SERVICES
MM | DD | YY   MM | DD | YY
FROM   TO

19. RESERVED FOR LOCAL USE

20. OUTSIDE LAB? $ CHARGES
☐ YES   ☐ NO

21. DIAGNOSIS OR NATURE OF ILLNESS OR INJURY. (RELATE ITEMS 1, 2, 3, OR 4 TO ITEM 24E BY LINE)

1. |___ . __| 3. |___ . __|

2. |___ . __| 4. |___ . __|

22. MEDICAID RESUBMISSION
CODE   ORIGINAL REF. NO.

23. PRIOR AUTHORIZATION NUMBER

24. A DATE(S) OF SERVICE			B Place of Service	C Type of Service	D PROCEDURES, SERVICES, OR SUPPLIES (Explain Unusual Circumstances)		E DIAGNOSIS CODE	F $ CHARGES	G DAYS OR UNITS	H EPSDT Family Plan	I EMG	J COB	K RESERVED FOR LOCAL USE
From MM DD YY	To MM DD YY				CPT/HCPCS	MODIFIER							
1													
2													
3													
4													
5													
6													

25. FEDERAL TAX I.D. NUMBER   SSN ☐ EIN ☐

26. PATIENT'S ACCOUNT NO.

27. ACCEPT ASSIGNMENT? (For govt. claims, see back)
☐ YES   ☐ NO

28. TOTAL CHARGE $

29. AMOUNT PAID $

30. BALANCE DUE $

31. SIGNATURE OF PHYSICIAN OR SUPPLIER INCLUDING DEGREES OR CREDENTIALS
(I certify that the statements on the reverse apply to this bill and are made a part thereof.)

SIGNED _____   DATE _____

32. NAME AND ADDRESS OF FACILITY WHERE SERVICES WERE RENDERED (If other than home or office)

33. PHYSICIAN'S, SUPPLIER'S BILLING NAME, ADDRESS, ZIP CODE & PHONE #

PIN#   GRP#

PHYSICIAN OR SUPPLIER INFORMATION

PLEASE PRINT OR TYPE

SAMPLE FORM 1500
SAMPLE FORM 1500   SAMPLE FORM 1500

Chapter 14
Medicare

MEDICARE ELIGIBILITY

1. General Medicare eligibility requires individuals or spouses to (fill in the blanks):
   a. have worked at least _____ years in Medicare-covered employment.
   b. be a minimum age of _____ years old.
   c. be a citizen or permanent resident of the _____ _____.

2. Individuals can also qualify for Medicare coverage if they are younger than 65 years old and have a _____ or chronic _____ disease.

MEDICARE ENROLLMENT

3. Individuals age ___ and over who do not qualify for Social Security benefits may "buy in" to Medicare Part A. (Circle the correct answer.).

   _____ a. 62

   _____ b. 64

   _____ c. 65

   _____ d. none of the above

Critical Thinking

4. Write a paragraph describing the difference between the *qualified Medicare beneficiary* program and the *specified low-income Medicare beneficiary* program.

   _____

   _____

   _____

   _____

MEDICARE PART A COVERAGE

5. Medicare pays only a portion of a patient's acute care hospitalization expenses, and the patient's out-of-pocket expenses are calculated on a _____ basis.

6. A benefit period begins on the first day of hospitalization and ends when the patient has been out of the hospital for ___ consecutive days. (Circle the correct answer.)
   a. 30
   b. 60
   c. 90
   d. none of the above

7. After 90 continuous days of hospitalization, the patient may elect to use some or all of the allotted ___ lifetime reserve days. (Circle the correct answer.)
   a. 30
   b. 60
   c. 90
   d. none of the above

8. Persons confined to a psychiatric hospital are allowed ___ lifetime reserve days. (Circle the correct answer.)
   a. 90
   b. 160
   c. 190
   d. none of the above

9. Inpatients admitted to a skilled nursing facility after a three-day minimum acute hospital stay, and who meet Medicare's qualified diagnosis and comprehensive treatment plan requirements, pay 2003 rates of (fill in the blanks):
   a. days 1-20   _____
   b. days 21-100   _____
   c. days 101+   _____

10. Match the insurance terms in the first column with the definitions in the second column. Write the correct letter in each blank.

   _____ Medicare Part A   a. used only once during a patient's lifetime

   _____ hospice care   b. the temporary hospitalization of a hospice patient

   _____ ESRD coverage   c. covers institutional care

   _____ lifetime reserve days   d. all terminally ill patients qualify for this

   _____ home health services   e. available to patients confined to the home

   _____ respite care   f. available to patients in need of renal dialysis or transplant

11. Kidney donor coverage includes ___. (Circle the correct answer.)
    a. preoperative testing
    b. surgery
    c. postoperative services
    d. all of the above

12. All payments for medical expenses incurred by a kidney donor are made directly to the ___. (Circle the correct answer.)
    a. health care providers
    b. kidney donor
    c. kidney recipient
    d. any of the above

13. Heart and heart-lung transplants are covered if the person is Medicare-eligible and the transplant takes place in a Medicare-certified regional ___. (Circle the correct answer.)
    a. hospital
    b. medical center
    c. transplant center
    d. any of the above

14. Liver transplants for adults are covered if the person is Medicare-eligible and does not have ___. (Circle the correct answer.)
    a. hepatitis B
    b. a malignancy
    c. surgery
    d. all of the above

MEDICARE PART B COVERAGE

15. Medicare Part B does not cover ___. (Circle the correct answer.)
    a. diagnostic testing
    b. routine physicals
    c. ambulance services
    d. physician services

16. Which of the following statements about Medicare Part B is NOT true? (Circle the correct answer.)
    a. Medicare pays for therapeutic shoes for hypertensive patients.
    b. Medicare pays for influenza, hepatitis B, and pneumococcal vaccines.
    c. Medicare pays for drugs that are not self-administered.
    d. none of the above

17. The following preventive screening services were added to the benefits under the Balanced Budget Act of 1997 (fill in the blanks):
    a. annual _____ screening for women over age 39
    b. annual colorectal screening/fecal-occult blood for patients age _____ and older
    c. colorectal screening/flexible sigmoidoscopies every _____ _____ for patients age 50 and over
    d. colorectal screening/colonoscopies every two years if the patient is at high risk for
       _____ _____
    e. screening _____ and clinical _____ examinations every three years

18. The patient is required to pay a $ _____ annual deductible and _____ percent of the Medicare allowed charges on all covered benefits, except in the outpatient setting.

19. Describe the possible consequences for providers who are in violation of Medicare regulations by routinely refraining from collecting the patient's deductible and coinsurance.
    _____

20. The coinsurance for outpatient mental health treatments is ___ of allowed charges. (Circle the correct answer.)
    a. 20%
    b. 50%
    c. 75%
    d. none

PARTICIPATING/NONPARTICIPATING PROVIDERS

21. Indicate whether each of the following applies to **PAR** or **nonPAR** providers on the line provided.

   a. _____ Providers may elect to accept assignment on a claim-by-claim basis.

   b. _____ Bonuses are provided to carriers for recruitment and enrollment of these providers.

   c. _____ Direct payment is made of all claims.

   d. _____ Faster processing of assigned claims occurs.

   e. _____ Patient must sign a Surgery Disclosure Notice for all nonassigned surgical fees over $500.

   f. _____ Provider fees are restricted to no more than the "limiting charge" on nonassigned claims.

   g. _____ A 5% higher fee schedule is used.

22. A nonPAR provider treats a patient for an office visit and the nonPAR limiting charge for that visit is $95. The nonPAR Medicare allowed fee is $80. Because the provider is nonPAR, he collects his payment from the patient at the time the service was delivered.
   How much money is the provider allowed to collect from the patient for this visit? $_____
   How much will Medicare reimburse the patient? $_____

23. A PAR provider treats a patient for an office visit and bills Medicare his usual fee of $100 for that visit. The PAR Medicare allowed fee is $75.
   How much will Medicare reimburse the provider assuming the patient's deductible has been satisfied? $_____
   How much will the provider be allowed to collect from the patient for this visit? $_____

24. If a nonPAR provider does not heed the carrier's warnings to desist from flagrant abuse of the "limiting charge" rules, the potential fine has been increased to ___. (Circle the correct answer.)

   a. $2,000

   b. $5,000

   c. $10,000

   d. $20,000

25. When is a nonPAR not restricted to billing the "limiting fee" on a specific claim?

   _____

Critical Thinking

26. Write a paragraph describing the use of the Surgery Disclosure Notice and the penalties for not using this form.

   _____

   _____

   _____

   _____

   _____

   _____

27. Federal law requires that all providers submit claims to Medicare if they provide a Medicare-covered service to a patient enrolled in Medicare Part B. This regulation does not apply if ___. (Circle the correct answer.)

    a. the patient disenrolled before the service was furnished

    b. the patient is not enrolled in Part B

    c. the patient or the patient's legal representative refuses to sign an authorization for release of medical information

    d. all of the above

28. The Privacy Act of 1979 forbids the regional carrier from disclosing the status of any unassigned claim beyond the ___. (Circle the correct answer.)

    a. date the claim was received by the carrier

    b. date the claim was paid, denied, or suspended

    c. general reason the claim was suspended

    d. all of the above

29. Which of the following Medicare-covered services are paid only on an assigned basis? (Circle the correct answer.)

    a. ambulatory surgery center facility fees

    b. clinical diagnostic laboratory services

    c. physician services provided to Medicaid-eligible recipients

    d. all of the above

30. Define *balance billing*. _____

_____

ADVANCE BENEFICIARY NOTICE

31. What is the purpose of obtaining an ABN? _____

_____

32. For each item, enter **T** for a true statement or **F** for a false statement on the line provided.

    _____ a. Medicare law requires payment only for services or supplies that are considered reasonable and necessary for the stated diagnosis.

    _____ b. Medicare may cover procedures deemed to be unproved, experimental, or investigational in nature.

    _____ c. The patient must pay the full cost of the procedures denied by Medicare as not medically necessary.

    _____ d. The patient must agree in writing, after receiving the services, to personally pay for services denied by Medicare as not medically necessary.

    _____ e. The provider must refund any payment received from a patient for a service denied by Medicare as not medically necessary unless the patient agreed verbally to personally pay for such services.

    _____ f. A refund is not required if the provider could not have known a specific treatment would be ruled unnecessary.

MEDICARE AS A SECONDARY PAYER

33. What should a provider do to prevent fines and penalties for routinely billing Medicare as primary payer when it is the secondary payer? _____

_____

34. The following statements apply to Medicare Secondary Payer fee schedule rules. (Fill in the blanks.)
    a. The primary insurance fee schedule overrules the Medicare schedule on _____ claims only.
    b. NonPARs who do not accept assignment are _____ from collecting amounts above the applicable limiting charge.
    c. Providers are not required to file Medicare secondary claims unless the _____ specifically requests it.

35. If a primary payer pays a claim after Medicare has already paid the claim as a "conditional primary payer," what action must the provider take? _____.

MEDICARE PLANS

36. List three forms of MSP Medicare beneficiaries often purchase to cover the Medicare deductible and coinsurance requirements.
    a. _____
    b. _____
    c. _____

37. Which of the following statements about a Medigap policy is NOT true? (Circle the correct answer.)
    a. A Medigap policy is a private, commercial plan that collects the premiums directly from the patient.
    b. Medigap premiums can widely vary even within the same geographic area.
    c. NonPAR providers are required to include Medigap information on the claim.
    d. The nonPAR provider does not receive an MSN directly from Medicare for nonassigned claims.

38. For each question, enter **Y** for yes or **N** for no on the line provided.

    _____ a. Is an employer-sponsored retirement plan regulated by the federal government?

    _____ b. Are premiums for an employer-sponsored retirement plan paid by the employer?

    _____ c. Are health care providers required to file employer-sponsored retirement plan claims?

    _____ d. If the employer-sponsored retirement claim is not forwarded electronically, will the patient need to file for benefits after the MSN is received?

39. The Medicare-Medicaid Crossover program is (fill in the blanks):
    a. a combination of the _____ and _____ programs.
    b. available to Medicare-eligible persons with incomes below the federal _____ level.

40. List five advantages of joining a Medicare HMO.
    a. _____
    b. _____
    c. _____
    d. _____
    e. _____

150

41. List three disadvantages of joining a Medicare HMO.

a. _____

b. _____

c. _____

42. For HMO-authorized fee-for-service specialty care, the claim is sent directly to ___. (Circle the correct answer.)

a. the HMO

b. the patient

c. Medicare

d. none of the above

43. What is the deadline for filing Medicare-HMO claims? (Circle the correct answer.)

a. 45 days

b. 90 days

c. one year

d. HMO specific

Critical Thinking

44. Why is it important that a practice's billing department be aware of each HMO's timely filing restrictions?

_____

_____

45. Provider Sponsored Organizations are managed care organizations owned and operated by a network of _____ and _____ rather than by an insurance company.

46. Preferred Provider Organizations provide care through a network of _____ and _____.

47. Medicare MSA is a special savings account that is used by the _____ to pay medical bills.

BILLING NOTES

48. Explain how the regional carrier for traditional Medicare claims is selected by CMS.

_____

_____

49. Complete the following sentences.

a. The words that appear on a Railroad Retirement Medicare card are _____
_____ .

b. On the Railroad Retirement Medicare card, the nine-digit identification number has a(n)

_____ .

c. Coal miners' claims are sent to the _____ .

d. The claim filing deadline for both regular Medicare and Railroad Retirement claims is

_____ .

e. A claim for services performed in late November 2002 must be postmarked on or before

_____ .

f. The claim that must be completed for all paper claims is the _____ .

g. All providers are required to file Medicare claims for their _____ .

h. When Medicare is the secondary payer, the _____ must be attached to the Medicare claim.

Know Your Acronyms

50. Define the following acronyms:

a. ABN _____

b. CLIA _____

c. DMERC _____

d. ESRD _____

e. FFS _____

f. GEP _____

g. HMO _____

h. IEP _____

i. LC _____

j. LLP _____

k. MSA _____

l. MSN _____

m. MSP _____

n. nonPAR _____

o. PAR _____

p. PFFS _____

q. PIN _____

r. PPO _____

s. PSO _____

t. QMB _____

u. RBRVS _____

v. RVUs _____

w. SCID _____

x. SEP _____

y. SLMB _____

z. SSA _____

aa. VA _____

EXERCISES

51. Complete Case Studies 14-a through 14-m using the blank claims provided. Follow the step-by-step instructions given in the textbook to properly complete each claim. If a patient has secondary coverage, complete an additional claim using secondary directions from the textbook. You may choose to use a pencil so corrections can be made.

DONALD L. GIVINGS, M.D.

11350 Medical Drive ■ Anywhere US 12345 ■ (101) 111-5555

EIN: 11-123456   SSN: 123-12-1234   MEDICARE: D1234
PIN: DG1234   GRP: DG12345   MEDICAID: DLG1234
BCBS: 12345

Encounter Form

PATIENT INFORMATION:

Name:	Alice E. Worthington
Address:	3301 Sunny Day Dr.
City:	Anywhere
State:	US
Zip Code:	12345
Telephone:	(101) 333-5555
Gender:	Female
Date of Birth:	02-16-1926
Occupation:	
Employer:	None
Spouse's Employer:	

INSURANCE INFORMATION:

Patient Number:	14-a
Place of Service:	Office
Primary Insurance Plan:	Medicare
Primary Insurance Plan ID #:	444-22-3333A
Group #:	
Primary Policyholder:	Alice E. Worthington
Policyholder Date of Birth:	02-16-1926
Relationship to Patient:	Self
Secondary Insurance Plan:	
Secondary Insurance Plan ID #:	
Secondary Policyholder:	

Patient Status ☐ Married ☐ Divorced ☒ Single ☐ Student ☐ Other

DIAGNOSIS INFORMATION

Diagnosis	Code	Diagnosis	Code
1. Breast lump	611.72	5.	
2. Breast pain	611.71	6.	
3. Family history of breast cancer	V16.3	7.	
4.		8.	

PROCEDURE INFORMATION

Description of Procedure or Service	Date	Code	Charge
1. Est. patient OV level II	07-12-YYYY	99212	$65.00
2.			
3.			
4.			
5.			

SPECIAL NOTES:

Refer to Dr. Kutter

(SAMPLE ONLY - NOT APPROVED FOR USE)

CARRIER

☐☐ PICA

HEALTH INSURANCE CLAIM FORM

PICA ☐☐☐

1. MEDICARE MEDICAID CHAMPUS CHAMPVA GROUP HEALTH PLAN FECA BLK LUNG OTHER	1a. INSURED'S I.D. NUMBER (FOR PROGRAM IN ITEM 1)

☐ (Medicare #) ☐ (Medicaid #) ☐ (Sponsor's SSN) ☐ (VA File #) ☐ (SSN or ID) ☐ (SSN) ☐ (ID)

2. PATIENT'S NAME (Last Name, First Name, Middle Initial)	3. PATIENT'S BIRTH DATE MM ⌇ DD ⌇ YY SEX M ☐ F ☐	4. INSURED'S NAME (Last Name, First Name, Middle Initial)
5. PATIENT'S ADDRESS (No. Street)	6. PATIENT RELATIONSHIP TO INSURED Self ☐ Spouse ☐ Child ☐ Other ☐	7. INSURED'S ADDRESS (No. Street)
CITY STATE	8. PATIENT STATUS Single ☐ Married ☐ Other ☐ Employed ☐ Full-Time Student ☐ Part-Time Student ☐	CITY STATE
ZIP CODE TELEPHONE (Include Area Code) ( )		ZIP CODE TELEPHONE (INCLUDE AREA CODE) ( )

9. OTHER INSURED'S NAME (Last Name, First Name, Middle Initial)	10. IS PATIENT'S CONDITION RELATED TO:	11. INSURED'S POLICY GROUP OR FECA NUMBER
a. OTHER INSURED'S POLICY OR GROUP NUMBER	a. EMPLOYMENT? (CURRENT OR PREVIOUS) ☐ YES ☐ NO	a. INSURED'S DATE OF BIRTH MM ⌇ DD ⌇ YY SEX M ☐ F ☐
b. OTHER INSURED'S DATE OF BIRTH MM ⌇ DD ⌇ YY SEX M ☐ F ☐	b. AUTO ACCIDENT? PLACE (State) ☐ YES ☐ NO	b. EMPLOYER'S NAME OR SCHOOL NAME
c. EMPLOYER'S NAME OR SCHOOL NAME	c. OTHER ACCIDENT? ☐ YES ☐ NO	c. INSURANCE PLAN NAME OR PROGRAM NAME
d. INSURANCE PLAN NAME OR PROGRAM NAME	10d. RESERVED FOR LOCAL USE	d. IS THERE ANOTHER HEALTH BENEFIT PLAN? ☐ YES ☐ NO If yes, return to and complete item 9 a – d.

READ BACK OF FORM BEFORE COMPLETING & SIGNING THIS FORM.
12. PATIENT'S OR AUTHORIZED PERSON'S SIGNATURE I authorize the release of any medical or other information necessary to process this claim. I also request payment of government benefits either to myself or to the party who accepts assignment below.

SIGNED _____   DATE _____

13. INSURED'S OR AUTHORIZED PERSON'S SIGNATURE I authorize payment of medical benefits to the undersigned physician or supplier for services described below.

SIGNED _____

PATIENT AND INSURED INFORMATION

14. DATE OF CURRENT: ILLNESS (First symptom) OR MM ⌇ DD ⌇ YY INJURY (Accident) OR PREGNANCY (LMP)	15. IF PATIENT HAS HAD SAME OR SIMILAR ILLNESS, GIVE FIRST DATE MM ⌇ DD ⌇ YY	16. DATES PATIENT UNABLE TO WORK IN CURRENT OCCUPATION MM ⌇ DD ⌇ YY MM ⌇ DD ⌇ YY FROM TO
17. NAME OF REFERRING PHYSICIAN OR OTHER SOURCE	17a. I.D. NUMBER OF REFERRING PHYSICIAN	18. HOSPITALIZATION DATES RELATED TO CURRENT SERVICES MM ⌇ DD ⌇ YY MM ⌇ DD ⌇ YY FROM TO
19. RESERVED FOR LOCAL USE		20. OUTSIDE LAB? $ CHARGES ☐ YES ☐ NO
21. DIAGNOSIS OR NATURE OF ILLNESS OR INJURY. (RELATE ITEMS 1, 2, 3, OR 4 TO ITEM 24E BY LINE) 1. └── . ── 2. └── . ── 3. └── . ── 4. └── . ──		22. MEDICAID RESUBMISSION CODE ORIGINAL REF. NO. 23. PRIOR AUTHORIZATION NUMBER

24. A DATE(S) OF SERVICE From To MM DD YY MM DD YY	B Place of Service	C Type of Service	D PROCEDURES, SERVICES, OR SUPPLIES (Explain Unusual Circumstances) CPT/HCPCS MODIFIER	E DIAGNOSIS CODE	F $ CHARGES	G DAYS OR UNITS	H EPSDT Family Plan	I EMG	J COB	K RESERVED FOR LOCAL USE
1										
2										
3										
4										
5										
6										

25. FEDERAL TAX I.D. NUMBER SSN ☐ EIN ☐	26. PATIENT'S ACCOUNT NO.	27. ACCEPT ASSIGNMENT? (For govt. claims, see back) ☐ YES ☐ NO	28. TOTAL CHARGE $	29. AMOUNT PAID $	30. BALANCE DUE $
31. SIGNATURE OF PHYSICIAN OR SUPPLIER INCLUDING DEGREES OR CREDENTIALS (I certify that the statements on the reverse apply to this bill and are made a part thereof.) SIGNED _____ DATE _____	32. NAME AND ADDRESS OF FACILITY WHERE SERVICES WERE RENDERED (If other than home or office)	33. PHYSICIAN'S, SUPPLIER'S BILLING NAME, ADDRESS, ZIP CODE & PHONE # PIN# GRP#			

PHYSICIAN OR SUPPLIER INFORMATION

(SAMPLE ONLY - NOT APPROVED FOR USE)   PLEASE PRINT OR TYPE   SAMPLE FORM 1500
SAMPLE FORM 1500 SAMPLE FORM 1500

Encounter Form

JONATHAN B. KUTTER, M.D. SURGERY

339 Woodland Place ■ Anywhere US 12345 ■ (101) 111-5555

EIN: 11-556677	SSN: 245-12-1234	MEDICARE: J1234
UPIN: JK1234	BCBS: 12885	MEDICAID: JBK1234

PATIENT INFORMATION:

Name:	Alice E. Worthington
Address:	3301 Sunny Day Dr.
City:	Anywhere
State:	US
Zip Code:	12345
Telephone:	(101) 333-5555
Gender:	Female
Date of Birth:	02-16-1926
Occupation:	
Employer:	None
Spouse's Employer:	

INSURANCE INFORMATION:

Patient Number:	14-b
Place of Service:	Office
Primary Insurance Plan:	Medicare
Primary Insurance Plan ID #:	444-22-3333A
Group #:	
Primary Policyholder:	Alice E. Worthington
Policyholder Date of Birth:	02-16-1926
Relationship to Patient:	Self
Secondary Insurance Plan:	
Secondary Insurance Plan ID #:	
Secondary Policyholder:	

Patient Status ☐ Married ☐ Divorced ☒ Single ☐ Student ☐ Other

DIAGNOSIS INFORMATION

Diagnosis	Code	Diagnosis	Code
1. Breast lump	611.72	5.	
2. Breast pain	611.71	6.	
3. Family history of breast cancer	V16.3	7.	
4.		8.	

PROCEDURE INFORMATION

Description of Procedure or Service	Date	Code	Charge
1. Office consult level II	07-15-YYYY	99242	$75.00
2.			
3.			
4.			
5.			

SPECIAL NOTES:

Referring physician: Donald L. Givings, M.D., UPIN/SSN: DG1234

(SAMPLE ONLY - NOT APPROVED FOR USE)

CARRIER

HEALTH INSURANCE CLAIM FORM

☐☐ PICA   PICA ☐☐

| 1. MEDICARE ☐ (Medicare #) MEDICAID ☐ (Medicaid #) CHAMPUS ☐ (Sponsor's SSN) CHAMPVA ☐ (VA File #) GROUP HEALTH PLAN ☐ (SSN or ID) FECA BLK LUNG ☐ (SSN) OTHER ☐ (ID) | 1a. INSURED'S I.D. NUMBER (FOR PROGRAM IN ITEM 1) |

2. PATIENT'S NAME (Last Name, First Name, Middle Initial)

3. PATIENT'S BIRTH DATE MM ╎ DD ╎ YY   SEX M ☐ F ☐

4. INSURED'S NAME (Last Name, First Name, Middle Initial)

5. PATIENT'S ADDRESS (No. Street)

6. PATIENT RELATIONSHIP TO INSURED
Self ☐ Spouse ☐ Child ☐ Other ☐

7. INSURED'S ADDRESS (No. Street)

CITY   STATE

8. PATIENT STATUS
Single ☐ Married ☐ Other ☐
Employed ☐ Full-Time Student ☐ Part-Time Student ☐

CITY   STATE

ZIP CODE   TELEPHONE (Include Area Code) (   )

ZIP CODE   TELEPHONE (INCLUDE AREA CODE) (   )

9. OTHER INSURED'S NAME (Last Name, First Name, Middle Initial)

10. IS PATIENT'S CONDITION RELATED TO:

11. INSURED'S POLICY GROUP OR FECA NUMBER

a. OTHER INSURED'S POLICY OR GROUP NUMBER

a. EMPLOYMENT? (CURRENT OR PREVIOUS)
☐ YES ☐ NO

a. INSURED'S DATE OF BIRTH MM ╎ DD ╎ YY   SEX M ☐ F ☐

b. OTHER INSURED'S DATE OF BIRTH MM ╎ DD ╎ YY   SEX M ☐ F ☐

b. AUTO ACCIDENT?   PLACE (State)
☐ YES ☐ NO

b. EMPLOYER'S NAME OR SCHOOL NAME

c. EMPLOYER'S NAME OR SCHOOL NAME

c. OTHER ACCIDENT?
☐ YES ☐ NO

c. INSURANCE PLAN NAME OR PROGRAM NAME

d. INSURANCE PLAN NAME OR PROGRAM NAME

10d. RESERVED FOR LOCAL USE

d. IS THERE ANOTHER HEALTH BENEFIT PLAN?
☐ YES ☐ NO   If yes, return to and complete item 9 a – d

READ BACK OF FORM BEFORE COMPLETING & SIGNING THIS FORM.
12. PATIENT'S OR AUTHORIZED PERSON'S SIGNATURE. I authorize the release of any medical or other information necessary to process this claim. I also request payment of government benefits either to myself or to the party who accepts assignment below.

SIGNED _____   DATE _____

13. INSURED'S OR AUTHORIZED PERSON'S SIGNATURE. I authorize payment of medical benefits to the undersigned physician or supplier for services described below.

SIGNED _____

PATIENT AND INSURED INFORMATION

14. DATE OF CURRENT: MM ╎ DD ╎ YY ◄ ILLNESS (First symptom) OR INJURY (Accident) OR PREGNANCY (LMP)

15. IF PATIENT HAS HAD SAME OR SIMILAR ILLNESS, GIVE FIRST DATE MM ╎ DD ╎ YY

16. DATES PATIENT UNABLE TO WORK IN CURRENT OCCUPATION MM ╎ DD ╎ YY   MM ╎ DD ╎ YY   FROM   TO

17. NAME OF REFERRING PHYSICIAN OR OTHER SOURCE

17a. I.D. NUMBER OF REFERRING PHYSICIAN

18. HOSPITALIZATION DATES RELATED TO CURRENT SERVICES MM ╎ DD ╎ YY   MM ╎ DD ╎ YY   FROM   TO

19. RESERVED FOR LOCAL USE

20. OUTSIDE LAB? $ CHARGES
☐ YES ☐ NO

21. DIAGNOSIS OR NATURE OF ILLNESS OR INJURY. (RELATE ITEMS 1, 2, 3, OR 4 TO ITEM 24E BY LINE)
1. └__ . __
2. └__ . __
3. └__ . __
4. └__ . __

22. MEDICAID RESUBMISSION CODE   ORIGINAL REF. NO.

23. PRIOR AUTHORIZATION NUMBER

24. A DATE(S) OF SERVICE From MM DD YY To MM DD YY	B Place of Service	C Type of Service	D PROCEDURES, SERVICES, OR SUPPLIES (Explain Unusual Circumstances) CPT/HCPCS ╎ MODIFIER	E DIAGNOSIS CODE	F $ CHARGES	G DAYS OR UNITS	H EPSDT Family Plan	I EMG	J COB	K RESERVED FOR LOCAL USE
1										
2										
3										
4										
5										
6										

25. FEDERAL TAX I.D. NUMBER SSN ☐ EIN ☐

26. PATIENT'S ACCOUNT NO.

27. ACCEPT ASSIGNMENT? (For govt. claims, see back) ☐ YES ☐ NO

28. TOTAL CHARGE $

29. AMOUNT PAID $

30. BALANCE DUE $

31. SIGNATURE OF PHYSICIAN OR SUPPLIER INCLUDING DEGREES OR CREDENTIALS (I certify that the statements on the reverse apply to this bill and are made a part thereof.)

SIGNED _____   DATE _____

32. NAME AND ADDRESS OF FACILITY WHERE SERVICES WERE RENDERED (If other than home or office)

33. PHYSICIAN'S, SUPPLIER'S BILLING NAME, ADDRESS, ZIP CODE & PHONE #

PIN#   GRP#

PHYSICIAN OR SUPPLIER INFORMATION

(SAMPLE ONLY - NOT APPROVED FOR USE)

PLEASE PRINT OR TYPE

SAMPLE FORM 1500
SAMPLE FORM 1500 SAMPLE FORM 1500

JONATHAN B. KUTTER, M.D. SURGERY

Encounter Form

339 Woodland Place ■ Anywhere US 12345 ■ (101) 111-5555

EIN: 11-556677   SSN: 245-12-1234   MEDICARE: J1234
UPIN: JK1234   BCBS: 12885   MEDICAID: JBK1234

PATIENT INFORMATION:

Name:	Alice E. Worthington
Address:	3301 Sunny Day Dr.
City:	Anywhere
State:	US
Zip Code:	12345
Telephone:	(101) 333-5555
Gender:	Female
Date of Birth:	02-16-1926
Occupation:	
Employer:	None
Spouse's Employer:	

INSURANCE INFORMATION:

Patient Number:	14-c
Place of Service:	Mercy Hospital PIN# M1234
Primary Insurance Plan:	Medicare
Primary Insurance Plan ID #:	444-22-3333A
Group #:	
Primary Policyholder:	Alice E. Worthington
Policyholder Date of Birth:	02-16-1926
Relationship to Patient:	Self
Secondary Insurance Plan:	
Secondary Insurance Plan ID #:	
Secondary Policyholder:	

Patient Status   ☐ Married   ☐ Divorced   ☒ Single   ☐ Student   ☐ Other

DIAGNOSIS INFORMATION

Diagnosis	Code	Diagnosis	Code
1. Breast cancer	174.8	5.	
2.		6.	
3.		7.	
4.		8.	

PROCEDURE INFORMATION

Description of Procedure or Service	Date	Code	Charge
1. Mastectomy, simple, complete	07-22-YYYY	19180	$1,200.00
2.			
3.			
4.			
5.			

SPECIAL NOTES:

Referring physician: Donald L. Givings, M.D., UPIN/SSN: DG1234

(SAMPLE ONLY - NOT APPROVED FOR USE)

CARRIER

| | PICA | | **HEALTH INSURANCE CLAIM FORM** | PICA | | |

| 1. | MEDICARE | MEDICAID | CHAMPUS | CHAMPVA | GROUP HEALTH PLAN | FECA BLK LUNG | OTHER | 1a. INSURED'S I.D. NUMBER (FOR PROGRAM IN ITEM 1) |
| | (Medicare #) | (Medicaid #) | (Sponsor's SSN) | (VA File #) | (SSN or ID) | (SSN) | (ID) | |

2. PATIENT'S NAME (Last Name, First Name, Middle Initial)

3. PATIENT'S BIRTH DATE MM DD YY SEX M F

4. INSURED'S NAME (Last Name, First Name, Middle Initial)

5. PATIENT'S ADDRESS (No. Street)

6. PATIENT RELATIONSHIP TO INSURED Self Spouse Child Other

7. INSURED'S ADDRESS (No. Street)

CITY STATE

8. PATIENT STATUS Single Married Other Employed Full-Time Student Part-Time Student

CITY STATE

ZIP CODE TELEPHONE (Include Area Code) ( )

ZIP CODE TELEPHONE (INCLUDE AREA CODE) ( )

9. OTHER INSURED'S NAME (Last Name, First Name, Middle Initial)

10. IS PATIENT'S CONDITION RELATED TO:

11. INSURED'S POLICY GROUP OR FECA NUMBER

a. OTHER INSURED'S POLICY OR GROUP NUMBER

a. EMPLOYMENT? (CURRENT OR PREVIOUS) YES NO

a. INSURED'S DATE OF BIRTH MM DD YY SEX M F

b. OTHER INSURED'S DATE OF BIRTH MM DD YY SEX M F

b. AUTO ACCIDENT? PLACE (State) YES NO

b. EMPLOYER'S NAME OR SCHOOL NAME

c. EMPLOYER'S NAME OR SCHOOL NAME

c. OTHER ACCIDENT? YES NO

c. INSURANCE PLAN NAME OR PROGRAM NAME

d. INSURANCE PLAN NAME OR PROGRAM NAME

10d. RESERVED FOR LOCAL USE

d. IS THERE ANOTHER HEALTH BENEFIT PLAN? YES NO If yes, return to and complete item 9 a – d.

READ BACK OF FORM BEFORE COMPLETING & SIGNING THIS FORM.
12. PATIENT'S OR AUTHORIZED PERSON'S SIGNATURE I authorize the release of any medical or other information necessary to process this claim. I also request payment of government benefits either to myself or to the party who accepts assignment below.

SIGNED _____ DATE _____

13. INSURED'S OR AUTHORIZED PERSON'S SIGNATURE I authorize payment of medical benefits to the undersigned physician or supplier for services described below.

SIGNED _____

PATIENT AND INSURED INFORMATION

14. DATE OF CURRENT: MM DD YY ILLNESS (First symptom) OR INJURY (Accident) OR PREGNANCY (LMP)

15. IF PATIENT HAS HAD SAME OR SIMILAR ILLNESS, GIVE FIRST DATE MM DD YY

16. DATES PATIENT UNABLE TO WORK IN CURRENT OCCUPATION MM DD YY FROM TO MM DD YY

17. NAME OF REFERRING PHYSICIAN OR OTHER SOURCE

17a. I.D. NUMBER OF REFERRING PHYSICIAN

18. HOSPITALIZATION DATES RELATED TO CURRENT SERVICES MM DD YY FROM TO MM DD YY

19. RESERVED FOR LOCAL USE

20. OUTSIDE LAB? YES NO $ CHARGES

21. DIAGNOSIS OR NATURE OF ILLNESS OR INJURY. (RELATE ITEMS 1, 2, 3, OR 4 TO ITEM 24E BY LINE)

1. _____ 3. _____

2. _____ 4. _____

22. MEDICAID RESUBMISSION CODE ORIGINAL REF. NO.

23. PRIOR AUTHORIZATION NUMBER

24. A DATE(S) OF SERVICE						B Place of Service	C Type of Service	D PROCEDURES, SERVICES, OR SUPPLIES (Explain Unusual Circumstances)		E DIAGNOSIS CODE	F $ CHARGES	G DAYS OR UNITS	H EPSDT Family Plan	I EMG	J COB	K RESERVED FOR LOCAL USE
From			To					CPT/HCPCS	MODIFIER							
MM	DD	YY	MM	DD	YY											
1																
2																
3																
4																
5																
6																

25. FEDERAL TAX I.D. NUMBER SSN EIN

26. PATIENT'S ACCOUNT NO.

27. ACCEPT ASSIGNMENT? (For govt. claims, see back) YES NO

28. TOTAL CHARGE $

29. AMOUNT PAID $

30. BALANCE DUE $

31. SIGNATURE OF PHYSICIAN OR SUPPLIER INCLUDING DEGREES OR CREDENTIALS (I certify that the statements on the reverse apply to this bill and are made a part thereof.)

SIGNED _____ DATE _____

32. NAME AND ADDRESS OF FACILITY WHERE SERVICES WERE RENDERED (If other than home or office)

33. PHYSICIAN'S, SUPPLIER'S BILLING NAME, ADDRESS, ZIP CODE & PHONE #

PIN# GRP#

PHYSICIAN OR SUPPLIER INFORMATION

(SAMPLE ONLY - NOT APPROVED FOR USE)

PLEASE PRINT OR TYPE

SAMPLE FORM 1500
SAMPLE FORM 1500 SAMPLE FORM 1500

Case Study 14-d

JONATHAN B. KUTTER, M.D. SURGERY

339 Woodland Place ■ Anywhere US 12345 ■ (101) 111-5555

EIN: 11-556677	SSN: 245-12-1234	MEDICARE: J1234
UPIN: JK1234	BCBS: 12885	MEDICAID: JBK1234

Encounter Form

PATIENT INFORMATION:

Name:	Alice E. Worthington
Address:	3301 Sunny Day Dr.
City:	Anywhere
State:	US
Zip Code:	12345
Telephone:	(101) 333-5555
Gender:	Female
Date of Birth:	02-16-1926
Occupation:	
Employer:	None
Spouse's Employer:	

INSURANCE INFORMATION:

Patient Number:	14-d
Place of Service:	Office
Primary Insurance Plan:	Medicare
Primary Insurance Plan ID #:	444-22-3333A
Group #:	
Primary Policyholder:	Alice E. Worthington
Policyholder Date of Birth:	02-16-1926
Relationship to Patient:	Self
Secondary Insurance Plan:	
Secondary Insurance Plan ID #:	
Secondary Policyholder:	

Patient Status ☐ Married ☐ Divorced ☒ Single ☐ Student ☐ Other

DIAGNOSIS INFORMATION

Diagnosis	Code	Diagnosis	Code
1. Breast cancer	174.8	5.	
2.		6.	
3.		7.	
4.		8.	

PROCEDURE INFORMATION

Description of Procedure or Service	Date	Code	Charge
1. Postoperative follow-up visit	08-12-YYYY	99024	$0.00
2.			
3.			
4.			
5.			

SPECIAL NOTES:

Referring physician: Donald L. Givings, M.D., UPIN/SSN: DG1234

PLEASE
DO NOT
STAPLE
IN THIS
AREA

CARRIER

PICA

HEALTH INSURANCE CLAIM FORM   PICA

1.	MEDICARE	MEDICAID	CHAMPUS	CHAMPVA	GROUP HEALTH PLAN	FECA BLK LUNG	OTHER	1a. INSURED'S I.D. NUMBER	(FOR PROGRAM IN ITEM 1)
	☐ (Medicare #)	☐ (Medicaid #)	☐ (Sponsor's SSN)	☐ (VA File #)	☐ (SSN or ID)	☐ (SSN)	☐ (ID)		

2. PATIENT'S NAME (Last Name, First Name, Middle Initial)

3. PATIENT'S BIRTH DATE   MM | DD | YY   SEX   M ☐   F ☐

4. INSURED'S NAME (Last Name, First Name, Middle Initial)

5. PATIENT'S ADDRESS (No. Street)

6. PATIENT RELATIONSHIP TO INSURED   Self ☐   Spouse ☐   Child ☐   Other ☐

7. INSURED'S ADDRESS (No. Street)

CITY   STATE

8. PATIENT STATUS   Single ☐   Married ☐   Other ☐
Employed ☐   Full-Time Student ☐   Part-Time Student ☐

CITY   STATE

ZIP CODE   TELEPHONE (Include Area Code) (   )

ZIP CODE   TELEPHONE (INCLUDE AREA CODE) (   )

9. OTHER INSURED'S NAME (Last Name, First Name, Middle Initial)

10. IS PATIENT'S CONDITION RELATED TO:

11. INSURED'S POLICY GROUP OR FECA NUMBER

a. OTHER INSURED'S POLICY OR GROUP NUMBER

a. EMPLOYMENT? (CURRENT OR PREVIOUS)   ☐ YES   ☐ NO

a. INSURED'S DATE OF BIRTH   MM | DD | YY   SEX   M ☐   F ☐

b. OTHER INSURED'S DATE OF BIRTH   MM | DD | YY   SEX   M ☐   F ☐

b. AUTO ACCIDENT?   PLACE (State)   ☐ YES   ☐ NO

b. EMPLOYER'S NAME OR SCHOOL NAME

c. EMPLOYER'S NAME OR SCHOOL NAME

c. OTHER ACCIDENT?   ☐ YES   ☐ NO

c. INSURANCE PLAN NAME OR PROGRAM NAME

d. INSURANCE PLAN NAME OR PROGRAM NAME

10d. RESERVED FOR LOCAL USE

d. IS THERE ANOTHER HEALTH BENEFIT PLAN?   ☐ YES   ☐ NO   If yes, return to and complete item 9 a – d.

READ BACK OF FORM BEFORE COMPLETING & SIGNING THIS FORM.
12. PATIENT'S OR AUTHORIZED PERSON'S SIGNATURE I authorize the release of any medical or other information necessary to process this claim. I also request payment of government benefits either to myself or to the party who accepts assignment below.

SIGNED _____   DATE _____

13. INSURED'S OR AUTHORIZED PERSON'S SIGNATURE I authorize payment of medical benefits to the undersigned physician or supplier for services described below.

SIGNED _____

PATIENT AND INSURED INFORMATION

14. DATE OF CURRENT: ILLNESS (First symptom) OR INJURY (Accident) OR PREGNANCY (LMP)   MM | DD | YY

15. IF PATIENT HAS HAD SAME OR SIMILAR ILLNESS, GIVE FIRST DATE   MM | DD | YY

16. DATES PATIENT UNABLE TO WORK IN CURRENT OCCUPATION   FROM MM | DD | YY   TO MM | DD | YY

17. NAME OF REFERRING PHYSICIAN OR OTHER SOURCE

17a. I.D. NUMBER OF REFERRING PHYSICIAN

18. HOSPITALIZATION DATES RELATED TO CURRENT SERVICES   FROM MM | DD | YY   TO MM | DD | YY

19. RESERVED FOR LOCAL USE

20. OUTSIDE LAB?   ☐ YES   ☐ NO $ CHARGES

21. DIAGNOSIS OR NATURE OF ILLNESS OR INJURY. (RELATE ITEMS 1, 2, 3, OR 4 TO ITEM 24E BY LINE)
1. |___ . __| 3. |___ . __|
2. |___ . __| 4. |___ . __|

22. MEDICAID RESUBMISSION CODE   ORIGINAL REF. NO.

23. PRIOR AUTHORIZATION NUMBER

24. A DATE(S) OF SERVICE						B Place of Service	C Type of Service	D PROCEDURES, SERVICES, OR SUPPLIES (Explain Unusual Circumstances) CPT/HCPCS	MODIFIER	E DIAGNOSIS CODE	F $ CHARGES	G DAYS OR UNITS	H EPSDT Family Plan	I EMG	J COB	K RESERVED FOR LOCAL USE
From MM	DD	YY	To MM	DD	YY											
1																
2																
3																
4																
5																
6																

25. FEDERAL TAX I.D. NUMBER   SSN ☐ EIN ☐

26. PATIENT'S ACCOUNT NO.

27. ACCEPT ASSIGNMENT? (For govt. claims, see back)   ☐ YES   ☐ NO

28. TOTAL CHARGE $

29. AMOUNT PAID $

30. BALANCE DUE $

31. SIGNATURE OF PHYSICIAN OR SUPPLIER INCLUDING DEGREES OR CREDENTIALS (I certify that the statements on the reverse apply to this bill and are made a part thereof.)

SIGNED _____   DATE _____

32. NAME AND ADDRESS OF FACILITY WHERE SERVICES WERE RENDERED (If other than home or office)

33. PHYSICIAN'S, SUPPLIER'S BILLING NAME, ADDRESS, ZIP CODE & PHONE #

PIN#   GRP#

PHYSICIAN OR SUPPLIER INFORMATION

DONALD L. GIVINGS, M.D.

Encounter Form

11350 Medical Drive ■ Anywhere US 12345 ■ (101) 111-5555

EIN: 11-123456	SSN: 123-12-1234	MEDICARE: D1234
PIN: DG1234	GRP: DG12345	MEDICAID: DLG1234
BCBS: 12345		

PATIENT INFORMATION:

Name:	Rebecca Nichols
Address:	384 Dean Street
City:	Anywhere
State:	US
Zip Code:	12345
Telephone:	(101) 333-5555
Gender:	Female
Date of Birth:	10-12-1925
Occupation:	
Employer:	None
Spouse's Employer:	

INSURANCE INFORMATION:

Patient Number:	14-e
Place of Service:	Mercy Hospital
Primary Insurance Plan:	Medicare
Primary Insurance Plan ID #:	667-14-3344A
Group #:	
Primary Policyholder:	Rebecca Nichols
Policyholder Date of Birth:	10-12-1925
Relationship to Patient:	Self
Secondary Insurance Plan:	
Secondary Insurance Plan ID #:	
Secondary Policyholder:	

Patient Status ☐ Married ☐ Divorced ☒ Single ☐ Student ☐ Other

DIAGNOSIS INFORMATION

Diagnosis	Code	Diagnosis	Code
1. Rectal bleeding	569.3	5.	
2. Diarrhea	787.91	6.	
3. Abnormal loss of weight	783.21	7.	
4.		8.	

PROCEDURE INFORMATION

Description of Procedure or Service	Date	Code	Charge
1. Initial hosp. level IV	08-06-YYYY	99224	$175.00
2. Subsq. hosp. level III	08-07-YYYY	99233	85.00
3. Subsq. hosp. level III	08-08-YYYY	99233	85.00
4. Subsq. hosp. level II	08-09-YYYY	99232	75.00
5. Hosp. discharge, 30 min.	08-10-YYYY	99238	75.00

SPECIAL NOTES:

Dr. Gestive saw the patient for a consult on August 7 & August 8.

PLEASE
DO NOT
STAPLE
IN THIS
AREA

CARRIER

[ ] [ ] PICA

HEALTH INSURANCE CLAIM FORM

PICA [ ] [ ]

| 1. | | | | GROUP | FECA | OTHER | 1a. INSURED'S I.D. NUMBER | (FOR PROGRAM IN ITEM 1) |

1. MEDICARE MEDICAID CHAMPUS CHAMPVA GROUP HEALTH PLAN FECA BLK LUNG OTHER

[ ] (Medicare #) [ ] (Medicaid #) [ ] (Sponsor's SSN) [ ] (VA File #) [ ] (SSN or ID) [ ] (SSN) [ ] (ID)

1a. INSURED'S I.D. NUMBER (FOR PROGRAM IN ITEM 1)

2. PATIENT'S NAME (Last Name, First Name, Middle Initial)

3. PATIENT'S BIRTH DATE
MM | DD | YY   SEX
M [ ]   F [ ]

4. INSURED'S NAME (Last Name, First Name, Middle Initial)

5. PATIENT'S ADDRESS (No. Street)

6. PATIENT RELATIONSHIP TO INSURED
Self [ ] Spouse [ ] Child [ ] Other [ ]

7. INSURED'S ADDRESS (No. Street)

CITY   STATE

8. PATIENT STATUS
Single [ ]   Married [ ]   Other [ ]

Employed [ ] Full-Time Student [ ] Part-Time Student [ ]

CITY   STATE

ZIP CODE   TELEPHONE (Include Area Code)
(   )

ZIP CODE   TELEPHONE (INCLUDE AREA CODE)
(   )

9. OTHER INSURED'S NAME (Last Name, First Name, Middle Initial)

10. IS PATIENT'S CONDITION RELATED TO:

11. INSURED'S POLICY GROUP OR FECA NUMBER

a. OTHER INSURED'S POLICY OR GROUP NUMBER

a. EMPLOYMENT? (CURRENT OR PREVIOUS)
[ ] YES [ ] NO

a. INSURED'S DATE OF BIRTH
MM | DD | YY   SEX
M [ ] F [ ]

b. OTHER INSURED'S DATE OF BIRTH
MM | DD | YY   SEX
M [ ] F [ ]

b. AUTO ACCIDENT?   PLACE (State)
[ ] YES [ ] NO

b. EMPLOYER'S NAME OR SCHOOL NAME

c. EMPLOYER'S NAME OR SCHOOL NAME

c. OTHER ACCIDENT?
[ ] YES [ ] NO

c. INSURANCE PLAN NAME OR PROGRAM NAME

d. INSURANCE PLAN NAME OR PROGRAM NAME

10d. RESERVED FOR LOCAL USE

d. IS THERE ANOTHER HEALTH BENEFIT PLAN?
[ ] YES [ ] NO   If yes, return to and complete item 9 a – d.

READ BACK OF FORM BEFORE COMPLETING & SIGNING THIS FORM.
12. PATIENT'S OR AUTHORIZED PERSON'S SIGNATURE I authorize the release of any medical or other information necessary to process this claim. I also request payment of government benefits either to myself or to the party who accepts assignment below.

SIGNED _____   DATE _____

13. INSURED'S OR AUTHORIZED PERSON'S SIGNATURE I authorize payment of medical benefits to the undersigned physician or supplier for services described below

SIGNED _____

PATIENT AND INSURED INFORMATION

14. DATE OF CURRENT:
MM | DD | YY
ILLNESS (First symptom) OR
INJURY (Accident) OR
PREGNANCY (LMP)

15. IF PATIENT HAS HAD SAME OR SIMILAR ILLNESS, GIVE FIRST DATE   MM | DD | YY

16. DATES PATIENT UNABLE TO WORK IN CURRENT OCCUPATION
MM | DD | YY   MM | DD | YY
FROM   TO

17. NAME OF REFERRING PHYSICIAN OR OTHER SOURCE

17a. I.D. NUMBER OF REFERRING PHYSICIAN

18. HOSPITALIZATION DATES RELATED TO CURRENT SERVICES
MM | DD | YY   MM | DD | YY
FROM   TO

19. RESERVED FOR LOCAL USE

20. OUTSIDE LAB? $ CHARGES
[ ] YES [ ] NO

21. DIAGNOSIS OR NATURE OF ILLNESS OR INJURY. (RELATE ITEMS 1, 2, 3, OR 4 TO ITEM 24E BY LINE)

1. |___.__   3. |___.__

2. |___.__   4. |___.__

22. MEDICAID RESUBMISSION
CODE   ORIGINAL REF. NO.

23. PRIOR AUTHORIZATION NUMBER

24. A				B	C	D	E	F	G	H	I	J	K
DATE(S) OF SERVICE				Place of Service	Type of Service	PROCEDURES, SERVICES, OR SUPPLIES (Explain Unusual Circumstances)	DIAGNOSIS CODE	$ CHARGES	DAYS OR UNITS	EPSDT Family Plan	EMG	COB	RESERVED FOR LOCAL USE
From		To				CPT/HCPCS	MODIFIER							
MM	DD	YY	MM	DD	YY										
1														
2														
3														
4														
5														
6														

25. FEDERAL TAX I.D. NUMBER   SSN EIN
[ ] [ ]

26. PATIENT'S ACCOUNT NO.

27. ACCEPT ASSIGNMENT?
(For govt. claims, see back)
[ ] YES [ ] NO

28. TOTAL CHARGE
$

29. AMOUNT PAID
$

30. BALANCE DUE
$

31. SIGNATURE OF PHYSICIAN OR SUPPLIER INCLUDING DEGREES OR CREDENTIALS
(I certify that the statements on the reverse apply to this bill and are made a part thereof.)

SIGNED _____ DATE _____

32. NAME AND ADDRESS OF FACILITY WHERE SERVICES WERE RENDERED (If other than home or office)

33. PHYSICIAN'S, SUPPLIER'S BILLING NAME, ADDRESS, ZIP CODE & PHONE #

PIN#   GRP#

PHYSICIAN OR SUPPLIER INFORMATION

COLIN D. GESTIVE, M.D. GASTROENTEROLOGY

35 Ulcer Place ■ Anywhere US 12345 ■ (101) 111-5555

EIN: 11-447766	SSN: 321-12-1234	MEDICARE: C1234
UPIN: CD1234	BCBS: 44345	MEDICAID: CDG1234

Encounter Form

PATIENT INFORMATION:

Name:	Rebecca Nichols
Address:	384 Dean Street
City:	Anywhere
State:	US
Zip Code:	12345
Telephone:	(101) 333-5555
Gender:	Female
Date of Birth:	10-12-1925
Occupation:	
Employer:	None
Spouse's Employer:	

INSURANCE INFORMATION:

Patient Number:	14-f
Place of Service:	Mercy Hospital
Primary Insurance Plan:	Medicare
Primary Insurance Plan ID #:	667-14-3344A
Group #:	
Primary Policyholder:	Rebecca Nichols
Policyholder Date of Birth:	10-12-1925
Relationship to Patient:	Self
Secondary Insurance Plan:	
Secondary Insurance Plan ID #:	
Secondary Policyholder:	

Patient Status ☐ Married   ☐ Divorced   ☒ Single   ☐ Student   ☐ Other

DIAGNOSIS INFORMATION

Diagnosis	Code	Diagnosis	Code
1. Diverticulitis of the colon with hemorrhage	562.13	5.	
2.		6.	
3.		7.	
4.		8.	

PROCEDURE INFORMATION

Description of Procedure or Service	Date	Code	Charge
1. Initial inpatient consult level IV	08-07-YYYY	99254	$220.00
2. Follow-up inpatient consult level III	08-08-YYYY	99263	80.00
3.			
4.			
5.			

SPECIAL NOTES:

Referring physician: Donald L. Givings, M.D.   UPIN/SSN: DG1234

PLEASE
DO NOT
STAPLE
IN THIS
AREA

CARRIER

[ ][ ] PICA

HEALTH INSURANCE CLAIM FORM

PICA [ ][ ][ ]

1. MEDICARE MEDICAID CHAMPUS CHAMPVA GROUP HEALTH PLAN FECA BLK LUNG OTHER
    [ ] (Medicare #) [ ] (Medicaid #) [ ] (Sponsor's SSN) [ ] (VA File #) [ ] (SSN or ID) [ ] (SSN) [ ] (ID)

1a. INSURED'S I.D. NUMBER (FOR PROGRAM IN ITEM 1)

2. PATIENT'S NAME (Last Name, First Name, Middle Initial)

3. PATIENT'S BIRTH DATE MM | DD | YY   SEX M [ ] F [ ]

4. INSURED'S NAME (Last Name, First Name, Middle Initial)

5. PATIENT'S ADDRESS (No. Street)

6. PATIENT RELATIONSHIP TO INSURED
    Self [ ] Spouse [ ] Child [ ] Other [ ]

7. INSURED'S ADDRESS (No. Street)

CITY STATE

8. PATIENT STATUS
    Single [ ] Married [ ] Other [ ]
    Employed [ ] Full-Time Student [ ] Part-Time Student [ ]

CITY STATE

ZIP CODE TELEPHONE (Include Area Code) (   )

ZIP CODE TELEPHONE (INCLUDE AREA CODE) (   )

9. OTHER INSURED'S NAME (Last Name, First Name, Middle Initial)

10. IS PATIENT'S CONDITION RELATED TO:

11. INSURED'S POLICY GROUP OR FECA NUMBER

a. OTHER INSURED'S POLICY OR GROUP NUMBER

a. EMPLOYMENT? (CURRENT OR PREVIOUS)
    [ ] YES [ ] NO

a. INSURED'S DATE OF BIRTH MM | DD | YY   SEX M [ ] F [ ]

b. OTHER INSURED'S DATE OF BIRTH MM | DD | YY   SEX M [ ] F [ ]

b. AUTO ACCIDENT? PLACE (State)
    [ ] YES [ ] NO

b. EMPLOYER'S NAME OR SCHOOL NAME

c. EMPLOYER'S NAME OR SCHOOL NAME

c. OTHER ACCIDENT?
    [ ] YES [ ] NO

c. INSURANCE PLAN NAME OR PROGRAM NAME

d. INSURANCE PLAN NAME OR PROGRAM NAME

10d. RESERVED FOR LOCAL USE

d. IS THERE ANOTHER HEALTH BENEFIT PLAN?
    [ ] YES [ ] NO If yes, return to and complete item 9 a – d.

READ BACK OF FORM BEFORE COMPLETING & SIGNING THIS FORM.

12. PATIENT'S OR AUTHORIZED PERSON'S SIGNATURE I authorize the release of any medical or other information necessary to process this claim. I also request payment of government benefits either to myself or to the party who accepts assignment below.

SIGNED _____ DATE _____

13. INSURED'S OR AUTHORIZED PERSON'S SIGNATURE I authorize payment of medical benefits to the undersigned physician or supplier for services described below.

SIGNED _____

PATIENT AND INSURED INFORMATION

14. DATE OF CURRENT: ILLNESS (First symptom) OR INJURY (Accident) OR PREGNANCY (LMP) MM | DD | YY

15. IF PATIENT HAS HAD SAME OR SIMILAR ILLNESS, GIVE FIRST DATE MM | DD | YY

16. DATES PATIENT UNABLE TO WORK IN CURRENT OCCUPATION MM | DD | YY FROM TO MM | DD | YY

17. NAME OF REFERRING PHYSICIAN OR OTHER SOURCE

17a. I.D. NUMBER OF REFERRING PHYSICIAN

18. HOSPITALIZATION DATES RELATED TO CURRENT SERVICES MM | DD | YY FROM TO MM | DD | YY

19. RESERVED FOR LOCAL USE

20. OUTSIDE LAB? $ CHARGES
    [ ] YES [ ] NO

21. DIAGNOSIS OR NATURE OF ILLNESS OR INJURY. (RELATE ITEMS 1, 2, 3, OR 4 TO ITEM 24E BY LINE)

1. |___.__|
2. |___.__|
3. |___.__|
4. |___.__|

22. MEDICAID RESUBMISSION CODE ORIGINAL REF. NO.

23. PRIOR AUTHORIZATION NUMBER

24. A DATE(S) OF SERVICE						B Place of Service	C Type of Service	D PROCEDURES, SERVICES, OR SUPPLIES (Explain Unusual Circumstances) CPT/HCPCS	MODIFIER	E DIAGNOSIS CODE	F $ CHARGES	G DAYS OR UNITS	H EPSDT Family Plan	I EMG	J COB	K RESERVED FOR LOCAL USE
From MM	DD	YY	To MM	DD	YY											
1																
2																
3																
4																
5																
6																

25. FEDERAL TAX I.D. NUMBER SSN [ ] EIN [ ]

26. PATIENT'S ACCOUNT NO.

27. ACCEPT ASSIGNMENT? (For govt. claims, see back) [ ] YES [ ] NO

28. TOTAL CHARGE $

29. AMOUNT PAID $

30. BALANCE DUE $

31. SIGNATURE OF PHYSICIAN OR SUPPLIER INCLUDING DEGREES OR CREDENTIALS (I certify that the statements on the reverse apply to this bill and are made a part thereof.)

SIGNED _____ DATE _____

32. NAME AND ADDRESS OF FACILITY WHERE SERVICES WERE RENDERED (If other than home or office)

33. PHYSICIAN'S, SUPPLIER'S BILLING NAME, ADDRESS, ZIP CODE & PHONE #

PIN# _____ GRP# _____

PHYSICIAN OR SUPPLIER INFORMATION

PLEASE PRINT OR TYPE

SAMPLE FORM 1500
SAMPLE FORM 1500 SAMPLE FORM 1500

LISA M. MASON, M.D., FAMILY PRACTICE

547 Antigua Road ■ Anywhere US 12345 ■ (101) 111-5555

| EIN: 11-495867 | SSN: 333-12-9484 | MEDICARE: L1234 |
| UPIN: LM4234 | BCBS: 39994 | MEDICAID: LMM1234 |

Encounter Form

PATIENT INFORMATION:

Name:	Samuel T. Mahoney Jr.
Address:	498 Meadow Lane
City:	Anywhere
State:	US
Zip Code:	12345
Telephone:	(101) 333-5555
Gender:	Male
Date of Birth:	09-04-1930
Occupation:	
Employer:	None
Spouse's Employer:	

INSURANCE INFORMATION:

Patient Number:	14-g
Place of Service:	Office
Primary Insurance Plan:	Medicare
Primary Insurance Plan ID #:	312-78-5894A
Group #:	
Primary Policyholder:	Samuel T. Mahoney Jr.
Policyholder Date of Birth:	09-04-1930
Relationship to Patient:	Self
Secondary Insurance Plan:	
Secondary Insurance Plan ID #:	
Secondary Policyholder:	

Patient Status ☒ Married   ☐ Divorced   ☐ Single   ☐ Student   ☐ Other

DIAGNOSIS INFORMATION

Diagnosis	Code	Diagnosis	Code
1. Asthma, unspecified	493.90	5.	
2. URI	465.9	6.	
3.		7.	
4.		8.	

PROCEDURE INFORMATION

Description of Procedure or Service	Date	Code	Charge
1. Est. patient OV level II	10-03-YYYY	99212	$25.16
2.			
3.			
4.			
5.			

SPECIAL NOTES:

Dr. Mason is nonPAR with Medicare

PLEASE
DO NOT
STAPLE
IN THIS
AREA

CARRIER

◻◻ PICA

HEALTH INSURANCE CLAIM FORM PICA ◻◻◻

1. MEDICARE MEDICAID CHAMPUS CHAMPVA GROUP HEALTH PLAN FECA BLK LUNG OTHER
◻ (Medicare #) ◻ (Medicaid #) ◻ (Sponsor's SSN) ◻ (VA File #) ◻ (SSN or ID) ◻ (SSN) ◻ (ID)

1a. INSURED'S I.D. NUMBER (FOR PROGRAM IN ITEM 1)

2. PATIENT'S NAME (Last Name, First Name, Middle Initial)

3. PATIENT'S BIRTH DATE MM │ DD │ YY SEX M ◻ F ◻

4. INSURED'S NAME (Last Name, First Name, Middle Initial)

5. PATIENT'S ADDRESS (No. Street)

6. PATIENT RELATIONSHIP TO INSURED Self ◻ Spouse ◻ Child ◻ Other ◻

7. INSURED'S ADDRESS (No. Street)

CITY STATE

8. PATIENT STATUS Single ◻ Married ◻ Other ◻
Employed ◻ Full-Time Student ◻ Part-Time Student ◻

CITY STATE

ZIP CODE TELEPHONE (Include Area Code) (   )

ZIP CODE TELEPHONE (INCLUDE AREA CODE) (   )

9. OTHER INSURED'S NAME (Last Name, First Name, Middle Initial)

10. IS PATIENT'S CONDITION RELATED TO:

11. INSURED'S POLICY GROUP OR FECA NUMBER

a. OTHER INSURED'S POLICY OR GROUP NUMBER

a. EMPLOYMENT? (CURRENT OR PREVIOUS) ◻ YES ◻ NO

a. INSURED'S DATE OF BIRTH MM │ DD │ YY SEX M ◻ F ◻

b. OTHER INSURED'S DATE OF BIRTH MM │ DD │ YY SEX M ◻ F ◻

b. AUTO ACCIDENT? PLACE (State) ◻ YES ◻ NO

b. EMPLOYER'S NAME OR SCHOOL NAME

c. EMPLOYER'S NAME OR SCHOOL NAME

c. OTHER ACCIDENT? ◻ YES ◻ NO

c. INSURANCE PLAN NAME OR PROGRAM NAME

d. INSURANCE PLAN NAME OR PROGRAM NAME

10d. RESERVED FOR LOCAL USE

d. IS THERE ANOTHER HEALTH BENEFIT PLAN? ◻ YES ◻ NO If yes, return to and complete item 9 a - d.

READ BACK OF FORM BEFORE COMPLETING & SIGNING THIS FORM.
12. PATIENT'S OR AUTHORIZED PERSON'S SIGNATURE I authorize the release of any medical or other information necessary to process this claim. I also request payment of government benefits either to myself or to the party who accepts assignment below.

SIGNED _____ DATE _____

13. INSURED'S OR AUTHORIZED PERSON'S SIGNATURE I authorize payment of medical benefits to the undersigned physician or supplier for services described below.

SIGNED _____

PATIENT AND INSURED INFORMATION

14. DATE OF CURRENT: ILLNESS (First symptom) OR INJURY (Accident) OR PREGNANCY (LMP) MM │ DD │ YY

15. IF PATIENT HAS HAD SAME OR SIMILAR ILLNESS, GIVE FIRST DATE MM │ DD │ YY

16. DATES PATIENT UNABLE TO WORK IN CURRENT OCCUPATION FROM MM │ DD │ YY TO MM │ DD │ YY

17. NAME OF REFERRING PHYSICIAN OR OTHER SOURCE

17a. I.D. NUMBER OF REFERRING PHYSICIAN

18. HOSPITALIZATION DATES RELATED TO CURRENT SERVICES FROM MM │ DD │ YY TO MM │ DD │ YY

19. RESERVED FOR LOCAL USE

20. OUTSIDE LAB? ◻ YES ◻ NO $ CHARGES

21. DIAGNOSIS OR NATURE OF ILLNESS OR INJURY. (RELATE ITEMS 1, 2, 3, OR 4 TO ITEM 24E BY LINE)
1. |___.__   3. |___.__
2. |___.__   4. |___.__

22. MEDICAID RESUBMISSION CODE ORIGINAL REF. NO.

23. PRIOR AUTHORIZATION NUMBER

24. A DATE(S) OF SERVICE						B Place of Service	C Type of Service	D PROCEDURES, SERVICES, OR SUPPLIES (Explain Unusual Circumstances)		E DIAGNOSIS CODE	F $ CHARGES	G DAYS OR UNITS	H EPSDT Family Plan	I EMG	J COB	K RESERVED FOR LOCAL USE
From MM	DD	YY	To MM	DD	YY			CPT/HCPCS	MODIFIER							
1																
2																
3																
4																
5																
6																

25. FEDERAL TAX I.D. NUMBER SSN ◻ EIN ◻

26. PATIENT'S ACCOUNT NO.

27. ACCEPT ASSIGNMENT? (For govt. claims, see back) ◻ YES ◻ NO

28. TOTAL CHARGE $

29. AMOUNT PAID $

30. BALANCE DUE $

31. SIGNATURE OF PHYSICIAN OR SUPPLIER INCLUDING DEGREES OR CREDENTIALS (I certify that the statements on the reverse apply to this bill and are made a part thereof.)

SIGNED _____ DATE _____

32. NAME AND ADDRESS OF FACILITY WHERE SERVICES WERE RENDERED (If other than home or office)

33. PHYSICIAN'S, SUPPLIER'S BILLING NAME, ADDRESS, ZIP CODE & PHONE #

PIN# GRP#

PHYSICIAN OR SUPPLIER INFORMATION

PLEASE PRINT OR TYPE

SAMPLE FORM 1500
SAMPLE FORM 1500 SAMPLE FORM 1500

DONALD L. GIVINGS, M.D.

11350 Medical Drive ■ Anywhere US 12345 ■ (101) 111-5555

EIN: 11-123456   SSN: 123-12-1234   MEDICARE: D1234
PIN: DG1234   GRP: DG12345   MEDICAID: DLG1234
BCBS: 12345

Encounter Form

PATIENT INFORMATION:

Name:	Abraham N. Freed
Address:	12 Nottingham Circle
City:	Anywhere
State:	US
Zip Code:	12345
Telephone:	(101) 333-5555
Gender:	Male
Date of Birth:	10-03-1922
Occupation:	
Employer:	Retired Johnson Steel
Spouse's Employer:	

INSURANCE INFORMATION:

Patient Number:	14-h
Place of Service:	Office
Primary Insurance Plan:	Medicare
Primary Insurance Plan ID #:	645-45-4545A
Group #:	
Primary Policyholder:	Abraham N. Freed
Policyholder Date of Birth:	10-03-1922
Relationship to Patient:	Self
Secondary Insurance Plan:	BCBS Medigap
Secondary Insurance Plan ID #:	NXY645-45-4545 987
Secondary Policyholder:	Abraham N. Freed

Patient Status   ☒ Married   ☐ Divorced   ☐ Single   ☐ Student   ☐ Other

DIAGNOSIS INFORMATION

Diagnosis	Code	Diagnosis	Code
1. Hypertension, malignant	401.0	5.	
2. Dizziness	780.2	6.	
3.		7.	
4.		8.	

PROCEDURE INFORMATION

Description of Procedure or Service	Date	Code	Charge
1. New patient OV level IV	03-07-YYYY	99204	$100.00
2. EKG	03-07-YYYY	93000	50.00
3. Venipuncture	03-07-YYYY	36415	8.00
4.			
5.			

SPECIAL NOTES:

Return visit: 2 weeks

PLEASE
DO NOT
STAPLE
IN THIS
AREA

CARRIER

HEALTH INSURANCE CLAIM FORM

PICA | | | PICA | |

1. MEDICARE	MEDICAID	CHAMPUS	CHAMPVA	GROUP HEALTH PLAN (SSN or ID)	FECA BLK LUNG (SSN)	OTHER	1a. INSURED'S I.D. NUMBER (FOR PROGRAM IN ITEM 1)
☐ (Medicare #)	☐ (Medicaid #)	☐ (Sponsor's SSN)	☐ (VA File #)	☐	☐	☐ (ID)	

2. PATIENT'S NAME (Last Name, First Name, Middle Initial)	3. PATIENT'S BIRTH DATE MM ¦ DD ¦ YY SEX M ☐ F ☐	4. INSURED'S NAME (Last Name, First Name, Middle Initial)

5. PATIENT'S ADDRESS (No. Street)	6. PATIENT RELATIONSHIP TO INSURED Self ☐ Spouse ☐ Child ☐ Other ☐	7. INSURED'S ADDRESS (No. Street)

CITY	STATE	8. PATIENT STATUS Single ☐ Married ☐ Other ☐	CITY	STATE

ZIP CODE	TELEPHONE (Include Area Code) ( )	Employed ☐ Full-Time Student ☐ Part-Time Student ☐	ZIP CODE	TELEPHONE (INCLUDE AREA CODE) ( )

9. OTHER INSURED'S NAME (Last Name, First Name, Middle Initial)	10. IS PATIENT'S CONDITION RELATED TO:	11. INSURED'S POLICY GROUP OR FECA NUMBER

a. OTHER INSURED'S POLICY OR GROUP NUMBER	a. EMPLOYMENT? (CURRENT OR PREVIOUS) ☐ YES ☐ NO	a. INSURED'S DATE OF BIRTH MM ¦ DD ¦ YY SEX M ☐ F ☐

b. OTHER INSURED'S DATE OF BIRTH MM ¦ DD ¦ YY SEX M ☐ F ☐	b. AUTO ACCIDENT? PLACE (State) ☐ YES ☐ NO	b. EMPLOYER'S NAME OR SCHOOL NAME

c. EMPLOYER'S NAME OR SCHOOL NAME	c. OTHER ACCIDENT? ☐ YES ☐ NO	c. INSURANCE PLAN NAME OR PROGRAM NAME

d. INSURANCE PLAN NAME OR PROGRAM NAME	10d. RESERVED FOR LOCAL USE	d. IS THERE ANOTHER HEALTH BENEFIT PLAN? ☐ YES ☐ NO If yes, return to and complete item 9 a – d.

READ BACK OF FORM BEFORE COMPLETING & SIGNING THIS FORM.
12. PATIENT'S OR AUTHORIZED PERSON'S SIGNATURE I authorize the release of any medical or other information necessary to process this claim. I also request payment of government benefits either to myself or to the party who accepts assignment below.

SIGNED _____ DATE _____

13. INSURED'S OR AUTHORIZED PERSON'S SIGNATURE I authorize payment of medical benefits to the undersigned physician or supplier for services described below.

SIGNED _____

14. DATE OF CURRENT: MM ¦ DD ¦ YY ◄ ILLNESS (First symptom) OR INJURY (Accident) OR PREGNANCY (LMP)	15. IF PATIENT HAS HAD SAME OR SIMILAR ILLNESS, GIVE FIRST DATE MM ¦ DD ¦ YY	16. DATES PATIENT UNABLE TO WORK IN CURRENT OCCUPATION MM ¦ DD ¦ YY MM ¦ DD ¦ YY FROM TO

17. NAME OF REFERRING PHYSICIAN OR OTHER SOURCE	17a. I.D. NUMBER OF REFERRING PHYSICIAN	18. HOSPITALIZATION DATES RELATED TO CURRENT SERVICES MM ¦ DD ¦ YY MM ¦ DD ¦ YY FROM TO

19. RESERVED FOR LOCAL USE	20. OUTSIDE LAB? $ CHARGES ☐ YES ☐ NO

21. DIAGNOSIS OR NATURE OF ILLNESS OR INJURY. (RELATE ITEMS 1, 2, 3, OR 4 TO ITEM 24E BY LINE)

1. └___ . __   3. └___ . __

2. └___ . __   4. └___ . __

22. MEDICAID RESUBMISSION CODE   ORIGINAL REF. NO.
23. PRIOR AUTHORIZATION NUMBER

24. A. DATE(S) OF SERVICE From To MM DD YY MM DD YY	B. Place of Service	C. Type of Service	D. PROCEDURES, SERVICES, OR SUPPLIES (Explain Unusual Circumstances) CPT/HCPCS MODIFIER	E. DIAGNOSIS CODE	F. $ CHARGES	G. DAYS OR UNITS	H. EPSDT Family Plan	I. EMG	J. COB	K. RESERVED FOR LOCAL USE
1										
2										
3										
4										
5										
6										

25. FEDERAL TAX I.D. NUMBER SSN ☐ EIN ☐	26. PATIENT'S ACCOUNT NO.	27. ACCEPT ASSIGNMENT? (For govt. claims, see back) ☐ YES ☐ NO	28. TOTAL CHARGE $	29. AMOUNT PAID $	30. BALANCE DUE $

31. SIGNATURE OF PHYSICIAN OR SUPPLIER INCLUDING DEGREES OR CREDENTIALS (I certify that the statements on the reverse apply to this bill and are made a part thereof.) SIGNED _____ DATE _____	32. NAME AND ADDRESS OF FACILITY WHERE SERVICES WERE RENDERED (If other than home or office)	33. PHYSICIAN'S, SUPPLIER'S BILLING NAME, ADDRESS, ZIP CODE & PHONE # PIN# GRP#

PATIENT AND INSURED INFORMATION

PHYSICIAN OR SUPPLIER INFORMATION

PLEASE PRINT OR TYPE   SAMPLE FORM 1500
SAMPLE FORM 1500 SAMPLE FORM 1500

169

CARRIER

☐☐☐ PICA

HEALTH INSURANCE CLAIM FORM

PICA ☐☐☐

| 1. | MEDICARE | MEDICAID | CHAMPUS | CHAMPVA | GROUP HEALTH PLAN | FECA BLK LUNG | OTHER | 1a. INSURED'S I.D. NUMBER (FOR PROGRAM IN ITEM 1) |

☐ (Medicare #) ☐ (Medicaid #) ☐ (Sponsor's SSN) ☐ (VA File #) ☐ (SSN or ID) ☐ (SSN) ☐ (ID)

2. PATIENT'S NAME (Last Name, First Name, Middle Initial)

3. PATIENT'S BIRTH DATE
MM ⎪ DD ⎪ YY   SEX
M ☐   F ☐

4. INSURED'S NAME (Last Name, First Name, Middle Initial)

5. PATIENT'S ADDRESS (No. Street)

6. PATIENT RELATIONSHIP TO INSURED
Self ☐ Spouse ☐ Child ☐ Other ☐

7. INSURED'S ADDRESS (No. Street)

CITY   STATE

8. PATIENT STATUS
Single ☐ Married ☐ Other ☐

CITY   STATE

ZIP CODE   TELEPHONE (Include Area Code)
(   )

Employed ☐ Full-Time Student ☐ Part-Time Student ☐

ZIP CODE   TELEPHONE (INCLUDE AREA CODE)
(   )

9. OTHER INSURED'S NAME (Last Name, First Name, Middle Initial)

10. IS PATIENT'S CONDITION RELATED TO:

11. INSURED'S POLICY GROUP OR FECA NUMBER

a. OTHER INSURED'S POLICY OR GROUP NUMBER

a. EMPLOYMENT? (CURRENT OR PREVIOUS)
☐ YES ☐ NO

a. INSURED'S DATE OF BIRTH
MM ⎪ DD ⎪ YY   SEX
M ☐ F ☐

b. OTHER INSURED'S DATE OF BIRTH
MM ⎪ DD ⎪ YY   SEX
M ☐ F ☐

b. AUTO ACCIDENT?   PLACE (State)
☐ YES ☐ NO

b. EMPLOYER'S NAME OR SCHOOL NAME

c. EMPLOYER'S NAME OR SCHOOL NAME

c. OTHER ACCIDENT?
☐ YES ☐ NO

c. INSURANCE PLAN NAME OR PROGRAM NAME

d. INSURANCE PLAN NAME OR PROGRAM NAME

10d. RESERVED FOR LOCAL USE

d. IS THERE ANOTHER HEALTH BENEFIT PLAN?
☐ YES ☐ NO   If yes, return to and complete item 9 a – d.

READ BACK OF FORM BEFORE COMPLETING & SIGNING THIS FORM.
12. PATIENT'S OR AUTHORIZED PERSON'S SIGNATURE I authorize the release of any medical or other information necessary to process this claim. I also request payment of government benefits either to myself or to the party who accepts assignment below.

SIGNED _____   DATE _____

13. INSURED'S OR AUTHORIZED PERSON'S SIGNATURE I authorize payment of medical benefits to the undersigned physician or supplier for services described below.

SIGNED _____

PATIENT AND INSURED INFORMATION

14. DATE OF CURRENT: ILLNESS (First symptom) OR
MM ⎪ DD ⎪ YY   INJURY (Accident) OR
PREGNANCY (LMP)

15. IF PATIENT HAS HAD SAME OR SIMILAR ILLNESS,
GIVE FIRST DATE MM ⎪ DD ⎪ YY

16. DATES PATIENT UNABLE TO WORK IN CURRENT OCCUPATION
MM ⎪ DD ⎪ YY   MM ⎪ DD ⎪ YY
FROM   TO

17. NAME OF REFERRING PHYSICIAN OR OTHER SOURCE

17a. I.D. NUMBER OF REFERRING PHYSICIAN

18. HOSPITALIZATION DATES RELATED TO CURRENT SERVICES
MM ⎪ DD ⎪ YY   MM ⎪ DD ⎪ YY
FROM   TO

19. RESERVED FOR LOCAL USE

20. OUTSIDE LAB? $ CHARGES
☐ YES ☐ NO

21. DIAGNOSIS OR NATURE OF ILLNESS OR INJURY. (RELATE ITEMS 1, 2, 3, OR 4 TO ITEM 24E BY LINE)

1. ⎣___ . __
2. ⎣___ . __
3. ⎣___ . __
4. ⎣___ . __

22. MEDICAID RESUBMISSION CODE   ORIGINAL REF. NO.

23. PRIOR AUTHORIZATION NUMBER

24. A DATE(S) OF SERVICE						B Place of Service	C Type of Service	D PROCEDURES, SERVICES, OR SUPPLIES (Explain Unusual Circumstances) CPT/HCPCS MODIFIER	E DIAGNOSIS CODE	F $ CHARGES	G DAYS OR UNITS	H EPSDT Family Plan	I EMG	J COB	K RESERVED FOR LOCAL USE
From MM	DD	YY	To MM	DD	YY										
1															
2															
3															
4															
5															
6															

PHYSICIAN OR SUPPLIER INFORMATION

25. FEDERAL TAX I.D. NUMBER   SSN ☐ EIN ☐

26. PATIENT'S ACCOUNT NO.

27. ACCEPT ASSIGNMENT?
(For govt. claims, see back)
☐ YES ☐ NO

28. TOTAL CHARGE
$

29. AMOUNT PAID
$

30. BALANCE DUE
$

31. SIGNATURE OF PHYSICIAN OR SUPPLIER INCLUDING DEGREES OR CREDENTIALS
(I certify that the statements on the reverse apply to this bill and are made a part thereof.)

SIGNED _____ DATE _____

32. NAME AND ADDRESS OF FACILITY WHERE SERVICES WERE RENDERED (If other than home or office)

33. PHYSICIAN'S, SUPPLIER'S BILLING NAME, ADDRESS, ZIP CODE & PHONE #

PIN#   GRP#

PLEASE PRINT OR TYPE

SAMPLE FORM 1500
SAMPLE FORM 1500 SAMPLE FORM 1500

DONALD L. GIVINGS, M.D.

11350 Medical Drive ■ Anywhere US 12345 ■ (101) 111-5555

EIN: 11-123456	SSN: 123-12-1234	MEDICARE: D1234
PIN: DG1234	GRP: DG12345	MEDICAID: DLG1234
BCBS: 12345		

Encounter Form

PATIENT INFORMATION:

Name:	Esther K. Freed
Address:	12 Nottingham Circle
City:	Anywhere
State:	US
Zip Code:	12345
Telephone:	(101) 333-5555
Gender:	Female
Date of Birth:	03-26-1925
Occupation:	
Employer:	
Spouse's Employer:	Retired Johnson Steel

INSURANCE INFORMATION:

Patient Number:	14-i
Place of Service:	Office
Primary Insurance Plan:	Medicare
Primary Insurance Plan ID #:	777-66-4444A
Group #:	
Primary Policyholder:	Abraham N. Freed
Policyholder Date of Birth:	10-03-1922
Relationship to Patient:	Spouse
Secondary Insurance Plan:	BCBS Medigap
Secondary Insurance Plan ID #:	NXY645-45-4545 987
Secondary Policyholder:	Abraham N. Freed

Patient Status   ☒ Married   ☐ Divorced   ☐ Single   ☐ Student   ☐ Other

DIAGNOSIS INFORMATION

Diagnosis	Code	Diagnosis	Code
1. Bronchopneumonia	485	5.	
2. Hemoptysis	786.3	6.	
3. Hematuria	599.7	7.	
4.		8.	

PROCEDURE INFORMATION

Description of Procedure or Service	Date	Code	Charge
1. New patient OV level IV	03-07-YYYY	99204	$100.00
2. Chest X-ray 2 views	03-07-YYYY	71020	50.00
3. Urinalysis, with microscopy	03-07-YYYY	81001	10.00
4.			
5.			

SPECIAL NOTES:

Return visit: 2 weeks

(SAMPLE ONLY - NOT APPROVED FOR USE)

CARRIER

☐☐ PICA

HEALTH INSURANCE CLAIM FORM

PICA ☐☐☐

1. MEDICARE	MEDICAID	CHAMPUS	CHAMPVA	GROUP HEALTH PLAN	FECA BLK LUNG	OTHER	1a. INSURED'S I.D. NUMBER	(FOR PROGRAM IN ITEM 1)
☐ (Medicare #)	☐ (Medicaid #)	☐ (Sponsor's SSN)	☐ (VA File #)	☐ (SSN or ID)	☐ (SSN)	☐ (ID)		

2. PATIENT'S NAME (Last Name, First Name, Middle Initial)

3. PATIENT'S BIRTH DATE
MM | DD | YY   SEX   M ☐   F ☐

4. INSURED'S NAME (Last Name, First Name, Middle Initial)

5. PATIENT'S ADDRESS (No. Street)

6. PATIENT RELATIONSHIP TO INSURED
Self ☐   Spouse ☐   Child ☐   Other ☐

7. INSURED'S ADDRESS (No. Street)

CITY   STATE

8. PATIENT STATUS
Single ☐   Married ☐   Other ☐

Employed ☐   Full-Time Student ☐   Part-Time Student ☐

CITY   STATE

ZIP CODE   TELEPHONE (Include Area Code)
(   )

ZIP CODE   TELEPHONE (INCLUDE AREA CODE)
(   )

9. OTHER INSURED'S NAME (Last Name, First Name, Middle Initial)

10. IS PATIENT'S CONDITION RELATED TO:

11. INSURED'S POLICY GROUP OR FECA NUMBER

a. OTHER INSURED'S POLICY OR GROUP NUMBER

a. EMPLOYMENT? (CURRENT OR PREVIOUS)
☐ YES   ☐ NO

a. INSURED'S DATE OF BIRTH
MM | DD | YY   SEX   M ☐   F ☐

b. OTHER INSURED'S DATE OF BIRTH
MM | DD | YY   SEX   M ☐   F ☐

b. AUTO ACCIDENT?   PLACE (State)
☐ YES   ☐ NO

b. EMPLOYER'S NAME OR SCHOOL NAME

c. EMPLOYER'S NAME OR SCHOOL NAME

c. OTHER ACCIDENT?
☐ YES   ☐ NO

c. INSURANCE PLAN NAME OR PROGRAM NAME

d. INSURANCE PLAN NAME OR PROGRAM NAME

10d. RESERVED FOR LOCAL USE

d. IS THERE ANOTHER HEALTH BENEFIT PLAN?
☐ YES   ☐ NO   If yes, return to and complete item 9 a – d.

READ BACK OF FORM BEFORE COMPLETING & SIGNING THIS FORM.
12. PATIENT'S OR AUTHORIZED PERSON'S SIGNATURE I authorize the release of any medical or other information necessary to process this claim. I also request payment of government benefits either to myself or to the party who accepts assignment below.

SIGNED _____   DATE _____

13. INSURED'S OR AUTHORIZED PERSON'S SIGNATURE I authorize payment of medical benefits to the undersigned physician or supplier for services described below.

SIGNED _____

PATIENT AND INSURED INFORMATION

14. DATE OF CURRENT:
MM | DD | YY
ILLNESS (First symptom) OR INJURY (Accident) OR PREGNANCY (LMP)

15. IF PATIENT HAS HAD SAME OR SIMILAR ILLNESS, GIVE FIRST DATE   MM | DD | YY

16. DATES PATIENT UNABLE TO WORK IN CURRENT OCCUPATION
MM | DD | YY   MM | DD | YY
FROM   TO

17. NAME OF REFERRING PHYSICIAN OR OTHER SOURCE

17a. I.D. NUMBER OF REFERRING PHYSICIAN

18. HOSPITALIZATION DATES RELATED TO CURRENT SERVICES
MM | DD | YY   MM | DD | YY
FROM   TO

19. RESERVED FOR LOCAL USE

20. OUTSIDE LAB? $ CHARGES
☐ YES   ☐ NO

21. DIAGNOSIS OR NATURE OF ILLNESS OR INJURY. (RELATE ITEMS 1, 2, 3, OR 4 TO ITEM 24E BY LINE)

1. └___ . ___   3. └___ . ___

2. └___ . ___   4. └___ . ___

22. MEDICAID RESUBMISSION CODE   ORIGINAL REF. NO.

23. PRIOR AUTHORIZATION NUMBER

24. A DATE(S) OF SERVICE						B Place of Service	C Type of Service	D PROCEDURES, SERVICES, OR SUPPLIES (Explain Unusual Circumstances)		E DIAGNOSIS CODE	F $ CHARGES	G DAYS OR UNITS	H EPSDT Family Plan	I EMG	J COB	K RESERVED FOR LOCAL USE
From			To					CPT/HCPCS	MODIFIER							
MM	DD	YY	MM	DD	YY											
1																
2																
3																
4																
5																
6																

25. FEDERAL TAX I.D. NUMBER   SSN ☐ EIN ☐

26. PATIENT'S ACCOUNT NO.

27. ACCEPT ASSIGNMENT? (For govt. claims, see back)
☐ YES   ☐ NO

28. TOTAL CHARGE
$

29. AMOUNT PAID
$

30. BALANCE DUE
$

31. SIGNATURE OF PHYSICIAN OR SUPPLIER INCLUDING DEGREES OR CREDENTIALS
(I certify that the statements on the reverse apply to this bill and are made a part thereof.)

SIGNED _____   DATE _____

32. NAME AND ADDRESS OF FACILITY WHERE SERVICES WERE RENDERED (If other than home or office)

33. PHYSICIAN'S, SUPPLIER'S BILLING NAME, ADDRESS, ZIP CODE & PHONE #

PIN#   GRP#

PHYSICIAN OR SUPPLIER INFORMATION

(SAMPLE ONLY - NOT APPROVED FOR USE)

PLEASE PRINT OR TYPE

SAMPLE FORM 1500
SAMPLE FORM 1500   SAMPLE FORM 1500

CARRIER

PLEASE
DO NOT
STAPLE
IN THIS
AREA

☐☐ PICA

HEALTH INSURANCE CLAIM FORM

PICA ☐☐☐

| 1. MEDICARE MEDICAID CHAMPUS CHAMPVA GROUP HEALTH PLAN FECA BLK LUNG OTHER | 1a. INSURED'S I.D. NUMBER (FOR PROGRAM IN ITEM 1) |

☐ (Medicare #) ☐ (Medicaid #) ☐ (Sponsor's SSN) ☐ (VA File #) ☐ (SSN or ID) ☐ (SSN) ☐ (ID)

2. PATIENT'S NAME (Last Name, First Name, Middle Initial)

3. PATIENT'S BIRTH DATE MM ┊ DD ┊ YY   SEX M ☐ F ☐

4. INSURED'S NAME (Last Name, First Name, Middle Initial)

5. PATIENT'S ADDRESS (No. Street)

6. PATIENT RELATIONSHIP TO INSURED Self ☐ Spouse ☐ Child ☐ Other ☐

7. INSURED'S ADDRESS (No. Street)

CITY   STATE

8. PATIENT STATUS Single ☐ Married ☐ Other ☐   Employed ☐ Full-Time Student ☐ Part-Time Student ☐

CITY   STATE

ZIP CODE   TELEPHONE (Include Area Code) (   )

ZIP CODE   TELEPHONE (INCLUDE AREA CODE) (   )

9. OTHER INSURED'S NAME (Last Name, First Name, Middle Initial)

10. IS PATIENT'S CONDITION RELATED TO:

11. INSURED'S POLICY GROUP OR FECA NUMBER

a. OTHER INSURED'S POLICY OR GROUP NUMBER

a. EMPLOYMENT? (CURRENT OR PREVIOUS) ☐ YES ☐ NO

a. INSURED'S DATE OF BIRTH MM ┊ DD ┊ YY   SEX M ☐ F ☐

b. OTHER INSURED'S DATE OF BIRTH MM ┊ DD ┊ YY SEX M ☐ F ☐

b. AUTO ACCIDENT? PLACE (State) ☐ YES ☐ NO

b. EMPLOYER'S NAME OR SCHOOL NAME

c. EMPLOYER'S NAME OR SCHOOL NAME

c. OTHER ACCIDENT? ☐ YES ☐ NO

c. INSURANCE PLAN NAME OR PROGRAM NAME

d. INSURANCE PLAN NAME OR PROGRAM NAME

10d. RESERVED FOR LOCAL USE

d. IS THERE ANOTHER HEALTH BENEFIT PLAN? ☐ YES ☐ NO If yes, return to and complete item 9 a – d.

READ BACK OF FORM BEFORE COMPLETING & SIGNING THIS FORM.
12. PATIENT'S OR AUTHORIZED PERSON'S SIGNATURE I authorize the release of any medical or other information necessary to process this claim. I also request payment of government benefits either to myself or to the party who accepts assignment below.

SIGNED _____ DATE _____

13. INSURED'S OR AUTHORIZED PERSON'S SIGNATURE I authorize payment of medical benefits to the undersigned physician or supplier for services described below.

SIGNED _____

PATIENT AND INSURED INFORMATION

14. DATE OF CURRENT: ◄ ILLNESS (First symptom) OR INJURY (Accident) OR PREGNANCY (LMP) MM ┊ DD ┊ YY

15. IF PATIENT HAS HAD SAME OR SIMILAR ILLNESS, GIVE FIRST DATE MM ┊ DD ┊ YY

16. DATES PATIENT UNABLE TO WORK IN CURRENT OCCUPATION MM ┊ DD ┊ YY   MM ┊ DD ┊ YY FROM   TO

17. NAME OF REFERRING PHYSICIAN OR OTHER SOURCE

17a. I.D. NUMBER OF REFERRING PHYSICIAN

18. HOSPITALIZATION DATES RELATED TO CURRENT SERVICES MM ┊ DD ┊ YY   MM ┊ DD ┊ YY FROM   TO

19. RESERVED FOR LOCAL USE

20. OUTSIDE LAB? $ CHARGES ☐ YES ☐ NO

21. DIAGNOSIS OR NATURE OF ILLNESS OR INJURY. (RELATE ITEMS 1, 2, 3, OR 4 TO ITEM 24E BY LINE)

1. └___ . __   3. └___ . __

2. └___ . __   4. └___ . __

22. MEDICAID RESUBMISSION CODE   ORIGINAL REF. NO.

23. PRIOR AUTHORIZATION NUMBER

24. A DATE(S) OF SERVICE						B Place of Service	C Type of Service	D PROCEDURES, SERVICES, OR SUPPLIES (Explain Unusual Circumstances) CPT/HCPCS ┊ MODIFIER	E DIAGNOSIS CODE	F $ CHARGES	G DAYS OR UNITS	H EPSDT Family Plan	I EMG	J COB	K RESERVED FOR LOCAL USE
From MM ┊ DD ┊ YY			To MM ┊ DD ┊ YY												
1															
2															
3															
4															
5															
6															

25. FEDERAL TAX I.D. NUMBER SSN ☐ EIN ☐

26. PATIENT'S ACCOUNT NO.

27. ACCEPT ASSIGNMENT? (For govt. claims, see back) ☐ YES ☐ NO

28. TOTAL CHARGE $

29. AMOUNT PAID $

30. BALANCE DUE $

31. SIGNATURE OF PHYSICIAN OR SUPPLIER INCLUDING DEGREES OR CREDENTIALS (I certify that the statements on the reverse apply to this bill and are made a part thereof.)

SIGNED _____ DATE _____

32. NAME AND ADDRESS OF FACILITY WHERE SERVICES WERE RENDERED (If other than home or office)

33. PHYSICIAN'S, SUPPLIER'S BILLING NAME, ADDRESS, ZIP CODE & PHONE #

PIN#   GRP#

PHYSICIAN OR SUPPLIER INFORMATION

PLEASE PRINT OR TYPE

SAMPLE FORM 1500
SAMPLE FORM 1500 SAMPLE FORM 1500

DONALD L. GIVINGS, M.D.

11350 Medical Drive ■ Anywhere US 12345 ■ (101) 111-5555

EIN: 11-123456   SSN: 123-12-1234   MEDICARE: D1234
PIN: DG1234   GRP: DG12345   MEDICAID: DLG1234
BCBS: 12345

Encounter Form

PATIENT INFORMATION:

Name:	Mary R. Booth
Address:	1007 Bond Avenue
City:	Anywhere
State:	US
Zip Code:	12345
Telephone:	(101) 333-5555
Gender:	Female
Date of Birth:	10-14-1933
Occupation:	
Employer:	Retired Mt. Royal Drugs
Spouse's Employer:	

INSURANCE INFORMATION:

Patient Number:	14-j
Place of Service:	Office
Primary Insurance Plan:	Medicare
Primary Insurance Plan ID #:	212-77-4444A
Group #:	
Primary Policyholder:	Mary R. Booth
Policyholder Date of Birth:	10-14-1933
Relationship to Patient:	Self
Secondary Insurance Plan:	AARP Medigap
Secondary Insurance Plan ID #:	212-77-4444
Secondary Policyholder:	Self

Patient Status   ☐ Married   ☐ Divorced   ☒ Single   ☐ Student   ☐ Other

DIAGNOSIS INFORMATION

Diagnosis	Code	Diagnosis	Code
1. Hypertension, benign	401.1	5.	
2.		6.	
3.		7.	
4.		8.	

PROCEDURE INFORMATION

Description of Procedure or Service	Date	Code	Charge
1. Est. patient OV level I	03-17-YYYY	99211	$55.00
2.			
3.			
4.			
5.			

SPECIAL NOTES:

Return visit: 3 months

PLEASE
DO NOT
STAPLE
IN THIS
AREA

CARRIER

HEALTH INSURANCE CLAIM FORM

PICA ☐☐☐

☐☐ PICA

1.						
MEDICARE	MEDICAID	CHAMPUS	CHAMPVA	GROUP HEALTH PLAN (SSN or ID)	FECA BLK LUNG (SSN)	OTHER (ID)
☐ (Medicare #)	☐ (Medicad #)	☐ (Sponsor's SSN)	☐ (VA File #)	☐	☐	☐

1a. INSURED'S I.D. NUMBER   (FOR PROGRAM IN ITEM 1)

2. PATIENT'S NAME (Last Name, First Name, Middle Initial)

3. PATIENT'S BIRTH DATE
MM   DD   YY   SEX
                M ☐   F ☐

4. INSURED'S NAME (Last Name, First Name, Middle Initial)

5. PATIENT'S ADDRESS (No. Street)

6. PATIENT RELATIONSHIP TO INSURED
Self ☐   Spouse ☐   Child ☐   Other ☐

7. INSURED'S ADDRESS (No. Street)

CITY   STATE

8. PATIENT STATUS
Single ☐   Married ☐   Other ☐

Employed ☐   Full-Time Student ☐   Part-Time Student ☐

CITY   STATE

ZIP CODE   TELEPHONE (Include Area Code)
(   )

ZIP CODE   TELEPHONE (INCLUDE AREA CODE)
(   )

9. OTHER INSURED'S NAME (Last Name, First Name, Middle Initial)

10. IS PATIENT'S CONDITION RELATED TO:

11. INSURED'S POLICY GROUP OR FECA NUMBER

a. OTHER INSURED'S POLICY OR GROUP NUMBER

a. EMPLOYMENT? (CURRENT OR PREVIOUS)
☐ YES   ☐ NO

a. INSURED'S DATE OF BIRTH
MM   DD   YY   SEX
                M ☐   F ☐

b. OTHER INSURED'S DATE OF BIRTH
MM   DD   YY   SEX
            M ☐   F ☐

b. AUTO ACCIDENT?   PLACE (State)
☐ YES   ☐ NO

b. EMPLOYER'S NAME OR SCHOOL NAME

c. EMPLOYER'S NAME OR SCHOOL NAME

c. OTHER ACCIDENT?
☐ YES   ☐ NO

c. INSURANCE PLAN NAME OR PROGRAM NAME

d. INSURANCE PLAN NAME OR PROGRAM NAME

10d. RESERVED FOR LOCAL USE

d. IS THERE ANOTHER HEALTH BENEFIT PLAN?
☐ YES   ☐ NO   If yes, return to and complete item 9 a – d.

READ BACK OF FORM BEFORE COMPLETING & SIGNING THIS FORM.
12. PATIENT'S OR AUTHORIZED PERSON'S SIGNATURE I authorize the release of any medical or other information necessary to process this claim. I also request payment of government benefits either to myself or to the party who accepts assignment below.

SIGNED _____   DATE _____

13. INSURED'S OR AUTHORIZED PERSON'S SIGNATURE I authorize payment of medical benefits to the undersigned physician or supplier for services described below.

SIGNED _____

PATIENT AND INSURED INFORMATION

14. DATE OF CURRENT: ◄ ILLNESS (First symptom) OR
MM   DD   YY   INJURY (Accident) OR
                    PREGNANCY (LMP)

15. IF PATIENT HAS HAD SAME OR SIMILAR ILLNESS,
GIVE FIRST DATE   MM   DD   YY

16. DATES PATIENT UNABLE TO WORK IN CURRENT OCCUPATION
MM   DD   YY   MM   DD   YY
FROM   TO

17. NAME OF REFERRING PHYSICIAN OR OTHER SOURCE

17a. I.D. NUMBER OF REFERRING PHYSICIAN

18. HOSPITALIZATION DATES RELATED TO CURRENT SERVICES
MM   DD   YY   MM   DD   YY
FROM   TO

19. RESERVED FOR LOCAL USE

20. OUTSIDE LAB? $ CHARGES
☐ YES   ☐ NO

21. DIAGNOSIS OR NATURE OF ILLNESS OR INJURY. (RELATE ITEMS 1, 2, 3, OR 4 TO ITEM 24E BY LINE)

1. ⌊___ . ___

3. ⌊___ . ___

2. ⌊___ . ___

4. ⌊___ . ___

22. MEDICAID RESUBMISSION
CODE   ORIGINAL REF. NO.

23. PRIOR AUTHORIZATION NUMBER

24.	A DATE(S) OF SERVICE						B Place of Service	C Type of Service	D PROCEDURES, SERVICES, OR SUPPLIES (Explain Unusual Circumstances)		E DIAGNOSIS CODE	F $ CHARGES	G DAYS OR UNITS	H EPSDT Family Plan	I EMG	J COB	K RESERVED FOR LOCAL USE
	From MM	DD	YY	To MM	DD	YY			CPT/HCPCS	MODIFIER							
1																	
2																	
3																	
4																	
5																	
6																	

25. FEDERAL TAX I.D. NUMBER   SSN ☐ EIN ☐

26. PATIENT'S ACCOUNT NO.

27. ACCEPT ASSIGNMENT?
(For govt. claims, see back)
☐ YES   ☐ NO

28. TOTAL CHARGE
$

29. AMOUNT PAID
$

30. BALANCE DUE
$

31. SIGNATURE OF PHYSICIAN OR SUPPLIER INCLUDING DEGREES OR CREDENTIALS
(I certify that the statements on the reverse apply to this bill and are made a part thereof.)

SIGNED _____   DATE _____

32. NAME AND ADDRESS OF FACILITY WHERE SERVICES WERE RENDERED (If other than home or office)

33. PHYSICIAN'S, SUPPLIER'S BILLING NAME, ADDRESS, ZIP CODE & PHONE #

PIN#   GRP#

PHYSICIAN OR SUPPLIER INFORMATION

PLEASE PRINT OR TYPE

SAMPLE FORM 1500
SAMPLE FORM 1500 SAMPLE FORM 1500

PLEASE
DO NOT
STAPLE
IN THIS
AREA

CARRIER

| | | PICA | | |

HEALTH INSURANCE CLAIM FORM

PICA | | |

1. MEDICARE MEDICAID CHAMPUS CHAMPVA GROUP HEALTH PLAN FECA BLK LUNG OTHER	1a. INSURED'S I.D. NUMBER (FOR PROGRAM IN ITEM 1)
(Medicare #) (Medicaid #) (Sponsor's SSN) (VA File #) (SSN or ID) (SSN) (ID)	

2. PATIENT'S NAME (Last Name, First Name, Middle Initial)	3. PATIENT'S BIRTH DATE MM DD YY SEX M F	4. INSURED'S NAME (Last Name, First Name, Middle Initial)

5. PATIENT'S ADDRESS (No. Street)	6. PATIENT RELATIONSHIP TO INSURED Self Spouse Child Other	7. INSURED'S ADDRESS (No. Street)
CITY STATE	8. PATIENT STATUS Single Married Other	CITY STATE
ZIP CODE TELEPHONE (Include Area Code) ( )	Employed Full-Time Student Part-Time Student	ZIP CODE TELEPHONE (INCLUDE AREA CODE) ( )

9. OTHER INSURED'S NAME (Last Name, First Name, Middle Initial)	10. IS PATIENT'S CONDITION RELATED TO:	11. INSURED'S POLICY GROUP OR FECA NUMBER
a. OTHER INSURED'S POLICY OR GROUP NUMBER	a. EMPLOYMENT? (CURRENT OR PREVIOUS) YES NO	a. INSURED'S DATE OF BIRTH MM DD YY SEX M F
b. OTHER INSURED'S DATE OF BIRTH MM DD YY SEX M F	b. AUTO ACCIDENT? PLACE (State) YES NO	b. EMPLOYER'S NAME OR SCHOOL NAME
c. EMPLOYER'S NAME OR SCHOOL NAME	c. OTHER ACCIDENT? YES NO	c. INSURANCE PLAN NAME OR PROGRAM NAME
d. INSURANCE PLAN NAME OR PROGRAM NAME	10d. RESERVED FOR LOCAL USE	d. IS THERE ANOTHER HEALTH BENEFIT PLAN? YES NO If yes, return to and complete item 9 a – d.

READ BACK OF FORM BEFORE COMPLETING & SIGNING THIS FORM.
12. PATIENT'S OR AUTHORIZED PERSON'S SIGNATURE I authorize the release of any medical or other information necessary to process this claim. I also request payment of government benefits either to myself or to the party who accepts assignment below.

SIGNED _____ DATE _____

13. INSURED'S OR AUTHORIZED PERSON'S SIGNATURE I authorize payment of medical benefits to the undersigned physician or supplier for services described below.

SIGNED _____

PATIENT AND INSURED INFORMATION

14. DATE OF CURRENT: ILLNESS (First symptom) OR INJURY (Accident) OR PREGNANCY (LMP) MM DD YY	15. IF PATIENT HAS HAD SAME OR SIMILAR ILLNESS, GIVE FIRST DATE MM DD YY	16. DATES PATIENT UNABLE TO WORK IN CURRENT OCCUPATION MM DD YY MM DD YY FROM TO
17. NAME OF REFERRING PHYSICIAN OR OTHER SOURCE	17a. I.D. NUMBER OF REFERRING PHYSICIAN	18. HOSPITALIZATION DATES RELATED TO CURRENT SERVICES MM DD YY MM DD YY FROM TO
19. RESERVED FOR LOCAL USE		20. OUTSIDE LAB? YES NO $ CHARGES

21. DIAGNOSIS OR NATURE OF ILLNESS OR INJURY. (RELATE ITEMS 1, 2, 3, OR 4 TO ITEM 24E BY LINE)	22. MEDICAID RESUBMISSION CODE ORIGINAL REF. NO.
1. ___ . __ 3. ___ . __	
2. ___ . __ 4. ___ . __	23. PRIOR AUTHORIZATION NUMBER

24. A DATE(S) OF SERVICE						B Place of Service	C Type of Service	D PROCEDURES, SERVICES, OR SUPPLIES (Explain Unusual Circumstances)		E DIAGNOSIS CODE	F $ CHARGES	G DAYS OR UNITS	H EPSDT Family Plan	I EMG	J COB	K RESERVED FOR LOCAL USE
From MM	DD	YY	To MM	DD	YY			CPT/HCPCS	MODIFIER							
1																
2																
3																
4																
5																
6																

25. FEDERAL TAX I.D. NUMBER SSN EIN	26. PATIENT'S ACCOUNT NO.	27. ACCEPT ASSIGNMENT? (For govt. claims, see back) YES NO	28. TOTAL CHARGE $	29. AMOUNT PAID $	30. BALANCE DUE $
31. SIGNATURE OF PHYSICIAN OR SUPPLIER INCLUDING DEGREES OR CREDENTIALS (I certify that the statements on the reverse apply to this bill and are made a part thereof.) SIGNED DATE	32. NAME AND ADDRESS OF FACILITY WHERE SERVICES WERE RENDERED (If other than home or office)		33. PHYSICIAN'S, SUPPLIER'S BILLING NAME, ADDRESS, ZIP CODE & PHONE # PIN# GRP#		

PHYSICIAN OR SUPPLIER INFORMATION

PLEASE PRINT OR TYPE

SAMPLE FORM 1500
SAMPLE FORM 1500 SAMPLE FORM 1500

176

DONALD L. GIVINGS, M.D.

11350 Medical Drive ■ Anywhere US 12345 ■ (101) 111-5555

EIN: 11-123456	SSN: 123-12-1234	MEDICARE: D1234
PIN: DG1234	GRP: DG12345	MEDICAID: DLG1234
BCBS: 12345		

Encounter Form

PATIENT INFORMATION:

Name:	Patricia S. Delaney
Address:	485 Garden Lane
City:	Anywhere
State:	US
Zip Code:	12345
Telephone:	(101) 333-5555
Gender:	Female
Date of Birth:	04-12-1931
Occupation:	
Employer:	
Spouse's Employer:	

INSURANCE INFORMATION:

Patient Number:	14-k
Place of Service:	Office
Primary Insurance Plan:	Medicare
Primary Insurance Plan ID #:	485375869A
Group #:	
Primary Policyholder:	Patricia S. Delaney
Policyholder Date of Birth:	04-12-1931
Relationship to Patient:	Self
Secondary Insurance Plan:	Medicaid
Secondary Insurance Plan ID #:	22886644XT
Secondary Policyholder:	Self

Patient Status ☐ Married ☐ Divorced ☒ Single ☐ Student ☐ Other

DIAGNOSIS INFORMATION

Diagnosis	Code	Diagnosis	Code
1. Rosacea	695.3	5.	
2.		6.	
3.		7.	
4.		8.	

PROCEDURE INFORMATION

Description of Procedure or Service	Date	Code	Charge
1. Est. patient OV level I	12-15-YYYY	99211	$55.00
2.			
3.			
4.			
5.			

SPECIAL NOTES:

Refer patient to dermatologist
Return visit: PRN

(SAMPLE ONLY - NOT APPROVED FOR USE)

CARRIER

☐☐ PICA

HEALTH INSURANCE CLAIM FORM

PICA ☐☐

1. ☐ MEDICARE (Medicare #) ☐ MEDICAID (Medicaid #) ☐ CHAMPUS (Sponsor's SSN) ☐ CHAMPVA (VA File #) ☐ GROUP HEALTH PLAN (SSN or ID) ☐ FECA BLK LUNG (SSN) ☐ OTHER (ID)

1a. INSURED'S I.D. NUMBER   (FOR PROGRAM IN ITEM 1)

2. PATIENT'S NAME (Last Name, First Name, Middle Initial)

3. PATIENT'S BIRTH DATE   MM | DD | YY   SEX   M ☐   F ☐

4. INSURED'S NAME (Last Name, First Name, Middle Initial)

5. PATIENT'S ADDRESS (No. Street)

6. PATIENT RELATIONSHIP TO INSURED   Self ☐   Spouse ☐   Child ☐   Other ☐

7. INSURED'S ADDRESS (No. Street)

CITY   STATE

8. PATIENT STATUS   Single ☐   Married ☐   Other ☐
Employed ☐   Full-Time Student ☐   Part-Time Student ☐

CITY   STATE

ZIP CODE   TELEPHONE (Include Area Code) (   )

ZIP CODE   TELEPHONE (INCLUDE AREA CODE) (   )

9. OTHER INSURED'S NAME (Last Name, First Name, Middle Initial)

10. IS PATIENT'S CONDITION RELATED TO:

11. INSURED'S POLICY GROUP OR FECA NUMBER

a. OTHER INSURED'S POLICY OR GROUP NUMBER

a. EMPLOYMENT? (CURRENT OR PREVIOUS)   ☐ YES   ☐ NO

a. INSURED'S DATE OF BIRTH   MM | DD | YY   SEX   M ☐   F ☐

b. OTHER INSURED'S DATE OF BIRTH   MM | DD | YY   SEX   M ☐   F ☐

b. AUTO ACCIDENT?   PLACE (State)   ☐ YES   ☐ NO

b. EMPLOYER'S NAME OR SCHOOL NAME

c. EMPLOYER'S NAME OR SCHOOL NAME

c. OTHER ACCIDENT?   ☐ YES   ☐ NO

c. INSURANCE PLAN NAME OR PROGRAM NAME

d. INSURANCE PLAN NAME OR PROGRAM NAME

10d. RESERVED FOR LOCAL USE

d. IS THERE ANOTHER HEALTH BENEFIT PLAN?   ☐ YES   ☐ NO   If yes, return to and complete item 9 a – d.

READ BACK OF FORM BEFORE COMPLETING & SIGNING THIS FORM.
12. PATIENT'S OR AUTHORIZED PERSON'S SIGNATURE I authorize the release of any medical or other information necessary to process this claim. I also request payment of government benefits either to myself or to the party who accepts assignment below.

SIGNED _____   DATE _____

13. INSURED'S OR AUTHORIZED PERSON'S SIGNATURE I authorize payment of medical benefits to the undersigned physician or supplier for services described below.

SIGNED _____

PATIENT AND INSURED INFORMATION

14. DATE OF CURRENT: MM | DD | YY   ◄ ILLNESS (First symptom) OR INJURY (Accident) OR PREGNANCY (LMP)

15. IF PATIENT HAS HAD SAME OR SIMILAR ILLNESS, GIVE FIRST DATE   MM | DD | YY

16. DATES PATIENT UNABLE TO WORK IN CURRENT OCCUPATION   FROM MM | DD | YY   TO MM | DD | YY

17. NAME OF REFERRING PHYSICIAN OR OTHER SOURCE

17a. I.D. NUMBER OF REFERRING PHYSICIAN

18. HOSPITALIZATION DATES RELATED TO CURRENT SERVICES   FROM MM | DD | YY   TO MM | DD | YY

19. RESERVED FOR LOCAL USE

20. OUTSIDE LAB?   ☐ YES   ☐ NO $ CHARGES

21. DIAGNOSIS OR NATURE OF ILLNESS OR INJURY. (RELATE ITEMS 1, 2, 3, OR 4 TO ITEM 24E BY LINE)
1. |___ . ___| 3. |___ . ___|
2. |___ . ___| 4. |___ . ___|

22. MEDICAID RESUBMISSION CODE   ORIGINAL REF. NO.

23. PRIOR AUTHORIZATION NUMBER

24. A DATE(S) OF SERVICE					B Place of Service	C Type of Service	D PROCEDURES, SERVICES, OR SUPPLIES (Explain Unusual Circumstances) CPT/HCPCS	MODIFIER	E DIAGNOSIS CODE	F $ CHARGES	G DAYS OR UNITS	H EPSDT Family Plan	I EMG	J COB	K RESERVED FOR LOCAL USE
From MM	DD	YY	To MM	DD	YY											
1															
2															
3															
4															
5															
6															

25. FEDERAL TAX I.D. NUMBER   ☐ SSN   ☐ EIN

26. PATIENT'S ACCOUNT NO.

27. ACCEPT ASSIGNMENT? (For govt. claims, see back)   ☐ YES   ☐ NO

28. TOTAL CHARGE $

29. AMOUNT PAID $

30. BALANCE DUE $

31. SIGNATURE OF PHYSICIAN OR SUPPLIER INCLUDING DEGREES OR CREDENTIALS (I certify that the statements on the reverse apply to this bill and are made a part thereof.)

SIGNED _____   DATE _____

32. NAME AND ADDRESS OF FACILITY WHERE SERVICES WERE RENDERED (If other than home or office)

33. PHYSICIAN'S, SUPPLIER'S BILLING NAME, ADDRESS, ZIP CODE & PHONE #

PIN# _____   GRP# _____

PHYSICIAN OR SUPPLIER INFORMATION

(SAMPLE ONLY - NOT APPROVED FOR USE)

PLEASE PRINT OR TYPE

SAMPLE FORM 1500
SAMPLE FORM 1500 SAMPLE FORM 1500

CLAIRE M. SKINNER, M.D. DERMATOLOGY

Encounter Form

50 Clear View Drive ■ Anywhere US 12345 ■ (101) 111-5555

EIN: 11-555555	SSN: 333-44-1234	MEDICARE: C1234
UPIN: CS1234	GRP: DG12345	MEDICAID: CMS1234
BCBS: 94949		

PATIENT INFORMATION:

Name:	Patricia S. Delaney
Address:	485 Garden Lane
City:	Anywhere
State:	US
Zip Code:	12345
Telephone:	(101) 333-5555
Gender:	Female
Date of Birth:	04-12-1931
Occupation:	
Employer:	
Spouse's Employer:	

INSURANCE INFORMATION:

Patient Number:	14-1
Place of Service:	Office
Primary Insurance Plan:	Medicare
Primary Insurance Plan ID #:	485375869A
Group #:	
Primary Policyholder:	Patricia S. Delaney
Policyholder Date of Birth:	04-12-1931
Relationship to Patient:	Self
Secondary Insurance Plan:	Medicaid
Secondary Insurance Plan ID #:	22886644XT
Secondary Policyholder:	Self

Patient Status ☐ Married ☐ Divorced ☒ Single ☐ Student ☐ Other

DIAGNOSIS INFORMATION

Diagnosis	Code	Diagnosis	Code
1. Rosacea	695.3	5.	
2.		6.	
3.		7.	
4.		8.	

PROCEDURE INFORMATION

Description of Procedure or Service	Date	Code	Charge
1. Office consult level III	12-15-YYYY	99243	$85.00
2.			
3.			
4.			
5.			

SPECIAL NOTES:

Referred by Donald L. Givings, M.D. UPIN/SSN: DG1234
Return visit: PRN

(SAMPLE ONLY - NOT APPROVED FOR USE)

CARRIER

[ ][ ] PICA

HEALTH INSURANCE CLAIM FORM

PICA [ ][ ]

1. MEDICARE MEDICAID CHAMPUS CHAMPVA GROUP FECA OTHER	1a. INSURED'S I.D. NUMBER (FOR PROGRAM IN ITEM 1)

1. MEDICARE ☐ (Medicare #) MEDICAID ☐ (Medicaid #) CHAMPUS ☐ (Sponsor's SSN) CHAMPVA ☐ (VA File #) GROUP HEALTH PLAN ☐ (SSN or ID) FECA BLK LUNG ☐ (SSN) OTHER ☐ (ID)

1a. INSURED'S I.D. NUMBER   (FOR PROGRAM IN ITEM 1)

2. PATIENT'S NAME (Last Name, First Name, Middle Initial)

3. PATIENT'S BIRTH DATE MM | DD | YY   SEX M ☐ F ☐

4. INSURED'S NAME (Last Name, First Name, Middle Initial)

5. PATIENT'S ADDRESS (No. Street)

6. PATIENT RELATIONSHIP TO INSURED Self ☐ Spouse ☐ Child ☐ Other ☐

7. INSURED'S ADDRESS (No. Street)

CITY   STATE

8. PATIENT STATUS Single ☐ Married ☐ Other ☐
Employed ☐ Full-Time Student ☐ Part-Time Student ☐

CITY   STATE

ZIP CODE   TELEPHONE (Include Area Code) (   )

ZIP CODE   TELEPHONE (INCLUDE AREA CODE) (   )

9. OTHER INSURED'S NAME (Last Name, First Name, Middle Initial)

10. IS PATIENT'S CONDITION RELATED TO:

11. INSURED'S POLICY GROUP OR FECA NUMBER

a. OTHER INSURED'S POLICY OR GROUP NUMBER

a. EMPLOYMENT? (CURRENT OR PREVIOUS) ☐ YES ☐ NO

a. INSURED'S DATE OF BIRTH MM | DD | YY   SEX M ☐ F ☐

b. OTHER INSURED'S DATE OF BIRTH MM | DD | YY   SEX M ☐ F ☐

b. AUTO ACCIDENT?   PLACE (State) ☐ YES ☐ NO

b. EMPLOYER'S NAME OR SCHOOL NAME

c. EMPLOYER'S NAME OR SCHOOL NAME

c. OTHER ACCIDENT? ☐ YES ☐ NO

c. INSURANCE PLAN NAME OR PROGRAM NAME

d. INSURANCE PLAN NAME OR PROGRAM NAME

10d. RESERVED FOR LOCAL USE

d. IS THERE ANOTHER HEALTH BENEFIT PLAN? ☐ YES ☐ NO If yes, return to and complete item 9 a – d.

READ BACK OF FORM BEFORE COMPLETING & SIGNING THIS FORM.
12. PATIENT'S OR AUTHORIZED PERSON'S SIGNATURE I authorize the release of any medical or other information necessary to process this claim. I also request payment of government benefits either to myself or to the party who accepts assignment below.

SIGNED _____   DATE _____

13. INSURED'S OR AUTHORIZED PERSON'S SIGNATURE I authorize payment of medical benefits to the undersigned physician or supplier for services described below.

SIGNED _____

PATIENT AND INSURED INFORMATION

14. DATE OF CURRENT: ILLNESS (First symptom) OR INJURY (Accident) OR PREGNANCY (LMP) MM | DD | YY

15. IF PATIENT HAS HAD SAME OR SIMILAR ILLNESS, GIVE FIRST DATE MM | DD | YY

16. DATES PATIENT UNABLE TO WORK IN CURRENT OCCUPATION FROM MM | DD | YY TO MM | DD | YY

17. NAME OF REFERRING PHYSICIAN OR OTHER SOURCE

17a. I.D. NUMBER OF REFERRING PHYSICIAN

18. HOSPITALIZATION DATES RELATED TO CURRENT SERVICES FROM MM | DD | YY TO MM | DD | YY

19. RESERVED FOR LOCAL USE

20. OUTSIDE LAB? ☐ YES ☐ NO $ CHARGES

21. DIAGNOSIS OR NATURE OF ILLNESS OR INJURY. (RELATE ITEMS 1, 2, 3, OR 4 TO ITEM 24E BY LINE)
1. |___ . ___   3. |___ . ___
2. |___ . ___   4. |___ . ___

22. MEDICAID RESUBMISSION CODE   ORIGINAL REF. NO.

23. PRIOR AUTHORIZATION NUMBER

24. A DATE(S) OF SERVICE From To MM DD YY MM DD YY	B Place of Service	C Type of Service	D PROCEDURES, SERVICES, OR SUPPLIES (Explain Unusual Circumstances) CPT/HCPCS MODIFIER	E DIAGNOSIS CODE	F $ CHARGES	G DAYS OR UNITS	H EPSDT Family Plan	I EMG	J COB	K RESERVED FOR LOCAL USE
1										
2										
3										
4										
5										
6										

25. FEDERAL TAX I.D. NUMBER   SSN ☐ EIN ☐

26. PATIENT'S ACCOUNT NO.

27. ACCEPT ASSIGNMENT? (For govt. claims, see back) ☐ YES ☐ NO

28. TOTAL CHARGE $

29. AMOUNT PAID $

30. BALANCE DUE $

31. SIGNATURE OF PHYSICIAN OR SUPPLIER INCLUDING DEGREES OR CREDENTIALS (I certify that the statements on the reverse apply to this bill and are made a part thereof.)

SIGNED _____ DATE _____

32. NAME AND ADDRESS OF FACILITY WHERE SERVICES WERE RENDERED (If other than home or office)

33. PHYSICIAN'S, SUPPLIER'S BILLING NAME, ADDRESS, ZIP CODE & PHONE #

PIN# _____ GRP# _____

PHYSICIAN OR SUPPLIER INFORMATION

(SAMPLE ONLY - NOT APPROVED FOR USE)   PLEASE PRINT OR TYPE

SAMPLE FORM 1500
SAMPLE FORM 1500 SAMPLE FORM 1500

180

_____

_____

_____

To My Medicare Patients:

My primary concern as your physician is to provide you with the best possible care. Medicare does not pay for all services and will only allow those which it determines, under the guidelines spelled out in the Omnibus Reconciliation Act of 1986 Section 1862(a)(1), to be reasonable and necessary. Under this law, a procedure or service deemed to be medically unreasonable or unnecessary will be denied. Since I believe each scheduled visit or planned procedure is both reasonable and necessary, I am required to notify you in advance that the following procedures or services listed below, which we have mutually agreed on, may be denied by Medicare.

Date of Service _____

Description of Service   Charge

_____   _____

_____   _____

_____   _____

Denial may be for the following reasons:

1. Medicare does not usually pay for this many visits or treatments,

2. Medicare does not usually pay for this many services within this period of time, and/or

3. Medicare does not usually pay for this type of service for your condition.

I, however, believe these procedures/services to be both reasonable and necessary for your condition, and will assist you in collecting payment from Medicare. In order for me to assist you in this matter, the law requires that you read the following agreement and sign it.

I have been informed by _____ that he/she believes, in my case, Medicare is likely to deny payment for the services and reasons stated above. If Medicare denies payment, I agree to be personally and fully responsible for payment.

Beneficiary's Name: _____ Medicare ID # _____

Beneficiary's Signature _____

or

Authorized Representative's Signature _____

DONALD L. GIVINGS, M.D.

11350 Medical Drive ■ Anywhere US 12345 ■ (101) 111-5555

EIN: 11-123456   SSN: 123-12-1234   MEDICARE: D1234
PIN: DG1234   GRP: DG12345   MEDICAID: DLG1234
BCBS: 12345

Encounter Form

PATIENT INFORMATION:

Name:	Danielle H. Ford
Address:	28 Delightful Drive
City:	Anywhere
State:	US
Zip Code:	12345
Telephone:	(101) 333-5555
Gender:	Female
Date of Birth:	12-10-1922
Occupation:	
Employer:	
Spouse's Employer:	

INSURANCE INFORMATION:

Patient Number:	14-m
Place of Service:	Office
Primary Insurance Plan:	Medicare
Primary Insurance Plan ID #:	756-66-7878W
Group #:	
Primary Policyholder:	
Policyholder Date of Birth:	
Relationship to Patient:	
Secondary Insurance Plan:	
Secondary Insurance Plan ID #:	
Secondary Policyholder:	

Patient Status   ☐ Married   ☐ Divorced   ☒ Single   ☐ Student   ☐ Other

DIAGNOSIS INFORMATION

Diagnosis	Code	Diagnosis	Code
1. Routine examination	V70.0	5.	
2.		6.	
3.		7.	
4.		8.	

PROCEDURE INFORMATION

Description of Procedure or Service	Date	Code	Charge
1. Preventive medicine, 65 years and over	08-09-YYYY	99397	$65.00
2.			
3.			
4.			
5.			

SPECIAL NOTES:

Have the patient sign a Medicare Medical Necessity form

Return visit: PRN

CARRIER

| | PICA | | **HEALTH INSURANCE CLAIM FORM** | PICA | | |

1. | MEDICARE | MEDICAID | CHAMPUS | CHAMPVA | GROUP HEALTH PLAN | FECA BLK LUNG | OTHER | **1a.** INSURED'S I.D. NUMBER | (FOR PROGRAM IN ITEM 1)
☐ (Medicare #) ☐ (Medicaid #) ☐ (Sponsor's SSN) ☐ (VA File #) ☐ (SSN or ID) ☐ (SSN) ☐ (ID)

2. PATIENT'S NAME (Last Name, First Name, Middle Initial)

3. PATIENT'S BIRTH DATE MM | DD | YY   SEX   M ☐   F ☐

4. INSURED'S NAME (Last Name, First Name, Middle Initial)

5. PATIENT'S ADDRESS (No. Street)

6. PATIENT RELATIONSHIP TO INSURED   Self ☐   Spouse ☐   Child ☐   Other ☐

7. INSURED'S ADDRESS (No. Street)

CITY | STATE

8. PATIENT STATUS   Single ☐   Married ☐   Other ☐   Employed ☐   Full-Time Student ☐   Part-Time Student ☐

CITY | STATE

ZIP CODE | TELEPHONE (Include Area Code) ( )

ZIP CODE | TELEPHONE (INCLUDE AREA CODE) ( )

9. OTHER INSURED'S NAME (Last Name, First Name, Middle Initial)

10. IS PATIENT'S CONDITION RELATED TO:

11. INSURED'S POLICY GROUP OR FECA NUMBER

a. OTHER INSURED'S POLICY OR GROUP NUMBER

a. EMPLOYMENT? (CURRENT OR PREVIOUS)   YES ☐   NO ☐

a. INSURED'S DATE OF BIRTH MM | DD | YY   SEX   M ☐   F ☐

b. OTHER INSURED'S DATE OF BIRTH MM | DD | YY   SEX   M ☐   F ☐

b. AUTO ACCIDENT?   PLACE (State)   YES ☐   NO ☐

b. EMPLOYER'S NAME OR SCHOOL NAME

c. EMPLOYER'S NAME OR SCHOOL NAME

c. OTHER ACCIDENT?   YES ☐   NO ☐

c. INSURANCE PLAN NAME OR PROGRAM NAME

d. INSURANCE PLAN NAME OR PROGRAM NAME

10d. RESERVED FOR LOCAL USE

d. IS THERE ANOTHER HEALTH BENEFIT PLAN?   YES ☐   NO ☐   If yes, return to and complete item 9 a – d.

READ BACK OF FORM BEFORE COMPLETING & SIGNING THIS FORM.
12. PATIENT'S OR AUTHORIZED PERSON'S SIGNATURE I authorize the release of any medical or other information necessary to process this claim. I also request payment of government benefits either to myself or to the party who accepts assignment below.

SIGNED _____ DATE _____

13. INSURED'S OR AUTHORIZED PERSON'S SIGNATURE I authorize payment of medical benefits to the undersigned physician or supplier for services described below.

SIGNED _____

PATIENT AND INSURED INFORMATION

14. DATE OF CURRENT: MM | DD | YY   ILLNESS (First symptom) OR INJURY (Accident) OR PREGNANCY (LMP)

15. IF PATIENT HAS HAD SAME OR SIMILAR ILLNESS, GIVE FIRST DATE MM | DD | YY

16. DATES PATIENT UNABLE TO WORK IN CURRENT OCCUPATION   FROM MM | DD | YY   TO MM | DD | YY

17. NAME OF REFERRING PHYSICIAN OR OTHER SOURCE

17a. I.D. NUMBER OF REFERRING PHYSICIAN

18. HOSPITALIZATION DATES RELATED TO CURRENT SERVICES   FROM MM | DD | YY   TO MM | DD | YY

19. RESERVED FOR LOCAL USE

20. OUTSIDE LAB?   YES ☐   NO ☐ $ CHARGES

21. DIAGNOSIS OR NATURE OF ILLNESS OR INJURY. (RELATE ITEMS 1, 2, 3, OR 4 TO ITEM 24E BY LINE)
1. └── . ──
2. └── . ──
3. └── . ──
4. └── . ──

22. MEDICAID RESUBMISSION CODE | ORIGINAL REF. NO.

23. PRIOR AUTHORIZATION NUMBER

24. A DATE(S) OF SERVICE						B Place of Service	C Type of Service	D PROCEDURES, SERVICES, OR SUPPLIES (Explain Unusual Circumstances)		E DIAGNOSIS CODE	F $ CHARGES	G DAYS OR UNITS	H EPSDT Family Plan	I EMG	J COB	K RESERVED FOR LOCAL USE
From MM	DD	YY	To MM	DD	YY			CPT/HCPCS	MODIFIER							
1																
2																
3																
4																
5																
6																

25. FEDERAL TAX I.D. NUMBER   SSN ☐   EIN ☐

26. PATIENT'S ACCOUNT NO.

27. ACCEPT ASSIGNMENT? (For govt. claims, see back)   YES ☐   NO ☐

28. TOTAL CHARGE $

29. AMOUNT PAID $

30. BALANCE DUE $

31. SIGNATURE OF PHYSICIAN OR SUPPLIER INCLUDING DEGREES OR CREDENTIALS (I certify that the statements on the reverse apply to this bill and are made a part thereof.)

SIGNED _____ DATE _____

32. NAME AND ADDRESS OF FACILITY WHERE SERVICES WERE RENDERED (If other than home or office)

33. PHYSICIAN'S, SUPPLIER'S BILLING NAME, ADDRESS, ZIP CODE & PHONE #

PIN# | GRP#

PHYSICIAN OR SUPPLIER INFORMATION

PLEASE PRINT OR TYPE   SAMPLE FORM 1500   SAMPLE FORM 1500 SAMPLE FORM 1500

183

Chapter 15
Medicaid

FEDERAL ELIGIBILITY REQUIREMENTS FOR MEDICAID

1. When a patient claims to be eligible for Medicaid benefits, what must be presented as proof? _____
   _____

2. In many cases, what does Medicaid eligibility depend on? _____

3. What do most states use for verification of Medicaid eligibility? _____

MEDICAID COVERED SERVICES

4. What does the EPSDT legislation mandate? _____
   _____

5. List six medical situations that require preauthorization from Medicaid.
   a. _____
   b. _____
   c. _____
   d. _____
   e. _____
   f. _____

6. Medicaid makes payment directly to ___. (Circle the correct answer.)
   a. Medicare
   b. patients
   c. providers
   d. all of the above

7. Who determines the reimbursement methodology and rates for Medicaid services? (Circle the correct answer.)
   a. federal government
   b. individual states
   c. Medicare
   d. none of the above

8. Emergency services and family planning services are exempt from ___. (Circle the correct answer.)

    a. copayments

    b. dual eligibles

    c. electronic submission

    d. none of the above

9. Medicaid recipients excluded from copayments include ___. (Circle the correct answer.)

    a. children over the age of 18

    b. hypertensive adults

    c. pregnant women

    d. all of the above

10. The portion of the Medicaid program paid by the federal government is known as the

    _____ _____ _____ _____.

MEDICARE-MEDICAID RELATIONSHIP

11. Define *dual eligibles*. _____

    _____

    _____

12. Services covered by both programs are paid first by _____ and the difference by _____.

MEDICAID AS A SECONDARY PAYER

13. Medicaid is always the ___. (Circle the correct answer.)

    a. primary insurance

    b. secondary insurance

    c. payer of last resort

    d. none of the above

14. Medicaid is billed only ___. (Circle the correct answer.)

    a. if other coverage denies responsibility for payment

    b. if other coverage pays less than the Medicaid fee schedule

    c. if Medicaid covers procedures not covered by another policy

    d. all of the above

PARTICIPATING PROVIDERS

15. If a patient has Medicaid and a service was performed that is a Medicaid-covered benefit, can the provider balance bill the patient? _____

16. Can a Medicaid patient be billed for a service that is not a Medicaid-covered benefit? _____

MEDICAID REMITTANCE ADVICE

17. A Medicaid remittance advice is sent to the ___. (Circle the correct answer.)

    a. patient

    b. provider

18. A Medicaid remittance advice contains ___. (Circle the correct answer.)

    a. adjusted claims

    b. status of claims

    c. voided claims

    d. all of the above

19. What option do providers have if they feel improper payment was issued? _____

    _____

BILLING INFORMATION NOTES

20. The required form for submitting Medicaid claims is the _____.

21. The deadline for filing claims for Medicaid patients ___. (Circle the correct answer.)
    a. varies from state to state
    b. is 30 days
    c. is 60 days
    d. is 90 days

22. Medicaid crossover claims follow the ___ deadlines for claims. (Circle the correct answer.)
    a. Medicaid
    b. secondary
    c. Medicare
    d. none of the above

23. State why collection of fees for uncovered services is difficult. _____

    _____

    _____

24. If the assignment of benefits is not marked on the CMS-1500 claim, what can happen to reimbursement?

    _____

    _____

25. For each question, enter **Y** for yes or **N** for no on the line provided.

    _____ a. Can a provider attempt to collect the difference between the Medicaid payment and the fee charged if the patient did not reveal that he/she was a Medicaid recipient at the time services were rendered?

    _____ b. Can there be a deductible for persons in the medically needy classification?

    _____ c. Are copayments required for some categories of Medicaid recipients?

    _____ d. Does the Medicaid recipient pay a premium for medical coverage?

    _____ e. If the patient's condition warrants extension of authorized inpatient days, should the hospital seek authorization for additional inpatient days?

    _____ f. Can Medicaid patients be eligible for Medicaid benefits one month and not the next?

    _____ g. Are cards issued for the "Unborn child of..." valid for services as soon as the child is born?

Know Your Acronyms

26. Define the following acronyms:

a. AFDC _____

b. CSRA _____

c. EPSDT _____

d. FMAP _____

e. FPL _____

f. MEVS _____

g. MMMNA _____

h. NBCCEDP _____

i. PCCM _____

j. PRA _____

k. QDWI _____

l. QI _____

m. QMB _____

n. REVS _____

o. SCHIP _____

p. SLMB _____

q. SSI _____

r. SURS _____

s. TANF _____

EXERCISES

27. Complete the Case Studies, 15-a through 15-f, using the blank claims provided. Follow the step-by-step instructions from the textbook to properly complete each claim. You may choose to use a pencil so corrections can be made.

DONALD L. GIVINGS, M.D.

11350 Medical Drive ■ Anywhere US 12345 ■ (101) 111-5555

EIN: 11-123456	SSN: 123-12-1234	MEDICARE: D1234
PIN: DG1234	GRP: DG12345	MEDICAID: DLG1234
BCBS: 12345		

Encounter Form

PATIENT INFORMATION:

Name:	Sharon W. Casey
Address:	483 Oakdale Avenue
City:	Anywhere
State:	US
Zip Code:	12345
Telephone:	(101) 333-5555
Gender:	Female
Date of Birth:	10-06-1970
Occupation:	
Employer:	
Spouse's Employer:	

INSURANCE INFORMATION:

Patient Number:	15-a
Place of Service:	Office
Primary Insurance Plan:	Medicaid
Primary Insurance Plan ID #:	22334455
Group #:	
Primary Policyholder:	Sharon W. Casey
Policyholder Date of Birth:	10-06-1970
Relationship to Patient:	Self
Secondary Insurance Plan:	
Secondary Insurance Plan ID #:	
Secondary Policyholder:	

Patient Status ☐ Married   ☐ Divorced   ☒ Single   ☐ Student   ☐ Other

DIAGNOSIS INFORMATION

Diagnosis	Code	Diagnosis	Code
1. Excessive menstruation	626.2	5.	
2. Irregular menstrual cycle	626.4	6.	
3.		7.	
4.		8.	

PROCEDURE INFORMATION

Description of Procedure or Service	Date	Code	Charge
1. Est. patient OV level III	11-13-YYYY	99213	$75.00
2.			
3.			
4.			
5.			

SPECIAL NOTES:

    Refer patient to GYN

    Return visit: PRN

(SAMPLE ONLY - NOT APPROVED FOR USE)

CARRIER

| | PICA | | **HEALTH INSURANCE CLAIM FORM** | PICA | | |

| 1. MEDICARE MEDICAID CHAMPUS CHAMPVA GROUP HEALTH PLAN FECA BLK LUNG OTHER | 1a. INSURED'S I.D. NUMBER (FOR PROGRAM IN ITEM 1) |
| (Medicare #) (Medicaid #) (Sponsor's SSN) (VA File #) (SSN or ID) (SSN) (ID) | |

| 2. PATIENT'S NAME (Last Name, First Name, Middle Initial) | 3. PATIENT'S BIRTH DATE MM DD YY SEX M F | 4. INSURED'S NAME (Last Name, First Name, Middle Initial) |

| 5. PATIENT'S ADDRESS (No. Street) | 6. PATIENT RELATIONSHIP TO INSURED Self Spouse Child Other | 7. INSURED'S ADDRESS (No. Street) |

| CITY STATE | 8. PATIENT STATUS Single Married Other | CITY STATE |

| ZIP CODE TELEPHONE (Include Area Code) ( ) | Employed Full-Time Student Part-Time Student | ZIP CODE TELEPHONE (INCLUDE AREA CODE) ( ) |

| 9. OTHER INSURED'S NAME (Last Name, First Name, Middle Initial) | 10. IS PATIENT'S CONDITION RELATED TO: | 11. INSURED'S POLICY GROUP OR FECA NUMBER |

| a. OTHER INSURED'S POLICY OR GROUP NUMBER | a. EMPLOYMENT? (CURRENT OR PREVIOUS) YES NO | a. INSURED'S DATE OF BIRTH MM DD YY SEX M F |

| b. OTHER INSURED'S DATE OF BIRTH MM DD YY SEX M F | b. AUTO ACCIDENT? PLACE (State) YES NO | b. EMPLOYER'S NAME OR SCHOOL NAME |

| c. EMPLOYER'S NAME OR SCHOOL NAME | c. OTHER ACCIDENT? YES NO | c. INSURANCE PLAN NAME OR PROGRAM NAME |

| d. INSURANCE PLAN NAME OR PROGRAM NAME | 10d. RESERVED FOR LOCAL USE | d. IS THERE ANOTHER HEALTH BENEFIT PLAN? YES NO If yes, return to and complete item 9 a – d. |

READ BACK OF FORM BEFORE COMPLETING & SIGNING THIS FORM.
12. PATIENT'S OR AUTHORIZED PERSON'S SIGNATURE I authorize the release of any medical or other information necessary to process this claim. I also request payment of government benefits either to myself or to the party who accepts assignment below.

SIGNED _____ DATE _____

13. INSURED'S OR AUTHORIZED PERSON'S SIGNATURE I authorize payment of medical benefits to the undersigned physician or supplier for services described below.

SIGNED _____

PATIENT AND INSURED INFORMATION

| 14. DATE OF CURRENT: ILLNESS (First symptom) OR INJURY (Accident) OR PREGNANCY (LMP) MM DD YY | 15. IF PATIENT HAS HAD SAME OR SIMILAR ILLNESS, GIVE FIRST DATE MM DD YY | 16. DATES PATIENT UNABLE TO WORK IN CURRENT OCCUPATION MM DD YY MM DD YY FROM TO |

| 17. NAME OF REFERRING PHYSICIAN OR OTHER SOURCE | 17a. I.D. NUMBER OF REFERRING PHYSICIAN | 18. HOSPITALIZATION DATES RELATED TO CURRENT SERVICES MM DD YY MM DD YY FROM TO |

| 19. RESERVED FOR LOCAL USE | 20. OUTSIDE LAB? $ CHARGES YES NO |

| 21. DIAGNOSIS OR NATURE OF ILLNESS OR INJURY. (RELATE ITEMS 1, 2, 3, OR 4 TO ITEM 24E BY LINE) 1. ___.___ 3. ___.___ 2. ___.___ 4. ___.___ | 22. MEDICAID RESUBMISSION CODE ORIGINAL REF. NO. |
| | 23. PRIOR AUTHORIZATION NUMBER |

24. A DATE(S) OF SERVICE					B Place of Service	C Type of Service	D PROCEDURES, SERVICES, OR SUPPLIES (Explain Unusual Circumstances)		E DIAGNOSIS CODE	F $ CHARGES	G DAYS OR UNITS	H EPSDT Family Plan	I EMG	J COB	K RESERVED FOR LOCAL USE
From MM	DD	YY	To MM	DD	YY			CPT/HCPCS	MODIFIER							
1																
2																
3																
4																
5																
6																

| 25. FEDERAL TAX I.D. NUMBER SSN EIN | 26. PATIENT'S ACCOUNT NO. | 27. ACCEPT ASSIGNMENT? (For govt. claims, see back) YES NO | 28. TOTAL CHARGE $ | 29. AMOUNT PAID $ | 30. BALANCE DUE $ |

| 31. SIGNATURE OF PHYSICIAN OR SUPPLIER INCLUDING DEGREES OR CREDENTIALS (I certify that the statements on the reverse apply to this bill and are made a part thereof.) SIGNED _____ DATE _____ | 32. NAME AND ADDRESS OF FACILITY WHERE SERVICES WERE RENDERED (If other than home or office) | 33. PHYSICIAN'S, SUPPLIER'S BILLING NAME, ADDRESS, ZIP CODE & PHONE # PIN# GRP# |

PHYSICIAN OR SUPPLIER INFORMATION

(SAMPLE ONLY - NOT APPROVED FOR USE) | *PLEASE PRINT OR TYPE* | SAMPLE FORM 1500 SAMPLE FORM 1500 SAMPLE FORM 1500

MARIA C. SECTION, M.D.   OB/GYN

Encounter Form

11 Maden Lane ■ Anywhere US 12345 ■ (101) 111-5555

EIN:	11-669977	SSN:	444-22-1234	MEDICARE:	M1234
UPIN:	MS1234	GRP:	DG12345	MEDICAID:	MCS1234
BCBS:	11223				

PATIENT INFORMATION:

Name:	Sharon W. Casey
Address:	483 Oakdale Avenue
City:	Anywhere
State:	US
Zip Code:	12345
Telephone:	(101) 333-5555
Gender:	Female
Date of Birth:	10-06-1970
Occupation:	
Employer:	
Spouse's Employer:	

INSURANCE INFORMATION:

Patient Number:	15-b
Place of Service:	Office
Primary Insurance Plan:	Medicaid
Primary Insurance Plan ID #:	22334455
Group #:	
Primary Policyholder:	Sharon W. Casey
Policyholder Date of Birth:	10-06-1970
Relationship to Patient:	Self
Secondary Insurance Plan:	
Secondary Insurance Plan ID #:	
Secondary Policyholder:	

Patient Status   ☐ Married   ☐ Divorced   ☒ Single   ☐ Student   ☐ Other

DIAGNOSIS INFORMATION

Diagnosis	Code	Diagnosis	Code
1. Excessive menstruation	626.2	5.	
2. Irregular menstrual cycle	626.4	6.	
3.		7.	
4.		8.	

PROCEDURE INFORMATION

Description of Procedure or Service	Date	Code	Charge
1. Office consult level III	11-20-YYYY	99243	$85.00
2.			
3.			
4.			
5.			

SPECIAL NOTES:

Referred by Donald L. Givings, M.D.,   UPI/SSN: DLG1234
Return visit: One month

(SAMPLE ONLY - NOT APPROVED FOR USE)

CARRIER

[ ][ ] PICA

HEALTH INSURANCE CLAIM FORM   PICA [ ][ ]

1. MEDICARE   MEDICAID   CHAMPUS   CHAMPVA   GROUP HEALTH PLAN   FECA BLK LUNG   OTHER
   [ ] (Medicare #)   [ ] (Medicaid #)   [ ] (Sponsor's SSN)   [ ] (VA File #)   [ ] (SSN or ID)   [ ] (SSN)   [ ] (ID)

1a. INSURED'S I.D. NUMBER   (FOR PROGRAM IN ITEM 1)

2. PATIENT'S NAME (Last Name, First Name, Middle Initial)

3. PATIENT'S BIRTH DATE   SEX
   MM | DD | YY   M [ ]   F [ ]

4. INSURED'S NAME (Last Name, First Name, Middle Initial)

5. PATIENT'S ADDRESS (No. Street)

6. PATIENT RELATIONSHIP TO INSURED
   Self [ ]   Spouse [ ]   Child [ ]   Other [ ]

7. INSURED'S ADDRESS (No. Street)

CITY   STATE

8. PATIENT STATUS
   Single [ ]   Married [ ]   Other [ ]
   Employed [ ]   Full-Time Student [ ]   Part-Time Student [ ]

CITY   STATE

ZIP CODE   TELEPHONE (Include Area Code)
                (   )

ZIP CODE   TELEPHONE (INCLUDE AREA CODE)
                (   )

9. OTHER INSURED'S NAME (Last Name, First Name, Middle Initial)

10. IS PATIENT'S CONDITION RELATED TO:

11. INSURED'S POLICY GROUP OR FECA NUMBER

a. OTHER INSURED'S POLICY OR GROUP NUMBER

a. EMPLOYMENT? (CURRENT OR PREVIOUS)
   [ ] YES   [ ] NO

a. INSURED'S DATE OF BIRTH   SEX
   MM | DD | YY   M [ ]   F [ ]

b. OTHER INSURED'S DATE OF BIRTH   SEX
   MM | DD | YY   M [ ]   F [ ]

b. AUTO ACCIDENT?   PLACE (State)
   [ ] YES   [ ] NO

b. EMPLOYER'S NAME OR SCHOOL NAME

c. EMPLOYER'S NAME OR SCHOOL NAME

c. OTHER ACCIDENT?
   [ ] YES   [ ] NO

c. INSURANCE PLAN NAME OR PROGRAM NAME

d. INSURANCE PLAN NAME OR PROGRAM NAME

10d. RESERVED FOR LOCAL USE

d. IS THERE ANOTHER HEALTH BENEFIT PLAN?
   [ ] YES   [ ] NO   If yes, return to and complete item 9 a - d.

READ BACK OF FORM BEFORE COMPLETING & SIGNING THIS FORM.
12. PATIENT'S OR AUTHORIZED PERSON'S SIGNATURE I authorize the release of any medical or other information necessary to process this claim. I also request payment of government benefits either to myself or to the party who accepts assignment below.

SIGNED _____   DATE _____

13. INSURED'S OR AUTHORIZED PERSON'S SIGNATURE I authorize payment of medical benefits to the undersigned physician or supplier for services described below.

SIGNED _____

PATIENT AND INSURED INFORMATION

14. DATE OF CURRENT: ILLNESS (First symptom) OR
    MM | DD | YY   INJURY (Accident) OR
                        PREGNANCY (LMP)

15. IF PATIENT HAS HAD SAME OR SIMILAR ILLNESS, GIVE FIRST DATE   MM | DD | YY

16. DATES PATIENT UNABLE TO WORK IN CURRENT OCCUPATION
    FROM   MM | DD | YY   TO   MM | DD | YY

17. NAME OF REFERRING PHYSICIAN OR OTHER SOURCE

17a. I.D. NUMBER OF REFERRING PHYSICIAN

18. HOSPITALIZATION DATES RELATED TO CURRENT SERVICES
    FROM   MM | DD | YY   TO   MM | DD | YY

19. RESERVED FOR LOCAL USE

20. OUTSIDE LAB? $ CHARGES
    [ ] YES   [ ] NO

21. DIAGNOSIS OR NATURE OF ILLNESS OR INJURY. (RELATE ITEMS 1, 2, 3, OR 4 TO ITEM 24E BY LINE)
    1. |___.___   3. |___.___
    2. |___.___   4. |___.___

22. MEDICAID RESUBMISSION CODE   ORIGINAL REF. NO.

23. PRIOR AUTHORIZATION NUMBER

24.

A DATE(S) OF SERVICE						B Place of Service	C Type of Service	D PROCEDURES, SERVICES, OR SUPPLIES (Explain Unusual Circumstances)		E DIAGNOSIS CODE	F $ CHARGES	G DAYS OR UNITS	H EPSDT Family Plan	I EMG	J COB	K RESERVED FOR LOCAL USE
From MM	DD	YY	To MM	DD	YY			CPT/HCPCS	MODIFIER							
1																
2																
3																
4																
5																
6																

25. FEDERAL TAX I.D. NUMBER   SSN [ ]   EIN [ ]

26. PATIENT'S ACCOUNT NO.

27. ACCEPT ASSIGNMENT? (For govt. claims, see back)
    [ ] YES   [ ] NO

28. TOTAL CHARGE $

29. AMOUNT PAID $

30. BALANCE DUE $

31. SIGNATURE OF PHYSICIAN OR SUPPLIER INCLUDING DEGREES OR CREDENTIALS
(I certify that the statements on the reverse apply to this bill and are made a part thereof.)

SIGNED _____   DATE _____

32. NAME AND ADDRESS OF FACILITY WHERE SERVICES WERE RENDERED (If other than home or office)

33. PHYSICIAN'S, SUPPLIER'S BILLING NAME, ADDRESS, ZIP CODE & PHONE #

PIN# _____   GRP# _____

PHYSICIAN OR SUPPLIER INFORMATION

(SAMPLE ONLY - NOT APPROVED FOR USE)   *PLEASE PRINT OR TYPE*   SAMPLE FORM 1500
SAMPLE FORM 1500 SAMPLE FORM 1500

DONALD L. GIVINGS, M.D.

Encounter Form

11350 Medical Drive ■ Anywhere US 12345 ■ (101) 111-5555

EIN: 11-123456	SSN: 123-12-1234	MEDICARE: D1234
PIN: DG1234	GRP: DG12345	MEDICAID: DLG1234
BCBS: 12345		

PATIENT INFORMATION:

Name:	Fred R. Jones
Address:	444 Taylor Avenue
City:	Anywhere
State:	US
Zip Code:	12345
Telephone:	(101) 333-5555
Gender:	Male
Date of Birth:	01-05-1949
Occupation:	
Employer:	
Spouse's Employer:	

INSURANCE INFORMATION:

Patient Number:	15-c
Place of Service:	Office
Primary Insurance Plan:	Medicaid
Primary Insurance Plan ID #:	55771122
Group #:	
Primary Policyholder:	
Policyholder Date of Birth:	
Relationship to Patient:	
Secondary Insurance Plan:	
Secondary Insurance Plan ID #:	
Secondary Policyholder:	

Patient Status ☐ Married ☒ Divorced ☐ Single ☐ Student ☐ Other

DIAGNOSIS INFORMATION

Diagnosis	Code	Diagnosis	Code
1. Difficulty in walking	719.70	5.	
2.		6.	
3.		7.	
4.		8.	

PROCEDURE INFORMATION

Description of Procedure or Service	Date	Code	Charge
1. Est. patient OV level III	06-19-YYYY	99213	$75.00
2.			
3.			
4.			
5.			

SPECIAL NOTES:

Refer patient to a podiatrist
Return visit: 3 months

PLEASE
DO NOT
STAPLE
IN THIS
AREA

| | PICA | | |

HEALTH INSURANCE CLAIM FORM

PICA | |

1.
MEDICARE MEDICAID CHAMPUS CHAMPVA GROUP HEALTH PLAN FECA BLK LUNG OTHER

(Medicare #) (Medicaid #) (Sponsor's SSN) (VA File #) (SSN or ID) (SSN) (ID)

1a. INSURED'S I.D. NUMBER (FOR PROGRAM IN ITEM 1)

2. PATIENT'S NAME (Last Name, First Name, Middle Initial)

3. PATIENT'S BIRTH DATE MM DD YY SEX M F

4. INSURED'S NAME (Last Name, First Name, Middle Initial)

5. PATIENT'S ADDRESS (No. Street)

6. PATIENT RELATIONSHIP TO INSURED Self Spouse Child Other

7. INSURED'S ADDRESS (No. Street)

CITY STATE

8. PATIENT STATUS Single Married Other

CITY STATE

ZIP CODE TELEPHONE (Include Area Code) ( )

Employed Full-Time Student Part-Time Student

ZIP CODE TELEPHONE (INCLUDE AREA CODE) ( )

9. OTHER INSURED'S NAME (Last Name, First Name, Middle Initial)

10. IS PATIENT'S CONDITION RELATED TO:

11. INSURED'S POLICY GROUP OR FECA NUMBER

a. OTHER INSURED'S POLICY OR GROUP NUMBER

a. EMPLOYMENT? (CURRENT OR PREVIOUS) YES NO

a. INSURED'S DATE OF BIRTH MM DD YY SEX M F

b. OTHER INSURED'S DATE OF BIRTH MM DD YY SEX M F

b. AUTO ACCIDENT? PLACE (State) YES NO

b. EMPLOYER'S NAME OR SCHOOL NAME

c. EMPLOYER'S NAME OR SCHOOL NAME

c. OTHER ACCIDENT? YES NO

c. INSURANCE PLAN NAME OR PROGRAM NAME

d. INSURANCE PLAN NAME OR PROGRAM NAME

10d. RESERVED FOR LOCAL USE

d. IS THERE ANOTHER HEALTH BENEFIT PLAN? YES NO If yes, return to and complete item 9 a – d.

READ BACK OF FORM BEFORE COMPLETING & SIGNING THIS FORM.
12. PATIENT'S OR AUTHORIZED PERSON'S SIGNATURE I authorize the release of any medical or other information necessary to process this claim. I also request payment of government benefits either to myself or to the party who accepts assignment below.

SIGNED _____ DATE _____

13. INSURED'S OR AUTHORIZED PERSON'S SIGNATURE I authorize payment of medical benefits to the undersigned physician or supplier for services described below.

SIGNED _____

14. DATE OF CURRENT: ILLNESS (First symptom) OR INJURY (Accident) OR PREGNANCY (LMP) MM DD YY

15. IF PATIENT HAS HAD SAME OR SIMILAR ILLNESS, GIVE FIRST DATE MM DD YY

16. DATES PATIENT UNABLE TO WORK IN CURRENT OCCUPATION MM DD YY FROM TO MM DD YY

17. NAME OF REFERRING PHYSICIAN OR OTHER SOURCE

17a. I.D. NUMBER OF REFERRING PHYSICIAN

18. HOSPITALIZATION DATES RELATED TO CURRENT SERVICES MM DD YY FROM TO MM DD YY

19. RESERVED FOR LOCAL USE

20. OUTSIDE LAB? YES NO $ CHARGES

21. DIAGNOSIS OR NATURE OF ILLNESS OR INJURY. (RELATE ITEMS 1, 2, 3, OR 4 TO ITEM 24E BY LINE)

1. _____ 3. _____

2. _____ 4. _____

22. MEDICAID RESUBMISSION CODE ORIGINAL REF. NO.

23. PRIOR AUTHORIZATION NUMBER

24. A DATE(S) OF SERVICE						B Place of Service	C Type of Service	D PROCEDURES, SERVICES, OR SUPPLIES (Explain Unusual Circumstances)		E DIAGNOSIS CODE	F $ CHARGES	G DAYS OR UNITS	H EPSDT Family Plan	I EMG	J COB	K RESERVED FOR LOCAL USE
From MM	DD	YY	To MM	DD	YY			CPT/HCPCS	MODIFIER							
1																
2																
3																
4																
5																
6																

25. FEDERAL TAX I.D. NUMBER SSN EIN

26. PATIENT'S ACCOUNT NO.

27. ACCEPT ASSIGNMENT? (For govt. claims, see back) YES NO

28. TOTAL CHARGE $

29. AMOUNT PAID $

30. BALANCE DUE $

31. SIGNATURE OF PHYSICIAN OR SUPPLIER INCLUDING DEGREES OR CREDENTIALS (I certify that the statements on the reverse apply to this bill and are made a part thereof.)

SIGNED _____ DATE _____

32. NAME AND ADDRESS OF FACILITY WHERE SERVICES WERE RENDERED (If other than home or office)

33. PHYSICIAN'S, SUPPLIER'S BILLING NAME, ADDRESS, ZIP CODE & PHONE #

PIN# GRP#

PLEASE PRINT OR TYPE

SAMPLE FORM 1500
SAMPLE FORM 1500 SAMPLE FORM 1500

194

JOHN F. WALKER, D.P.M. PODIATRY

546 Foothill Place ■ Anywhere US 12345 ■ (101) 111-5555

EIN:	11-993377	SSN: 657-12-4454	MEDICARE: J1234
UPIN:	JW1234	GRP: DG12345	MEDICAID: JFW1234
BCBS:			

Encounter Form

PATIENT INFORMATION:

Name:	Fred R. Jones
Address:	444 Taylor Avenue
City:	Anywhere
State:	US
Zip Code:	12345
Telephone:	(101) 333-5555
Gender:	Male
Date of Birth:	01-05-1949
Occupation:	
Employer:	
Spouse's Employer:	

INSURANCE INFORMATION:

Patient Number:	15-d
Place of Service:	Office
Primary Insurance Plan:	Medicaid
Primary Insurance Plan ID #:	55771122
Group #:	
Primary Policyholder:	
Policyholder Date of Birth:	
Relationship to Patient:	
Secondary Insurance Plan:	
Secondary Insurance Plan ID #:	
Secondary Policyholder:	

Patient Status ☐ Married ☒ Divorced ☐ Single ☐ Student ☐ Other

DIAGNOSIS INFORMATION

Diagnosis	Code	Diagnosis	Code
1. Fracture, great toe	826.0	5.	
2.		6.	
3.		7.	
4.		8.	

PROCEDURE INFORMATION

Description of Procedure or Service	Date	Code	Charge
1. Office consult level II	06-23-YYYY	99242	$75.00
2. Toe X-ray 2 views	06-23-YYYY	73660	50.00
3. Closed treatment of fracture, great toe	06-23-YYYY	28490	65.00
4.			
5.			

SPECIAL NOTES:

Referred by Donald L. Givings, M.D., UPI/SSN: DLG1234

(SAMPLE ONLY - NOT APPROVED FOR USE)

☐☐ PICA

HEALTH INSURANCE CLAIM FORM   PICA ☐☐

1. MEDICARE ☐ (Medicare #) MEDICAID ☐ (Medicaid #) CHAMPUS ☐ (Sponsor's SSN) CHAMPVA ☐ (VA File #) GROUP HEALTH PLAN ☐ (SSN or ID) FECA BLK LUNG ☐ (SSN) OTHER ☐ (ID)	1a. INSURED'S I.D. NUMBER (FOR PROGRAM IN ITEM 1)

2. PATIENT'S NAME (Last Name, First Name, Middle Initial)

3. PATIENT'S BIRTH DATE
MM ┆ DD ┆ YY   SEX   M ☐   F ☐

4. INSURED'S NAME (Last Name, First Name, Middle Initial)

5. PATIENT'S ADDRESS (No. Street)

6. PATIENT RELATIONSHIP TO INSURED
Self ☐   Spouse ☐   Child ☐   Other ☐

7. INSURED'S ADDRESS (No. Street)

CITY   STATE

8. PATIENT STATUS
Single ☐   Married ☐   Other ☐
Employed ☐   Full-Time Student ☐   Part-Time Student ☐

CITY   STATE

ZIP CODE   TELEPHONE (Include Area Code)
(   )

ZIP CODE   TELEPHONE (INCLUDE AREA CODE)
(   )

9. OTHER INSURED'S NAME (Last Name, First Name, Middle Initial)

10. IS PATIENT'S CONDITION RELATED TO:

11. INSURED'S POLICY GROUP OR FECA NUMBER

a. OTHER INSURED'S POLICY OR GROUP NUMBER

a. EMPLOYMENT? (CURRENT OR PREVIOUS)
☐ YES   ☐ NO

a. INSURED'S DATE OF BIRTH
MM ┆ DD ┆ YY   SEX   M ☐   F ☐

b. OTHER INSURED'S DATE OF BIRTH
MM ┆ DD ┆ YY   SEX   M ☐   F ☐

b. AUTO ACCIDENT?   PLACE (State)
☐ YES   ☐ NO

b. EMPLOYER'S NAME OR SCHOOL NAME

c. EMPLOYER'S NAME OR SCHOOL NAME

c. OTHER ACCIDENT?
☐ YES   ☐ NO

c. INSURANCE PLAN NAME OR PROGRAM NAME

d. INSURANCE PLAN NAME OR PROGRAM NAME

10d. RESERVED FOR LOCAL USE

d. IS THERE ANOTHER HEALTH BENEFIT PLAN?
☐ YES   ☐ NO   If yes, return to and complete item 9 a – d.

READ BACK OF FORM BEFORE COMPLETING & SIGNING THIS FORM.
12. PATIENT'S OR AUTHORIZED PERSON'S SIGNATURE I authorize the release of any medical or other information necessary to process this claim. I also request payment of government benefits either to myself or to the party who accepts assignment below.

SIGNED _____   DATE _____

13. INSURED'S OR AUTHORIZED PERSON'S SIGNATURE I authorize payment of medical benefits to the undersigned physician or supplier for services described below.

SIGNED _____

14. DATE OF CURRENT: ILLNESS (First symptom) OR
MM ┆ DD ┆ YY   INJURY (Accident) OR
PREGNANCY (LMP)

15. IF PATIENT HAS HAD SAME OR SIMILAR ILLNESS, GIVE FIRST DATE   MM ┆ DD ┆ YY

16. DATES PATIENT UNABLE TO WORK IN CURRENT OCCUPATION
MM ┆ DD ┆ YY   MM ┆ DD ┆ YY
FROM   TO

17. NAME OF REFERRING PHYSICIAN OR OTHER SOURCE

17a. I.D. NUMBER OF REFERRING PHYSICIAN

18. HOSPITALIZATION DATES RELATED TO CURRENT SERVICES
MM ┆ DD ┆ YY   MM ┆ DD ┆ YY
FROM   TO

19. RESERVED FOR LOCAL USE

20. OUTSIDE LAB? $ CHARGES
☐ YES   ☐ NO

21. DIAGNOSIS OR NATURE OF ILLNESS OR INJURY. (RELATE ITEMS 1, 2, 3, OR 4 TO ITEM 24E BY LINE)
1. └___ . ___
2. └___ . ___
3. └___ . ___
4. └___ . ___

22. MEDICAID RESUBMISSION
CODE   ORIGINAL REF. NO.

23. PRIOR AUTHORIZATION NUMBER

24. A DATE(S) OF SERVICE From MM DD YY To MM DD YY	B Place of Service	C Type of Service	D PROCEDURES, SERVICES, OR SUPPLIES (Explain Unusual Circumstances) CPT/HCPCS MODIFIER	E DIAGNOSIS CODE	F $ CHARGES	G DAYS OR UNITS	H EPSDT Family Plan	I EMG	J COB	K RESERVED FOR LOCAL USE
1										
2										
3										
4										
5										
6										

25. FEDERAL TAX I.D. NUMBER   SSN ☐ EIN ☐

26. PATIENT'S ACCOUNT NO.

27. ACCEPT ASSIGNMENT? (For govt. claims, see back)
☐ YES   ☐ NO

28. TOTAL CHARGE
$

29. AMOUNT PAID
$

30. BALANCE DUE
$

31. SIGNATURE OF PHYSICIAN OR SUPPLIER INCLUDING DEGREES OR CREDENTIALS
(I certify that the statements on the reverse apply to this bill and are made a part thereof.)

SIGNED _____   DATE _____

32. NAME AND ADDRESS OF FACILITY WHERE SERVICES WERE RENDERED (If other than home or office)

33. PHYSICIAN'S, SUPPLIER'S BILLING NAME, ADDRESS, ZIP CODE & PHONE #

PIN# _____   GRP# _____

(SAMPLE ONLY - NOT APPROVED FOR USE)

PLEASE PRINT OR TYPE

SAMPLE FORM 1500
SAMPLE FORM 1500 SAMPLE FORM 1500

CARRIER
PATIENT AND INSURED INFORMATION
PHYSICIAN OR SUPPLIER INFORMATION

196

DONALD L. GIVINGS, M.D.

11350 Medical Drive ■ Anywhere US 12345 ■ (101) 111-5555

EIN: 11-123456	SSN: 123-12-1234	MEDICARE: D1234
PIN: DG1234	GRP: DG12345	MEDICAID: DLG1234
BCBS: 12345		

Encounter Form

PATIENT INFORMATION:

Name:	Richard J. Davis
Address:	3764 Ravenwood Ave.
City:	Anywhere
State:	US
Zip Code:	12345
Telephone:	(101) 333-5555
Gender:	Male
Date of Birth:	03-10-1994
Occupation:	
Employer:	
Spouse's Employer:	

INSURANCE INFORMATION:

Patient Number:	15-e
Place of Service:	Office
Primary Insurance Plan:	Medicaid
Primary Insurance Plan ID #:	77557755
Group #:	
Primary Policyholder:	
Policyholder Date of Birth:	
Relationship to Patient:	
Secondary Insurance Plan:	
Secondary Insurance Plan ID #:	
Secondary Policyholder:	

Patient Status ☐ Married ☐ Divorced ☐ Single ☐ Student ☐ Other

DIAGNOSIS INFORMATION

Diagnosis	Code	Diagnosis	Code
1. Routine child health check	V20.2	5.	
2.		6.	
3.		7.	
4.		8.	

PROCEDURE INFORMATION

Description of Procedure or Service	Date	Code	Charge
1. Preventive medicine est. patient 5-11 years	07-18-YYYY	99393	$60.00
2. DTaP	07-18-YYYY	90700	40.00
3. MMR	07-18-YYYY	90707	55.00
4. OPV	07-18-YYYY	90712	25.00
5. Immunization administration (x3)	07-18-YYYY	90471	25.00
		90471	25.00
		90471	25.00

SPECIAL NOTES:

(SAMPLE ONLY - NOT APPROVED FOR USE)

CARRIER

| | PICA

HEALTH INSURANCE CLAIM FORM

PICA | | |

1. MEDICARE   MEDICAID   CHAMPUS   CHAMPVA   GROUP HEALTH PLAN   FECA BLK LUNG   OTHER
    ☐ (Medicare #) ☐ (Medicaid #) ☐ (Sponsor's SSN) ☐ (VA File #) ☐ (SSN or ID) ☐ (SSN) ☐ (ID)

1a. INSURED'S I.D. NUMBER   (FOR PROGRAM IN ITEM 1)

2. PATIENT'S NAME (Last Name, First Name, Middle Initial)

3. PATIENT'S BIRTH DATE   SEX
    MM | DD | YY   M ☐   F ☐

4. INSURED'S NAME (Last Name, First Name, Middle Initial)

5. PATIENT'S ADDRESS (No. Street)

6. PATIENT RELATIONSHIP TO INSURED
    Self ☐   Spouse ☐   Child ☐   Other ☐

7. INSURED'S ADDRESS (No. Street)

CITY   STATE

8. PATIENT STATUS
    Single ☐   Married ☐   Other ☐
    Employed ☐   Full-Time Student ☐   Part-Time Student ☐

CITY   STATE

ZIP CODE   TELEPHONE (Include Area Code) ( )

ZIP CODE   TELEPHONE (INCLUDE AREA CODE) ( )

9. OTHER INSURED'S NAME (Last Name, First Name, Middle Initial)

10. IS PATIENT'S CONDITION RELATED TO:

11. INSURED'S POLICY GROUP OR FECA NUMBER

a. OTHER INSURED'S POLICY OR GROUP NUMBER

a. EMPLOYMENT? (CURRENT OR PREVIOUS)
    ☐ YES   ☐ NO

a. INSURED'S DATE OF BIRTH   SEX
    MM | DD | YY   M ☐   F ☐

b. OTHER INSURED'S DATE OF BIRTH   SEX
    MM | DD | YY   M ☐   F ☐

b. AUTO ACCIDENT?   PLACE (State)
    ☐ YES   ☐ NO

b. EMPLOYER'S NAME OR SCHOOL NAME

c. EMPLOYER'S NAME OR SCHOOL NAME

c. OTHER ACCIDENT?
    ☐ YES   ☐ NO

c. INSURANCE PLAN NAME OR PROGRAM NAME

d. INSURANCE PLAN NAME OR PROGRAM NAME

10d. RESERVED FOR LOCAL USE

d. IS THERE ANOTHER HEALTH BENEFIT PLAN?
    ☐ YES   ☐ NO   If yes, return to and complete item 9 a – d.

READ BACK OF FORM BEFORE COMPLETING & SIGNING THIS FORM.
12. PATIENT'S OR AUTHORIZED PERSON'S SIGNATURE I authorize the release of any medical or other information necessary to process this claim. I also request payment of government benefits either to myself or to the party who accepts assignment below.

SIGNED _____   DATE _____

13. INSURED'S OR AUTHORIZED PERSON'S SIGNATURE I authorize payment of medical benefits to the undersigned physician or supplier for services described below.

SIGNED _____

PATIENT AND INSURED INFORMATION

14. DATE OF CURRENT: ILLNESS (First symptom) OR
    MM | DD | YY   INJURY (Accident) OR
                    PREGNANCY (LMP)

15. IF PATIENT HAS HAD SAME OR SIMILAR ILLNESS, GIVE FIRST DATE   MM | DD | YY

16. DATES PATIENT UNABLE TO WORK IN CURRENT OCCUPATION
    MM | DD | YY   MM | DD | YY
    FROM   TO

17. NAME OF REFERRING PHYSICIAN OR OTHER SOURCE

17a. I.D. NUMBER OF REFERRING PHYSICIAN

18. HOSPITALIZATION DATES RELATED TO CURRENT SERVICES
    MM | DD | YY   MM | DD | YY
    FROM   TO

19. RESERVED FOR LOCAL USE

20. OUTSIDE LAB? $ CHARGES
    ☐ YES   ☐ NO

21. DIAGNOSIS OR NATURE OF ILLNESS OR INJURY. (RELATE ITEMS 1, 2, 3, OR 4 TO ITEM 24E BY LINE)

1. |___.___| 3. |___.___|

2. |___.___| 4. |___.___|

22. MEDICAID RESUBMISSION CODE   ORIGINAL REF. NO.

23. PRIOR AUTHORIZATION NUMBER

24. A						B	C	D		E	F	G	H	I	J	K
DATE(S) OF SERVICE						Place of Service	Type of Service	PROCEDURES, SERVICES, OR SUPPLIES (Explain Unusual Circumstances)		DIAGNOSIS CODE	$ CHARGES	DAYS OR UNITS	EPSDT Family Plan	EMG	COB	RESERVED FOR LOCAL USE
From			To					CPT/HCPCS	MODIFIER							
MM	DD	YY	MM	DD	YY											
1																
2																
3																
4																
5																
6																

25. FEDERAL TAX I.D. NUMBER   SSN ☐ EIN ☐

26. PATIENT'S ACCOUNT NO.

27. ACCEPT ASSIGNMENT? (For govt. claims, see back)   ☐ YES   ☐ NO

28. TOTAL CHARGE $

29. AMOUNT PAID $

30. BALANCE DUE $

31. SIGNATURE OF PHYSICIAN OR SUPPLIER INCLUDING DEGREES OR CREDENTIALS
    (I certify that the statements on the reverse apply to this bill and are made a part thereof.)

SIGNED _____   DATE _____

32. NAME AND ADDRESS OF FACILITY WHERE SERVICES WERE RENDERED (If other than home or office)

33. PHYSICIAN'S, SUPPLIER'S BILLING NAME, ADDRESS, ZIP CODE & PHONE #

PIN# _____   GRP# _____

PHYSICIAN OR SUPPLIER INFORMATION

(SAMPLE ONLY - NOT APPROVED FOR USE)   *PLEASE PRINT OR TYPE*   SAMPLE FORM 1500
SAMPLE FORM 1500 SAMPLE FORM 1500

DONALD L. GIVINGS, M.D.

11350 Medical Drive ■ Anywhere US 12345 ■ (101) 111-5555

EIN: 11-123456   SSN: 123-12-1234   MEDICARE: D1234

PIN: DG1234   GRP: DG12345   MEDICAID: DLG1234

BCBS: 12345

Encounter Form

PATIENT INFORMATION:

Name:	Dolores Giovanni
Address:	384 Beverly Avenue
City:	Anywhere
State:	US
Zip Code:	12345
Telephone:	(101) 333-5555
Gender:	Female
Date of Birth:	10-22-1966
Occupation:	
Employer:	
Spouse's Employer:	

INSURANCE INFORMATION:

Patient Number:	15-f
Place of Service:	Mercy Hospital, Medicaid PIN# MHS2244
Primary Insurance Plan:	Medicare
Primary Insurance Plan ID #:	88776655
Group #:	
Primary Policyholder:	
Policyholder Date of Birth:	
Relationship to Patient:	
Secondary Insurance Plan:	
Secondary Insurance Plan ID #:	
Secondary Policyholder:	

Patient Status   ☐ Married   ☒ Divorced   ☐ Single   ☐ Student   ☐ Other

DIAGNOSIS INFORMATION

Diagnosis	Code	Diagnosis	Code
1. E. coli, unspecified	008.00	5.	
2.		6.	
3.		7.	
4.		8.	

PROCEDURE INFORMATION

Description of Procedure or Service	Date	Code	Charge
1. Initial hosp. level III	09-13-YYYY	99223	$175.00
2. Subsq. hosp. level III	09-14-YYYY, 09-15-YYYY, 09-16-YYYY	99233	Each @ $85.00
3. Hosp. discharge more than 30 min.	09-17-YYYY	99239	100.00
4.			
5.			

SPECIAL NOTES:

PLEASE
DO NOT
STAPLE
IN THIS
AREA

CARRIER

☐☐ PICA

HEALTH INSURANCE CLAIM FORM PICA ☐☐

1. ☐ MEDICARE (Medicare #) ☐ MEDICAID (Medicaid #) ☐ CHAMPUS (Sponsor's SSN) ☐ CHAMPVA (VA File #) ☐ GROUP HEALTH PLAN (SSN or ID) ☐ FECA BLK LUNG (SSN) ☐ OTHER (ID) | 1a. INSURED'S I.D. NUMBER (FOR PROGRAM IN ITEM 1)

2. PATIENT'S NAME (Last Name, First Name, Middle Initial) | 3. PATIENT'S BIRTH DATE MM ¦ DD ¦ YY SEX M ☐ F ☐ | 4. INSURED'S NAME (Last Name, First Name, Middle Initial)

5. PATIENT'S ADDRESS (No. Street) | 6. PATIENT RELATIONSHIP TO INSURED Self ☐ Spouse ☐ Child ☐ Other ☐ | 7. INSURED'S ADDRESS (No. Street)

CITY | STATE | 8. PATIENT STATUS Single ☐ Married ☐ Other ☐ | CITY | STATE

ZIP CODE | TELEPHONE (Include Area Code) ( ) | Employed ☐ Full-Time Student ☐ Part-Time Student ☐ | ZIP CODE | TELEPHONE (INCLUDE AREA CODE) ( )

9. OTHER INSURED'S NAME (Last Name, First Name, Middle Initial) | 10. IS PATIENT'S CONDITION RELATED TO: | 11. INSURED'S POLICY GROUP OR FECA NUMBER

a. OTHER INSURED'S POLICY OR GROUP NUMBER | a. EMPLOYMENT? (CURRENT OR PREVIOUS) ☐ YES ☐ NO | a. INSURED'S DATE OF BIRTH MM ¦ DD ¦ YY SEX M ☐ F ☐

b. OTHER INSURED'S DATE OF BIRTH MM ¦ DD ¦ YY SEX M ☐ F ☐ | b. AUTO ACCIDENT? PLACE (State) ☐ YES ☐ NO | b. EMPLOYER'S NAME OR SCHOOL NAME

c. EMPLOYER'S NAME OR SCHOOL NAME | c. OTHER ACCIDENT? ☐ YES ☐ NO | c. INSURANCE PLAN NAME OR PROGRAM NAME

d. INSURANCE PLAN NAME OR PROGRAM NAME | 10d. RESERVED FOR LOCAL USE | d. IS THERE ANOTHER HEALTH BENEFIT PLAN? ☐ YES ☐ NO If yes, return to and complete item 9 a – d.

READ BACK OF FORM BEFORE COMPLETING & SIGNING THIS FORM.
12. PATIENT'S OR AUTHORIZED PERSON'S SIGNATURE I authorize the release of any medical or other information necessary to process this claim. I also request payment of government benefits either to myself or to the party who accepts assignment below.

SIGNED _____ DATE _____

13. INSURED'S OR AUTHORIZED PERSON'S SIGNATURE I authorize payment of medical benefits to the undersigned physician or supplier for services described below.

SIGNED _____

PATIENT AND INSURED INFORMATION

14. DATE OF CURRENT: MM ¦ DD ¦ YY ◄ ILLNESS (First symptom) OR INJURY (Accident) OR PREGNANCY (LMP) | 15. IF PATIENT HAS HAD SAME OR SIMILAR ILLNESS, GIVE FIRST DATE MM ¦ DD ¦ YY | 16. DATES PATIENT UNABLE TO WORK IN CURRENT OCCUPATION MM ¦ DD ¦ YY MM ¦ DD ¦ YY FROM TO

17. NAME OF REFERRING PHYSICIAN OR OTHER SOURCE | 17a. I.D. NUMBER OF REFERRING PHYSICIAN | 18. HOSPITALIZATION DATES RELATED TO CURRENT SERVICES MM ¦ DD ¦ YY MM ¦ DD ¦ YY FROM TO

19. RESERVED FOR LOCAL USE | 20. OUTSIDE LAB? ☐ YES ☐ NO $ CHARGES

21. DIAGNOSIS OR NATURE OF ILLNESS OR INJURY. (RELATE ITEMS 1, 2, 3, OR 4 TO ITEM 24E BY LINE)
1. └____ . __   3. └____ . __
2. └____ . __   4. └____ . __

22. MEDICAID RESUBMISSION CODE ORIGINAL REF. NO.

23. PRIOR AUTHORIZATION NUMBER

24. A DATE(S) OF SERVICE					B Place of Service	C Type of Service	D PROCEDURES, SERVICES, OR SUPPLIES (Explain Unusual Circumstances)		E DIAGNOSIS CODE	F $ CHARGES	G DAYS OR UNITS	H EPSDT Family Plan	I EMG	J COB	K RESERVED FOR LOCAL USE
From MM	DD	YY	To MM	DD	YY			CPT/HCPCS	MODIFIER							
1															
2															
3															
4															
5															
6															

25. FEDERAL TAX I.D. NUMBER ☐ SSN ☐ EIN | 26. PATIENT'S ACCOUNT NO. | 27. ACCEPT ASSIGNMENT? (For govt. claims, see back) ☐ YES ☐ NO | 28. TOTAL CHARGE $ | 29. AMOUNT PAID $ | 30. BALANCE DUE $

31. SIGNATURE OF PHYSICIAN OR SUPPLIER INCLUDING DEGREES OR CREDENTIALS (I certify that the statements on the reverse apply to this bill and are made a part thereof.) SIGNED _____ DATE _____ | 32. NAME AND ADDRESS OF FACILITY WHERE SERVICES WERE RENDERED (If other than home or office) | 33. PHYSICIAN'S, SUPPLIER'S BILLING NAME, ADDRESS, ZIP CODE & PHONE # PIN# GRP#

PHYSICIAN OR SUPPLIER INFORMATION

(SAMPLE ONLY - NOT APPROVED FOR USE) | *PLEASE PRINT OR TYPE* | SAMPLE FORM 1500 SAMPLE FORM 1500 SAMPLE FORM 1500

Chapter 16
TRICARE

TRICARE BACKGROUND

1. Complete the following sentences.

    a. CHAMPUS resulted from an initiative to provide military medical care for families of

    _____.

    b. TRICARE supplements the health care resources of the uniformed services with networks of

    _____.

    c. The number of TRICARE regions in the United States is _____.

TRICARE ADMINISTRATION

2. What is the name of the office that coordinates and administers the TRICARE program?

_____

3. Where do you send TRICARE claims? _____

TRICARE OPTIONS

4. List three TRICARE health care options.

    a. _____

    b. _____

    c. _____

5. Match the insurance terms in the first column with the definitions in the second column. Write the correct letter in each blank.

    _____ TRICARE Prime   a. PPO

    _____ TRICARE Extra   b. fee-for-service

    _____ TRICARE Standard   c. similar to a civilian HMO

6. Which of the three TRICARE options provides comprehensive health care benefits at the lowest cost?

_____

7. Who guides TRICARE Prime members through the health care system and coordinates all specialty medical needs? _____

8. Briefly describe the *catastrophic cap benefit.* _____

   _____

9. No enrollment is required to be covered by _____.

10. When is the Point-of-Service option activated for a TRICARE Prime Beneficiary?

    _____

11. For each question, enter **Y** for yes or **N** for no on the line provided.

    _____ a. Are TRICARE Extra network providers allowed to balance bill?

    _____ b. Are TRICARE Extra enrollees allowed to seek health care services from a military treatment facility?

    _____ c. Are TRICARE Standard enrollees responsible for deductibles and copayments?

    _____ d. Are there any enrollment requirements for TRICARE Standard?

    _____ e. Do TRICARE Standard participating providers have to accept the TRICARE Standard allowable charge as payment in full?

12. Which TRICARE plan provides beneficiaries with the greatest freedom in selecting civilian providers? (Circle the correct answer.)
    a. TRICARE Prime
    b. TRICARE Extra
    c. TRICARE Standard
    d. none of the above

13. Which TRICARE plan has the highest out-of-pocket costs? (Circle the correct answer.)
    a. TRICARE Prime
    b. TRICARE Extra
    c. TRICARE Standard
    d. none of the above

TRICARE BILLING INFORMATION

14. When sending claims to the TRICARE carrier, be sure to use both the _____ _____ _____ number and its associated zip code.

15. How would you obtain the current address of the TRICARE carrier assigned to your area?

    _____

    _____

16. Changes in general benefits are enacted by ___. (Circle the correct answer.)
    a. CMS
    b. the military
    c. the United States Congress
    d. none of the above

17. The form used to file a TRICARE claim is ___. (Circle the correct answer.)

    a. HCFA-1450

    b. CMS-1500

    c. different for each catchment area

    d. any of the above

18. For mental health cases, a TRICARE Treatment Report must be filed with a claim for more than ___ outpatient visits in any calendar year. (Circle the correct answer.)

    a. 12

    b. 23

    c. 30

    d. none of the above

19. Claims will be denied if they are filed more than ___ months after the date of service for outpatient care. (Circle the correct answer.)

    a. 6

    b. 9

    c. 12

    d. 18

20. Which of the following TRICARE plans require(s) payment of enrollment fees? (Circle the correct answer.)

    a. TRICARE Prime

    b. TRICARE Standard

    c. TRICARE Extra

    d. all of the above

21. All deductibles are applied in the government's fiscal year which runs from ___. (Circle the correct answer.)

    a. July 1 of one year to June 30 of the next

    b. October 1 of one year to September 30 of the next

    c. January 1 to December 31 of the same year

    d. none of the above

Critical Thinking

22. Write a paragraph describing the *Good Faith Policy*.

    _____

    _____

    _____

    _____

    _____

    _____

23. All TRICARE nonPAR providers are subject to a limiting charge of 15% ____ the TRICARE Fee Schedule for PAR providers. (Circle the correct answer.)

    a. above

    b. below

24. State the exceptions to the 15% limiting charge. _____

    _____

25. What words should be written at the top of the claim for services that fall under the special handicap benefits? _____

26. What words should be written on the envelope when filing services for hospice care?

    _____

27. If a TRICARE claim has been filed with no response for 45 days, who should be contacted?

    _____

Know Your Acronyms

28. Define the following acronyms:

    a. BSR _____

    b. CHAMPVA _____

    c. CRI _____

    d. DEERS _____

    e. DoD _____

    f. DSM _____

    g. HA _____

    h. HCF _____

    i. LA _____

    j. MHSS _____

    k. MTF _____

    l. NAS _____

    m. OHI _____

    n. PCM _____

    o. PFP _____

    p. PMO _____

    q. TDP _____

    r. TRDP _____

    s. TMA _____

    t. TSC _____

EXERCISES

29. Complete Case Studies 16-a through 16-e using the blank claims provided. Follow the step-by-step instructions in the textbook to properly complete each claim. If a patient has secondary coverage, complete an additional claim using secondary directions from the textbook. You may choose to use a pencil so corrections can be made.

DONALD L. GIVINGS, M.D.

11350 Medical Drive ■ Anywhere US 12345 ■ (101) 111-5555

EIN: 11-123456	SSN: 123-12-1234	MEDICARE: D1234
UPIN: DG1234	GRP: DG12345	MEDICAID: DLG1234
BCBS: 12345	TRICARE: 5555	

Encounter Form

PATIENT INFORMATION:

Name:	Jeffrey D. Heem
Address:	333 Heavenly Place
City:	Anywhere
State:	US
Zip Code:	12345
Telephone:	(101) 333-5555
Gender:	Male
Date of Birth:	05-05-1964
Occupation:	
Employer:	US Army
Spouse's Employer:	

INSURANCE INFORMATION:

Patient Number:	16-a
Place of Service:	Office
Primary Insurance Plan:	TRICARE Standard
Primary Insurance Plan ID #:	234-55-6789
Group #:	
Primary Policyholder:	
Policyholder Date of Birth:	
Relationship to Patient:	
Secondary Insurance Plan:	
Secondary Insurance Plan ID #:	
Secondary Policyholder:	

Patient Status   ☒ Married   ☐ Divorced   ☐ Single   ☐ Student   ☐ Other

DIAGNOSIS INFORMATION

Diagnosis	Code	Diagnosis	Code
1. Acute sinusitis, frontal	461.1	5.	
2. Sore throat	784.1	6.	
3.		7.	
4.		8.	

PROCEDURE INFORMATION

Description of Procedure or Service	Date	Code	Charge
1. New patient OV level II	11-05-YYYY	99202	$70.00
2.			
3.			
4.			
5.			

SPECIAL NOTES:

PLEASE
DO NOT
STAPLE
IN THIS
AREA

CARRIER

| | PICA | | **HEALTH INSURANCE CLAIM FORM** | PICA | | |

1. MEDICARE MEDICAID CHAMPUS CHAMPVA GROUP HEALTH PLAN FECA BLK LUNG OTHER	1a. INSURED'S I.D. NUMBER	(FOR PROGRAM IN ITEM 1)

☐ (Medicare #) ☐ (Medicaid #) ☐ (Sponsor's SSN) ☐ (VA File #) ☐ (SSN or ID) ☐ (SSN) ☐ (ID)

2. PATIENT'S NAME (Last Name, First Name, Middle Initial)

3. PATIENT'S BIRTH DATE
MM   DD   YY   SEX   M ☐   F ☐

4. INSURED'S NAME (Last Name, First Name, Middle Initial)

5. PATIENT'S ADDRESS (No. Street)

6. PATIENT RELATIONSHIP TO INSURED
Self ☐   Spouse ☐   Child ☐   Other ☐

7. INSURED'S ADDRESS (No. Street)

CITY   STATE

8. PATIENT STATUS
Single ☐   Married ☐   Other ☐
Employed ☐   Full-Time Student ☐   Part-Time Student ☐

CITY   STATE

ZIP CODE   TELEPHONE (Include Area Code)
(   )

ZIP CODE   TELEPHONE (INCLUDE AREA CODE)
(   )

9. OTHER INSURED'S NAME (Last Name, First Name, Middle Initial)

10. IS PATIENT'S CONDITION RELATED TO:

11. INSURED'S POLICY GROUP OR FECA NUMBER

a. OTHER INSURED'S POLICY OR GROUP NUMBER

a. EMPLOYMENT? (CURRENT OR PREVIOUS)
☐ YES   ☐ NO

a. INSURED'S DATE OF BIRTH
MM   DD   YY   SEX   M ☐   F ☐

b. OTHER INSURED'S DATE OF BIRTH
MM   DD   YY   SEX   M ☐   F ☐

b. AUTO ACCIDENT?   PLACE (State)
☐ YES   ☐ NO

b. EMPLOYER'S NAME OR SCHOOL NAME

c. EMPLOYER'S NAME OR SCHOOL NAME

c. OTHER ACCIDENT?
☐ YES   ☐ NO

c. INSURANCE PLAN NAME OR PROGRAM NAME

d. INSURANCE PLAN NAME OR PROGRAM NAME

10d. RESERVED FOR LOCAL USE

d. IS THERE ANOTHER HEALTH BENEFIT PLAN?
☐ YES   ☐ NO   If yes, return to and complete item 9 a – d.

READ BACK OF FORM BEFORE COMPLETING & SIGNING THIS FORM.
12. PATIENT'S OR AUTHORIZED PERSON'S SIGNATURE I authorize the release of any medical or other information necessary to process this claim. I also request payment of government benefits either to myself or to the party who accepts assignment below.

SIGNED _____   DATE _____

13. INSURED'S OR AUTHORIZED PERSON'S SIGNATURE I authorize payment of medical benefits to the undersigned physician or supplier for services described below.

SIGNED _____

PATIENT AND INSURED INFORMATION

14. DATE OF CURRENT: ILLNESS (First symptom) OR
MM   DD   YY   INJURY (Accident) OR PREGNANCY (LMP)

15. IF PATIENT HAS HAD SAME OR SIMILAR ILLNESS, GIVE FIRST DATE   MM   DD   YY

16. DATES PATIENT UNABLE TO WORK IN CURRENT OCCUPATION
MM   DD   YY   MM   DD   YY
FROM   TO

17. NAME OF REFERRING PHYSICIAN OR OTHER SOURCE

17a. I.D. NUMBER OF REFERRING PHYSICIAN

18. HOSPITALIZATION DATES RELATED TO CURRENT SERVICES
MM   DD   YY   MM   DD   YY
FROM   TO

19. RESERVED FOR LOCAL USE

20. OUTSIDE LAB? $ CHARGES
☐ YES   ☐ NO

21. DIAGNOSIS OR NATURE OF ILLNESS OR INJURY. (RELATE ITEMS 1, 2, 3, OR 4 TO ITEM 24E BY LINE)
1. ____ . __   3. ____ . __
2. ____ . __   4. ____ . __

22. MEDICAID RESUBMISSION
CODE   ORIGINAL REF. NO.

23. PRIOR AUTHORIZATION NUMBER

24. A DATE(S) OF SERVICE					B Place of Service	C Type of Service	D PROCEDURES, SERVICES, OR SUPPLIES (Explain Unusual Circumstances)		E DIAGNOSIS CODE	F $ CHARGES	G DAYS OR UNITS	H EPSDT Family Plan	I EMG	J COB	K RESERVED FOR LOCAL USE
From MM DD YY			To MM DD YY				CPT/HCPCS	MODIFIER							
1															
2															
3															
4															
5															
6															

25. FEDERAL TAX I.D. NUMBER   SSN ☐ EIN ☐

26. PATIENT'S ACCOUNT NO.

27. ACCEPT ASSIGNMENT? (For govt. claims, see back)
☐ YES   ☐ NO

28. TOTAL CHARGE $

29. AMOUNT PAID $

30. BALANCE DUE $

31. SIGNATURE OF PHYSICIAN OR SUPPLIER INCLUDING DEGREES OR CREDENTIALS
(I certify that the statements on the reverse apply to this bill and are made a part thereof.)

SIGNED _____   DATE _____

32. NAME AND ADDRESS OF FACILITY WHERE SERVICES WERE RENDERED (If other than home or office)

33. PHYSICIAN'S, SUPPLIER'S BILLING NAME, ADDRESS, ZIP CODE & PHONE #

PIN# _____   GRP# _____

PHYSICIAN OR SUPPLIER INFORMATION

(SAMPLE ONLY - NOT APPROVED FOR USE)

PLEASE PRINT OR TYPE

SAMPLE FORM 1500
SAMPLE FORM 1500   SAMPLE FORM 1500

DONALD L. GIVINGS, M.D.

11350 Medical Drive ■ Anywhere US 12345 ■ (101) 111-5555

EIN: 11-123456	SSN: 123-12-1234	MEDICARE: D1234
UPIN: DG1234	GRP: DG12345	MEDICAID: DLG1234
BCBS: 12345	TRICARE: 5555	

Encounter Form

PATIENT INFORMATION:

Name:	Dana S. Bright
Address:	28 Upton Circle
City:	Anywhere
State:	US
Zip Code:	12345
Telephone:	(101) 333-5555
Gender:	Female
Date of Birth:	07-05-1971
Occupation:	
Employer:	
Spouse's Employer:	US Navy (See duty address below)

INSURANCE INFORMATION:

Patient Number:	16-b
Place of Service:	Office
Primary Insurance Plan:	TRICARE Extra
Primary Insurance Plan ID #:	567-56-5757
Group #:	
Primary Policyholder:	Ron L. Bright
Policyholder Date of Birth:	08-12-70
Relationship to Patient:	Spouse
Secondary Insurance Plan:	
Secondary Insurance Plan ID #:	
Secondary Policyholder:	

Patient Status   ☒ Married   ☐ Divorced   ☐ Single   ☐ Student   ☐ Other

DIAGNOSIS INFORMATION

Diagnosis	Code	Diagnosis	Code
1. Chronic cholecystitis	575.11	5.	
2.		6.	
3.		7.	
4.		8.	

PROCEDURE INFORMATION

Description of Procedure or Service	Date	Code	Charge
1. Est. patient OV level IV	06-22-YYYY	99214	$85.00
2.			
3.			
4.			
5.			

SPECIAL NOTES:

Spouse's Employer's Address: Duty Station Address Dept. 21 Naval Station, Anywhere US 23456

Refer patient to Dr. Kutter

PLEASE
DO NOT
STAPLE
IN THIS
AREA

CARRIER

☐☐ PICA

HEALTH INSURANCE CLAIM FORM

PICA ☐☐☐

1. ☐ MEDICARE (Medicare #) ☐ MEDICAID (Medicaid #) ☐ CHAMPUS (Sponsor's SSN) ☐ CHAMPVA (VA File #) ☐ GROUP HEALTH PLAN (SSN or ID) ☐ FECA BLK LUNG (SSN) ☐ OTHER (ID)

1a. INSURED'S I.D. NUMBER (FOR PROGRAM IN ITEM 1)

2. PATIENT'S NAME (Last Name, First Name, Middle Initial)

3. PATIENT'S BIRTH DATE MM | DD | YY   SEX M ☐ F ☐

4. INSURED'S NAME (Last Name, First Name, Middle Initial)

5. PATIENT'S ADDRESS (No. Street)

6. PATIENT RELATIONSHIP TO INSURED Self ☐ Spouse ☐ Child ☐ Other ☐

7. INSURED'S ADDRESS (No. Street)

CITY   STATE

8. PATIENT STATUS Single ☐ Married ☐ Other ☐
Employed ☐ Full-Time Student ☐ Part-Time Student ☐

CITY   STATE

ZIP CODE   TELEPHONE (Include Area Code) ( )

ZIP CODE   TELEPHONE (INCLUDE AREA CODE) ( )

9. OTHER INSURED'S NAME (Last Name, First Name, Middle Initial)

10. IS PATIENT'S CONDITION RELATED TO:

11. INSURED'S POLICY GROUP OR FECA NUMBER

a. OTHER INSURED'S POLICY OR GROUP NUMBER

a. EMPLOYMENT? (CURRENT OR PREVIOUS) ☐ YES ☐ NO

a. INSURED'S DATE OF BIRTH MM | DD | YY   SEX M ☐ F ☐

b. OTHER INSURED'S DATE OF BIRTH MM | DD | YY   SEX M ☐ F ☐

b. AUTO ACCIDENT?   PLACE (State) ☐ YES ☐ NO

b. EMPLOYER'S NAME OR SCHOOL NAME

c. EMPLOYER'S NAME OR SCHOOL NAME

c. OTHER ACCIDENT? ☐ YES ☐ NO

c. INSURANCE PLAN NAME OR PROGRAM NAME

d. INSURANCE PLAN NAME OR PROGRAM NAME

10d. RESERVED FOR LOCAL USE

d. IS THERE ANOTHER HEALTH BENEFIT PLAN? ☐ YES ☐ NO If yes, return to and complete item 9 a – d.

READ BACK OF FORM BEFORE COMPLETING & SIGNING THIS FORM.
12. PATIENT'S OR AUTHORIZED PERSON'S SIGNATURE I authorize the release of any medical or other information necessary to process this claim. I also request payment of government benefits either to myself or to the party who accepts assignment below.

SIGNED _____ DATE _____

13. INSURED'S OR AUTHORIZED PERSON'S SIGNATURE I authorize payment of medical benefits to the undersigned physician or supplier for services described below.

SIGNED _____

PATIENT AND INSURED INFORMATION

14. DATE OF CURRENT: MM | DD | YY ◄ ILLNESS (First symptom) OR INJURY (Accident) OR PREGNANCY (LMP)

15. IF PATIENT HAS HAD SAME OR SIMILAR ILLNESS, GIVE FIRST DATE MM | DD | YY

16. DATES PATIENT UNABLE TO WORK IN CURRENT OCCUPATION MM | DD | YY FROM   TO MM | DD | YY

17. NAME OF REFERRING PHYSICIAN OR OTHER SOURCE

17a. I.D. NUMBER OF REFERRING PHYSICIAN

18. HOSPITALIZATION DATES RELATED TO CURRENT SERVICES MM | DD | YY FROM   TO MM | DD | YY

19. RESERVED FOR LOCAL USE

20. OUTSIDE LAB? ☐ YES ☐ NO $ CHARGES

21. DIAGNOSIS OR NATURE OF ILLNESS OR INJURY. (RELATE ITEMS 1, 2, 3, OR 4 TO ITEM 24E BY LINE)

1. └____ . ____
2. └____ . ____
3. └____ . ____
4. └____ . ____

22. MEDICAID RESUBMISSION CODE   ORIGINAL REF. NO.

23. PRIOR AUTHORIZATION NUMBER

24. A. DATE(S) OF SERVICE						B. Place of Service	C. Type of Service	D. PROCEDURES, SERVICES, OR SUPPLIES (Explain Unusual Circumstances) CPT/HCPCS	MODIFIER	E. DIAGNOSIS CODE	F. $ CHARGES	G. DAYS OR UNITS	H. EPSDT Family Plan	I. EMG	J. COB	K. RESERVED FOR LOCAL USE
From MM	DD	YY	To MM	DD	YY											
1																
2																
3																
4																
5																
6																

25. FEDERAL TAX I.D. NUMBER SSN ☐ EIN ☐

26. PATIENT'S ACCOUNT NO.

27. ACCEPT ASSIGNMENT? (For govt. claims, see back) ☐ YES ☐ NO

28. TOTAL CHARGE $

29. AMOUNT PAID $

30. BALANCE DUE $

31. SIGNATURE OF PHYSICIAN OR SUPPLIER INCLUDING DEGREES OR CREDENTIALS (I certify that the statements on the reverse apply to this bill and are made a part thereof.)

SIGNED _____ DATE _____

32. NAME AND ADDRESS OF FACILITY WHERE SERVICES WERE RENDERED (If other than home or office)

33. PHYSICIAN'S, SUPPLIER'S BILLING NAME, ADDRESS, ZIP CODE & PHONE #

PIN#   GRP#

PHYSICIAN OR SUPPLIER INFORMATION

JONATHAN B. KUTTER, M.D. SURGERY

Encounter Form

339 Woodland Place ■ Anywhere US 12345 ■ (101) 111-5555

EIN: 11-556677	SSN: 245-12-1234	MEDICARE:J1234
UPIN: JK1234	BCBS: 12885	MEDICAID: JBK1234
TRICARE: 5555		

PATIENT INFORMATION:

Name:	Dana S. Bright
Address:	28 Upton Circle
City:	Anywhere
State:	US
Zip Code:	12345
Telephone:	(101) 333-5555
Gender:	Female
Date of Birth:	07-05-1971
Occupation:	
Employer:	
Spouse's Employer:	US Navy (See duty address below)

INSURANCE INFORMATION:

Patient Number:	16-c
Place of Service:	Mercy Hospital (Outpatient)
Primary Insurance Plan:	TRICARE Extra
Primary Insurance Plan ID #:	567-56-5757
Group #:	
Primary Policyholder:	Ron L. Bright
Policyholder Date of Birth:	08-12-70
Relationship to Patient:	Spouse
Secondary Insurance Plan:	
Secondary Insurance Plan ID #:	
Secondary Policyholder:	

Patient Status   ☒ Married   ☐ Divorced   ☐ Single   ☐ Student   ☐ Other

DIAGNOSIS INFORMATION

Diagnosis	Code	Diagnosis	Code
1. Chronic cholecystitis	575.11	5.	
2.		6.	
3.		7.	
4.		8.	

PROCEDURE INFORMATION

Description of Procedure or Service	Date	Code	Charge
1. Laparoscopic cholecystectomy	06-29-YYYY	56340	$2,300.00
2.			
3.			
4.			
5.			

SPECIAL NOTES:

Referred by Donald L. Givings, M.D., EIN: 11123456

Admitted   06/29/YYYY

Discharged 06/30/YYYY

PLEASE
DO NOT
STAPLE
IN THIS
AREA

CARRIER

☐☐ PICA

HEALTH INSURANCE CLAIM FORM

PICA ☐☐☐

1. MEDICARE ☐ (Medicare #)   **MEDICAID** ☐ (Medicaid #)   **CHAMPUS** ☐ (Sponsor's SSN)   **CHAMPVA** ☐ (VA File #)   **GROUP HEALTH PLAN** ☐ (SSN or ID)   **FECA BLK LUNG** ☐ (SSN)   **OTHER** ☐ (ID)

1a. INSURED'S I.D. NUMBER (FOR PROGRAM IN ITEM 1)

2. PATIENT'S NAME (Last Name, First Name, Middle Initial)

3. PATIENT'S BIRTH DATE MM | DD | YY   **SEX** M ☐ F ☐

4. INSURED'S NAME (Last Name, First Name, Middle Initial)

5. PATIENT'S ADDRESS (No. Street)

6. PATIENT RELATIONSHIP TO INSURED Self ☐ Spouse ☐ Child ☐ Other ☐

7. INSURED'S ADDRESS (No. Street)

CITY   STATE

8. PATIENT STATUS Single ☐ Married ☐ Other ☐

Employed ☐ Full-Time Student ☐ Part-Time Student ☐

CITY   STATE

ZIP CODE   TELEPHONE (Include Area Code) ( )

ZIP CODE   TELEPHONE (INCLUDE AREA CODE) ( )

9. OTHER INSURED'S NAME (Last Name, First Name, Middle Initial)

10. IS PATIENT'S CONDITION RELATED TO:

11. INSURED'S POLICY GROUP OR FECA NUMBER

a. OTHER INSURED'S POLICY OR GROUP NUMBER

a. EMPLOYMENT? (CURRENT OR PREVIOUS) ☐ YES ☐ NO

a. INSURED'S DATE OF BIRTH MM | DD | YY   **SEX** M ☐ F ☐

b. OTHER INSURED'S DATE OF BIRTH MM | DD | YY   **SEX** M ☐ F ☐

b. AUTO ACCIDENT? ☐ YES ☐ NO   PLACE (State)

b. EMPLOYER'S NAME OR SCHOOL NAME

c. EMPLOYER'S NAME OR SCHOOL NAME

c. OTHER ACCIDENT? ☐ YES ☐ NO

c. INSURANCE PLAN NAME OR PROGRAM NAME

d. INSURANCE PLAN NAME OR PROGRAM NAME

10d. RESERVED FOR LOCAL USE

d. IS THERE ANOTHER HEALTH BENEFIT PLAN? ☐ YES ☐ NO If yes, return to and complete item 9 a – d.

READ BACK OF FORM BEFORE COMPLETING & SIGNING THIS FORM.
12. PATIENT'S OR AUTHORIZED PERSON'S SIGNATURE I authorize the release of any medical or other information necessary to process this claim. I also request payment of government benefits either to myself or to the party who accepts assignment below.

SIGNED _____ DATE _____

13. INSURED'S OR AUTHORIZED PERSON'S SIGNATURE I authorize payment of medical benefits to the undersigned physician or supplier for services described below.

SIGNED _____

PATIENT AND INSURED INFORMATION

14. DATE OF CURRENT: MM | DD | YY   ILLNESS (First symptom) OR INJURY (Accident) OR PREGNANCY (LMP)

15. IF PATIENT HAS HAD SAME OR SIMILAR ILLNESS, GIVE FIRST DATE MM | DD | YY

16. DATES PATIENT UNABLE TO WORK IN CURRENT OCCUPATION MM | DD | YY   FROM   TO   MM | DD | YY

17. NAME OF REFERRING PHYSICIAN OR OTHER SOURCE

17a. I.D. NUMBER OF REFERRING PHYSICIAN

18. HOSPITALIZATION DATES RELATED TO CURRENT SERVICES MM | DD | YY   FROM   TO   MM | DD | YY

19. RESERVED FOR LOCAL USE

20. OUTSIDE LAB? ☐ YES ☐ NO $ CHARGES

21. DIAGNOSIS OR NATURE OF ILLNESS OR INJURY. (RELATE ITEMS 1, 2, 3, OR 4 TO ITEM 24E BY LINE)
1. |___.___
2. |___.___
3. |___.___
4. |___.___

22. MEDICAID RESUBMISSION CODE   ORIGINAL REF. NO.

23. PRIOR AUTHORIZATION NUMBER

24. A. DATE(S) OF SERVICE From MM DD YY	To MM DD YY	B. Place of Service	C. Type of Service	D. PROCEDURES, SERVICES, OR SUPPLIES (Explain Unusual Circumstances) CPT/HCPCS	MODIFIER	E. DIAGNOSIS CODE	F. $ CHARGES	G. DAYS OR UNITS	H. EPSDT Family Plan	I. EMG	J. COB	K. RESERVED FOR LOCAL USE
1												
2												
3												
4												
5												
6												

25. FEDERAL TAX I.D. NUMBER SSN ☐ EIN ☐

26. PATIENT'S ACCOUNT NO.

27. ACCEPT ASSIGNMENT? (For govt. claims, see back) ☐ YES ☐ NO

28. TOTAL CHARGE $

29. AMOUNT PAID $

30. BALANCE DUE $

31. SIGNATURE OF PHYSICIAN OR SUPPLIER INCLUDING DEGREES OR CREDENTIALS (I certify that the statements on the reverse apply to this bill and are made a part thereof.)

SIGNED _____ DATE _____

32. NAME AND ADDRESS OF FACILITY WHERE SERVICES WERE RENDERED (if other than home or office)

33. PHYSICIAN'S, SUPPLIER'S BILLING NAME, ADDRESS, ZIP CODE & PHONE #

PIN#   GRP#

PHYSICIAN OR SUPPLIER INFORMATION

PLEASE PRINT OR TYPE

SAMPLE FORM 1500
SAMPLE FORM 1500 SAMPLE FORM 1500

DONALD L. GIVINGS, M.D.

11350 Medical Drive ■ Anywhere US 12345 ■ (101) 111-5555

EIN: 11-123456	SSN: 123-12-1234	MEDICARE: D1234
UPIN: DG1234	GRP: DG12345	MEDICAID: DLG1234
BCBS: 12345	TRICARE: 5555	

Encounter Form

PATIENT INFORMATION:

Name:	Odel M. Ryer, Jr.
Address:	484 Pinewood Ave.
City:	Anywhere
State:	US
Zip Code:	12345
Telephone:	(101) 333-5555
Gender:	Male
Date of Birth:	04-28-1949
Occupation:	
Employer:	US Air Force Retired
Spouse's Employer:	

INSURANCE INFORMATION:

Patient Number:	16-d
Place of Service:	Office
Primary Insurance Plan:	TRICARE Standard
Primary Insurance Plan ID #:	464-44-4646
Group #:	
Primary Policyholder:	Odel M. Ryer, Jr.
Policyholder Date of Birth:	04-28-1949
Relationship to Patient:	Self
Secondary Insurance Plan:	
Secondary Insurance Plan ID #:	
Secondary Policyholder:	

Patient Status ☒ Married ☐ Divorced ☐ Single ☐ Student ☐ Other

DIAGNOSIS INFORMATION

Diagnosis	Code	Diagnosis	Code
1. Heartburn	787.1	5.	
2.		6.	
3.		7.	
4.		8.	

PROCEDURE INFORMATION

Description of Procedure or Service	Date	Code	Charge
1. Est. patient OV level I	04-12-YYYY	99211	$55.00
2.			
3.			
4.			
5.			

SPECIAL NOTES:

Return visit: PRN

(SAMPLE ONLY - NOT APPROVED FOR USE)

CARRIER

HEALTH INSURANCE CLAIM FORM

PICA □□□

□□ PICA

1. MEDICARE	MEDICAID	CHAMPUS	CHAMPVA	GROUP HEALTH PLAN	FECA BLK LUNG	OTHER	1a. INSURED'S I.D. NUMBER	(FOR PROGRAM IN ITEM 1)
□ (Medicare #)	□ (Medicaid #)	□ (Sponsor's SSN)	□ (VA File #)	□ (SSN or ID)	□ (SSN)	□ (ID)		

2. PATIENT'S NAME (Last Name, First Name, Middle Initial)

3. PATIENT'S BIRTH DATE
MM ¦ DD ¦ YY   SEX
M □   F □

4. INSURED'S NAME (Last Name, First Name, Middle Initial)

5. PATIENT'S ADDRESS (No. Street)

6. PATIENT RELATIONSHIP TO INSURED
Self □   Spouse □   Child □   Other □

7. INSURED'S ADDRESS (No. Street)

CITY   STATE

8. PATIENT STATUS
Single □   Married □   Other □

CITY   STATE

ZIP CODE   TELEPHONE (Include Area Code)
(   )

Employed □   Full-Time Student □   Part-Time Student □

ZIP CODE   TELEPHONE (INCLUDE AREA CODE)
(   )

9. OTHER INSURED'S NAME (Last Name, First Name, Middle Initial)

10. IS PATIENT'S CONDITION RELATED TO:

11. INSURED'S POLICY GROUP OR FECA NUMBER

a. OTHER INSURED'S POLICY OR GROUP NUMBER

a. EMPLOYMENT? (CURRENT OR PREVIOUS)
□ YES   □ NO

a. INSURED'S DATE OF BIRTH
MM ¦ DD ¦ YY   SEX
M □   F □

b. OTHER INSURED'S DATE OF BIRTH
MM ¦ DD ¦ YY   SEX
M □   F □

b. AUTO ACCIDENT?   PLACE (State)
□ YES   □ NO

b. EMPLOYER'S NAME OR SCHOOL NAME

c. EMPLOYER'S NAME OR SCHOOL NAME

c. OTHER ACCIDENT?
□ YES   □ NO

c. INSURANCE PLAN NAME OR PROGRAM NAME

d. INSURANCE PLAN NAME OR PROGRAM NAME

10d. RESERVED FOR LOCAL USE

d. IS THERE ANOTHER HEALTH BENEFIT PLAN?
□ YES   □ NO   If yes, return to and complete item 9 a – d.

READ BACK OF FORM BEFORE COMPLETING & SIGNING THIS FORM.
12. PATIENT'S OR AUTHORIZED PERSON'S SIGNATURE I authorize the release of any medical or other information necessary to process this claim. I also request payment of government benefits either to myself or to the party who accepts assignment below.

SIGNED _____   DATE _____

13. INSURED'S OR AUTHORIZED PERSON'S SIGNATURE I authorize payment of medical benefits to the undersigned physician or supplier for services described below.

SIGNED _____

PATIENT AND INSURED INFORMATION

14. DATE OF CURRENT:
MM ¦ DD ¦ YY   ILLNESS (First symptom) OR INJURY (Accident) OR PREGNANCY (LMP)

15. IF PATIENT HAS HAD SAME OR SIMILAR ILLNESS, GIVE FIRST DATE   MM ¦ DD ¦ YY

16. DATES PATIENT UNABLE TO WORK IN CURRENT OCCUPATION
MM ¦ DD ¦ YY   MM ¦ DD ¦ YY
FROM   TO

17. NAME OF REFERRING PHYSICIAN OR OTHER SOURCE

17a. I.D. NUMBER OF REFERRING PHYSICIAN

18. HOSPITALIZATION DATES RELATED TO CURRENT SERVICES
MM ¦ DD ¦ YY   MM ¦ DD ¦ YY
FROM   TO

19. RESERVED FOR LOCAL USE

20. OUTSIDE LAB? $ CHARGES
□ YES   □ NO

21. DIAGNOSIS OR NATURE OF ILLNESS OR INJURY. (RELATE ITEMS 1, 2, 3, OR 4 TO ITEM 24E BY LINE)

1. └___ ¦ __   3. └___ ¦ __

2. └___ ¦ __   4. └___ ¦ __

22. MEDICAID RESUBMISSION
CODE   ORIGINAL REF. NO.

23. PRIOR AUTHORIZATION NUMBER

24. A DATE(S) OF SERVICE						B Place of Service	C Type of Service	D PROCEDURES, SERVICES, OR SUPPLIES (Explain Unusual Circumstances) CPT/HCPCS ¦ MODIFIER	E DIAGNOSIS CODE	F $ CHARGES	G DAYS OR UNITS	H EPSDT Family Plan	I EMG	J COB	K RESERVED FOR LOCAL USE
From			To												
MM	DD	YY	MM	DD	YY										
1															
2															
3															
4															
5															
6															

25. FEDERAL TAX I.D. NUMBER   SSN EIN
□   □

26. PATIENT'S ACCOUNT NO.

27. ACCEPT ASSIGNMENT?
(For govt. claims, see back)
□ YES   □ NO

28. TOTAL CHARGE
$

29. AMOUNT PAID
$

30. BALANCE DUE
$

31. SIGNATURE OF PHYSICIAN OR SUPPLIER INCLUDING DEGREES OR CREDENTIALS
(I certify that the statements on the reverse apply to this bill and are made a part thereof.)

SIGNED _____ DATE _____

32. NAME AND ADDRESS OF FACILITY WHERE SERVICES WERE RENDERED (If other than home or office)

33. PHYSICIAN'S, SUPPLIER'S BILLING NAME, ADDRESS, ZIP CODE & PHONE #

PIN#   GRP#

PHYSICIAN OR SUPPLIER INFORMATION

(SAMPLE ONLY - NOT APPROVED FOR USE)

PLEASE PRINT OR TYPE

SAMPLE FORM 1500
SAMPLE FORM 1500 SAMPLE FORM 1500

DONALD L. GIVINGS, M.D.

11350 Medical Drive ■ Anywhere US 12345 ■ (101) 111-5555

EIN: 11-123456	SSN: 123-12-1234	MEDICARE: D1234
UPIN: DG1234	GRP: DG12345	MEDICAID: DLG1234
BCBS: 12345	TRICARE: 5555	

Encounter Form

PATIENT INFORMATION:

Name:	Annalisa M. Faris
Address:	394 Myriam Court
City:	Anywhere
State:	US
Zip Code:	12345
Telephone:	(101) 333-5555
Gender:	Female
Date of Birth:	04-04-1999
Occupation:	
Employer:	
Spouse's Employer:	

INSURANCE INFORMATION:

Patient Number:	16-e
Place of Service:	Mercy Hospital
Primary Insurance Plan:	TRICARE Prime
Primary Insurance Plan ID #:	323-23-3333
Group #:	
Primary Policyholder:	Nacir R. Faris
Policyholder Date of Birth:	06-21-1975
Relationship to Patient:	Father
Secondary Insurance Plan:	
Secondary Insurance Plan ID #:	
Secondary Policyholder:	

Patient Status ☐ Married ☐ Divorced ☒ Single ☐ Student ☐ Other

DIAGNOSIS INFORMATION

Diagnosis	Code	Diagnosis	Code
1. Chills with fever	780.6	5.	
2. Lethargy	780.7	6.	
3. Loss of appetite	783.0	7.	
4. Loss of weight	783.2	8.	

PROCEDURE INFORMATION

Description of Procedure or Service	Date	Code	Charge
1. Initial hosp. level IV	06-02-YYYY	99224	$200.00
2. Subsq. hosp. level III	06-03-YYYY	99233	$85.00
3. Subsq. hosp. level III	06-04-YYYY	99233	$85.00
4. Subsq. hosp. level III	06-06-YYYY	99233	$85.00
5. Subsq. hosp. level II	06-07-YYYY	99232	$75.00
6. Subsq. hosp. level II	06-09-YYYY	99232	$75.00
7. Subsq. hosp. level II	06-10-YYYY	99232	$75.00

SPECIAL NOTES:

Father is stationed at 555 Regiment Way, Anywhere US 12345

Admission authorization # D50123

Patient was discharged 06/11/YYYY but not seen

PLEASE
DO NOT
STAPLE
IN THIS
AREA

CARRIER

HEALTH INSURANCE CLAIM FORM

| | PICA | | PICA | | |

| | | | | | PICA | | | |

1. MEDICARE ☐ (Medicare #) MEDICAID ☐ (Medicaid #) CHAMPUS ☐ (Sponsor's SSN) CHAMPVA ☐ (VA File #) GROUP HEALTH PLAN ☐ (SSN or ID) FECA BLK LUNG ☐ (SSN) OTHER ☐ (ID)

1a. INSURED'S I.D. NUMBER (FOR PROGRAM IN ITEM 1)

2. PATIENT'S NAME (Last Name, First Name, Middle Initial)

3. PATIENT'S BIRTH DATE MM | DD | YY SEX M ☐ F ☐

4. INSURED'S NAME (Last Name, First Name, Middle Initial)

5. PATIENT'S ADDRESS (No. Street)

6. PATIENT RELATIONSHIP TO INSURED Self ☐ Spouse ☐ Child ☐ Other ☐

7. INSURED'S ADDRESS (No. Street)

CITY   STATE

8. PATIENT STATUS Single ☐ Married ☐ Other ☐ Employed ☐ Full-Time Student ☐ Part-Time Student ☐

CITY   STATE

ZIP CODE   TELEPHONE (Include Area Code) (   )

ZIP CODE   TELEPHONE (INCLUDE AREA CODE) (   )

9. OTHER INSURED'S NAME (Last Name, First Name, Middle Initial)

10. IS PATIENT'S CONDITION RELATED TO:

11. INSURED'S POLICY GROUP OR FECA NUMBER

a. OTHER INSURED'S POLICY OR GROUP NUMBER

a. EMPLOYMENT? (CURRENT OR PREVIOUS) YES ☐ NO ☐

a. INSURED'S DATE OF BIRTH MM | DD | YY SEX M ☐ F ☐

b. OTHER INSURED'S DATE OF BIRTH MM | DD | YY SEX M ☐ F ☐

b. AUTO ACCIDENT? PLACE (State) YES ☐ NO ☐

b. EMPLOYER'S NAME OR SCHOOL NAME

c. EMPLOYER'S NAME OR SCHOOL NAME

c. OTHER ACCIDENT? YES ☐ NO ☐

c. INSURANCE PLAN NAME OR PROGRAM NAME

d. INSURANCE PLAN NAME OR PROGRAM NAME

10d. RESERVED FOR LOCAL USE

d. IS THERE ANOTHER HEALTH BENEFIT PLAN? YES ☐ NO ☐ If yes, return to and complete item 9 a – d.

READ BACK OF FORM BEFORE COMPLETING & SIGNING THIS FORM.
12. PATIENT'S OR AUTHORIZED PERSON'S SIGNATURE I authorize the release of any medical or other information necessary to process this claim. I also request payment of government benefits either to myself or to the party who accepts assignment below.

SIGNED _____ DATE _____

13. INSURED'S OR AUTHORIZED PERSON'S SIGNATURE I authorize payment of medical benefits to the undersigned physician or supplier for services described below.

SIGNED _____

PATIENT AND INSURED INFORMATION

14. DATE OF CURRENT: ILLNESS (First symptom) OR INJURY (Accident) OR PREGNANCY (LMP) MM | DD | YY

15. IF PATIENT HAS HAD SAME OR SIMILAR ILLNESS, GIVE FIRST DATE MM | DD | YY

16. DATES PATIENT UNABLE TO WORK IN CURRENT OCCUPATION FROM MM | DD | YY TO MM | DD | YY

17. NAME OF REFERRING PHYSICIAN OR OTHER SOURCE

17a. I.D. NUMBER OF REFERRING PHYSICIAN

18. HOSPITALIZATION DATES RELATED TO CURRENT SERVICES FROM MM | DD | YY TO MM | DD | YY

19. RESERVED FOR LOCAL USE

20. OUTSIDE LAB? YES ☐ NO ☐ $ CHARGES

21. DIAGNOSIS OR NATURE OF ILLNESS OR INJURY. (RELATE ITEMS 1, 2, 3, OR 4 TO ITEM 24E BY LINE)

1. |___ . ___| 3. |___ . ___|
2. |___ . ___| 4. |___ . ___|

22. MEDICAID RESUBMISSION CODE   ORIGINAL REF. NO.

23. PRIOR AUTHORIZATION NUMBER

24. A DATE(S) OF SERVICE						B Place of Service	C Type of Service	D PROCEDURES, SERVICES, OR SUPPLIES (Explain Unusual Circumstances)		E DIAGNOSIS CODE	F $ CHARGES	G DAYS OR UNITS	H EPSDT Family Plan	I EMG	J COB	K RESERVED FOR LOCAL USE
From MM	DD	YY	To MM	DD	YY			CPT/HCPCS	MODIFIER							
1																
2																
3																
4																
5																
6																

25. FEDERAL TAX I.D. NUMBER SSN ☐ EIN ☐

26. PATIENT'S ACCOUNT NO.

27. ACCEPT ASSIGNMENT? (For govt. claims, see back) YES ☐ NO ☐

28. TOTAL CHARGE $

29. AMOUNT PAID $

30. BALANCE DUE $

31. SIGNATURE OF PHYSICIAN OR SUPPLIER INCLUDING DEGREES OR CREDENTIALS (I certify that the statements on the reverse apply to this bill and are made a part thereof.)

SIGNED _____ DATE _____

32. NAME AND ADDRESS OF FACILITY WHERE SERVICES WERE RENDERED (if other than home or office)

33. PHYSICIAN'S, SUPPLIER'S BILLING NAME, ADDRESS, ZIP CODE & PHONE #

PIN#   GRP#

PHYSICIAN OR SUPPLIER INFORMATION

PLEASE PRINT OR TYPE

SAMPLE FORM 1500
SAMPLE FORM 1500 SAMPLE FORM 1500

Chapter 17
Workers' Compensation

FEDERAL WORKERS' COMPENSATION PROGRAMS

1. The U.S. Department of Labor's OWCP administers programs to assist those who are injured at _____ or acquire a(n) _____ disease.

2. List two programs designed to prevent work-related injuries and illnesses.

   a. _____

   b. _____

3. The Black Lung Benefits Act provides medical treatment for respiratory conditions related to former ___. (Circle the correct answer.)
   a. coal miners
   b. longshoremen
   c. postal workers
   d. all of the above

4. The Federal Employees' Compensation Act provides workers' compensation coverage to all ___. (Circle the correct answer.)
   a. coal miners
   b. longshoremen
   c. postal workers
   d. all of the above

5. The Longshore and Harbor Workers' Compensation Program provides medical benefits to ___. (Circle the correct answer.)
   a. coal miners
   b. maritime workers
   c. postal workers
   d. all of the above

STATE WORKERS' COMPENSATION PROGRAM

6. A Workers' Compensation Board or Commission is established by each _____.

7. The State Insurance Fund must offer workers' compensation insurance to any _____ requesting it.

ELIGIBILITY FOR COVERAGE

8. List three occupations in which coverage for stress-related disorders has been awarded.

   a. _____

   b. _____

   c. _____

9. Give two situations of when an employee would qualify for workers' compensation even though he/she was not physically on company property. (Do not use examples given in the textbook.)

   _____

   _____

   _____

   _____

   _____

   _____

   _____

   _____

10. A worker will lose the right to workers' compensation coverage if injury results solely from
   _____ from _____ or _____.

CLASSIFICATION OF WORKERS' COMPENSATION CASES

11. List five classifications of workers' compensation cases mandated by federal law.

   a. _____

   b. _____

   c. _____

   d. _____

   e. _____

12. For each item, enter **T** for a true statement or **F** for a false statement on the line provided.

   _____ a. Medical treatment claims are filed for minor illness or injuries when the worker is treated and able to return to work within a few days.

   _____ b. Temporary disability claims cover medical treatment for illness and injuries but not payment for lost wages.

   _____ c. Permanent disability refers to the employee's degree of injury.

   _____ d. Vocational rehabilitation claims cover the expense of vocational retraining.

13. Describe the difference between *permanent total disability* and *permanent partial disability.*

   _____

   _____

14. How are survivor benefits calculated? _____

_____

SPECIAL HANDLING OF WORKERS' COMPENSATION CASES

15. If a patient has workers' compensation and the amount charged for the treatment is greater than the approved reimbursement for the treatment, can the provider balance bill the patient? _____

Critical Thinking

16. Why is it important to maintain separate files on patients who receive treatment from the same provider for both work-related disorders and regular medical care?

_____

_____

_____

_____

_____

FIRST REPORT OF INJURY

17. When should the First Report of Injury form be completed? _____

_____

18. List four parties who should receive a copy of a First Report of Injury form.
    a. _____
    b. _____
    c. _____
    d. _____

19. Explain why there is no patient signature line on the First Report of Injury form.

_____

_____

_____

20. What is the time limit for filing the First Report of Injury form? _____

_____

21. Should the patient's health insurance carrier be contacted to obtain the name and mailing address of the workers' compensation carrier? _____

22. Should the provider's office ask for a faxed confirmation from the employer of the worker with on-the-job injuries? _____

23. If an employer disputes the legitimacy of a claim, should the provider still file the First Report of Injury form? _____

24. Is the physician responsible for completing the First Report of Injury form? _____

PROGRESS REPORTS

25. What is the purpose of the Progress Report? _____

_____

26. What should be done with a file/claim number once it is assigned by the carrier or the Workers' Compensation Commission/Board? _____

_____

BILLING INFORMATION NOTES

27. Which of the following injured workers may be eligible for federal compensation plans? (Circle the correct answer/answers.)
    a. coal miners
    b. military employees
    c. federal employees
    d. all of the above

28. Which of the following can be designated a fiscal agent by state law and the corporation involved? (Circle the correct answer.)
    a. the State Compensation Fund
    b. a private, commercial insurance carrier
    c. the employer's special company capital funds set aside for compensation cases
    d. any of the above

29. What is the deductible for workers' compensation claims? _____

30. What is the copayment for workers' compensation claims? _____

31. Who pays workers' compensation premiums? _____

32. Which providers must accept the workers' compensation payment as payment in full? _____

_____

Know Your Acronyms

33. Define the following acronyms:

    a. DFEC   _____

    b. DOL   _____

    c. FECA   _____

    d. FELA   _____

    e. MSDS   _____

    f. MSHA   _____

g. OSHA _____

h. OWCP _____

● EXERCISES

34. Complete Case Studies 17-a through 17-f using the blank claims provided. Follow the step-by-step instructions in the textbook to properly complete each claim. If a patient has secondary coverage, complete an additional claim using secondary directions from the textbook. You may choose to use a pencil so corrections can be made.

DONALD L. GIVINGS, M.D.

11350 Medical Drive ■ Anywhere US 12345 ■ (101) 111-5555

EIN: 11-123456	SSN: 123-12-1234	MEDICARE: D1234
UPIN: DG1234	GRP: DG12345	MEDICAID: DLG1234
BCBS: 12345	TRICARE: 5555	

Encounter Form

PATIENT INFORMATION:

Name:	Sandy S. Grand
Address:	109 Darling Road
City:	Anywhere
State:	US
Zip Code:	12345
Telephone:	(101) 333-5555
Gender:	Female
Date of Birth:	12-03-1972
Occupation:	
Employer:	Starport Fitness Center
Spouse's Employer:	

INSURANCE INFORMATION:

Patient Number:	17-a
Place of Service:	Office
Primary Insurance Plan:	Workers Trust
Primary Insurance Plan ID #:	CLR5457
Group #:	
Primary Policyholder:	Sandy S. Grand
Policyholder Date of Birth:	12-03-1972
Relationship to Patient:	Self
Secondary Insurance Plan:	
Secondary Insurance Plan ID #:	
Secondary Policyholder:	

Patient Status ☐ Married ☐ Divorced ☒ Single ☐ Student ☐ Other

DIAGNOSIS INFORMATION

Diagnosis	Code	Diagnosis	Code
1. Wrist fracture, closed	814.00	5.	
2. Fall from chair	E884.2	6.	
3.		7.	
4.		8.	

PROCEDURE INFORMATION

Description of Procedure or Service	Date	Code	Charge
1. New patient OV level IV	02-03-YYYY	99204	$100.00
2.			
3.			
4.			
5.			

SPECIAL NOTES:

Patient cannot return to work until seen by the orthopedist, Dr. Breaker

(SAMPLE ONLY - NOT APPROVED FOR USE)

CARRIER

☐☐ PICA

HEALTH INSURANCE CLAIM FORM PICA ☐☐

1. MEDICARE MEDICAID CHAMPUS CHAMPVA GROUP HEALTH PLAN FECA BLK LUNG OTHER	1a. INSURED'S I.D. NUMBER (FOR PROGRAM IN ITEM 1)

☐ (Medicare #) ☐ (Medicaid #) ☐ (Sponsor's SSN) ☐ (VA File #) ☐ (SSN or ID) ☐ (SSN) ☐ (ID)

2. PATIENT'S NAME (Last Name, First Name, Middle Initial)

3. PATIENT'S BIRTH DATE MM | DD | YY SEX M ☐ F ☐

4. INSURED'S NAME (Last Name, First Name, Middle Initial)

5. PATIENT'S ADDRESS (No. Street)

6. PATIENT RELATIONSHIP TO INSURED Self ☐ Spouse ☐ Child ☐ Other ☐

7. INSURED'S ADDRESS (No. Street)

CITY STATE

8. PATIENT STATUS Single ☐ Married ☐ Other ☐

CITY STATE

ZIP CODE TELEPHONE (Include Area Code) ( )

Employed ☐ Full-Time Student ☐ Part-Time Student ☐

ZIP CODE TELEPHONE (INCLUDE AREA CODE) ( )

9. OTHER INSURED'S NAME (Last Name, First Name, Middle Initial)

10. IS PATIENT'S CONDITION RELATED TO:

11. INSURED'S POLICY GROUP OR FECA NUMBER

a. OTHER INSURED'S POLICY OR GROUP NUMBER

a. EMPLOYMENT? (CURRENT OR PREVIOUS) ☐ YES ☐ NO

a. INSURED'S DATE OF BIRTH MM | DD | YY SEX M ☐ F ☐

b. OTHER INSURED'S DATE OF BIRTH MM | DD | YY SEX M ☐ F ☐

b. AUTO ACCIDENT? PLACE (State) ☐ YES ☐ NO

b. EMPLOYER'S NAME OR SCHOOL NAME

c. EMPLOYER'S NAME OR SCHOOL NAME

c. OTHER ACCIDENT? ☐ YES ☐ NO

c. INSURANCE PLAN NAME OR PROGRAM NAME

d. INSURANCE PLAN NAME OR PROGRAM NAME

10d. RESERVED FOR LOCAL USE

d. IS THERE ANOTHER HEALTH BENEFIT PLAN? ☐ YES ☐ NO If yes, return to and complete item 9 a – d.

READ BACK OF FORM BEFORE COMPLETING & SIGNING THIS FORM.
12. PATIENT'S OR AUTHORIZED PERSON'S SIGNATURE I authorize the release of any medical or other information necessary to process this claim. I also request payment of government benefits either to myself or to the party who accepts assignment below.

SIGNED _____ DATE _____

13. INSURED'S OR AUTHORIZED PERSON'S SIGNATURE I authorize payment of medical benefits to the undersigned physician or supplier for services described below.

SIGNED _____

PATIENT AND INSURED INFORMATION

14. DATE OF CURRENT: MM | DD | YY ◄ ILLNESS (First symptom) OR INJURY (Accident) OR PREGNANCY (LMP)

15. IF PATIENT HAS HAD SAME OR SIMILAR ILLNESS, GIVE FIRST DATE MM | DD | YY

16. DATES PATIENT UNABLE TO WORK IN CURRENT OCCUPATION MM | DD | YY FROM TO MM | DD | YY

17. NAME OF REFERRING PHYSICIAN OR OTHER SOURCE

17a. I.D. NUMBER OF REFERRING PHYSICIAN

18. HOSPITALIZATION DATES RELATED TO CURRENT SERVICES MM | DD | YY FROM TO MM | DD | YY

19. RESERVED FOR LOCAL USE

20. OUTSIDE LAB? ☐ YES ☐ NO $ CHARGES

21. DIAGNOSIS OR NATURE OF ILLNESS OR INJURY. (RELATE ITEMS 1, 2, 3, OR 4 TO ITEM 24E BY LINE)

1. |___.___ 3. |___.___

2. |___.___ 4. |___.___

22. MEDICAID RESUBMISSION CODE ORIGINAL REF. NO.

23. PRIOR AUTHORIZATION NUMBER

24. A. DATE(S) OF SERVICE		B. Place of Service	C. Type of Service	D. PROCEDURES, SERVICES, OR SUPPLIES (Explain Unusual Circumstances)	E. DIAGNOSIS CODE	F. $ CHARGES	G. DAYS OR UNITS	H. EPSDT Family Plan	I. EMG	J. COB	K. RESERVED FOR LOCAL USE
From MM DD YY	To MM DD YY			CPT/HCPCS	MODIFIER							
1											
2											
3											
4											
5											
6											

25. FEDERAL TAX I.D. NUMBER SSN ☐ EIN ☐

26. PATIENT'S ACCOUNT NO.

27. ACCEPT ASSIGNMENT? (For govt. claims, see back) ☐ YES ☐ NO

28. TOTAL CHARGE $

29. AMOUNT PAID $

30. BALANCE DUE $

31. SIGNATURE OF PHYSICIAN OR SUPPLIER INCLUDING DEGREES OR CREDENTIALS (I certify that the statements on the reverse apply to this bill and are made a part thereof.)

SIGNED DATE

32. NAME AND ADDRESS OF FACILITY WHERE SERVICES WERE RENDERED (If other than home or office)

33. PHYSICIAN'S, SUPPLIER'S BILLING NAME, ADDRESS, ZIP CODE & PHONE #

PIN# GRP#

PHYSICIAN OR SUPPLIER INFORMATION

(SAMPLE ONLY - NOT APPROVED FOR USE)

PLEASE PRINT OR TYPE

SAMPLE FORM 1500
SAMPLE FORM 1500 SAMPLE FORM 1500

ELLIOT A. BREAKER, M.D. ORTHOPEDIST

5124 Pharmacy Drive ■ Anywhere US 12345 ■ (101) 111-5555

EIN: 11-997755	SSN: 223-22-1222	MEDICARE: E1234
UPIN: EB1234	GRP: EB12345	MEDICAID: EAB1234
BCBS: 48489	TRICARE: 5555	

Encounter Form

PATIENT INFORMATION:

Name:	Sandy S. Grand
Address:	109 Darling Road
City:	Anywhere
State:	US
Zip Code:	12345
Telephone:	(101) 333-5555
Gender:	Female
Date of Birth:	12-03-1972
Occupation:	
Employer:	Starport Fitness Center
Spouse's Employer:	

INSURANCE INFORMATION:

Patient Number:	17-b
Place of Service:	Office
Primary Insurance Plan:	Workers Trust
Primary Insurance Plan ID #:	CLR5457
Group #:	
Primary Policyholder:	Sandy S. Grand
Policyholder Date of Birth:	12-03-1972
Relationship to Patient:	Self
Secondary Insurance Plan:	
Secondary Insurance Plan ID #:	
Secondary Policyholder:	

Patient Status   ☐ Married   ☐ Divorced   ☒ Single   ☐ Student   ☐ Other

DIAGNOSIS INFORMATION

Diagnosis	Code	Diagnosis	Code
1. Wrist fracture, closed	814.00	5.	
2. Fall from chair	E884.2	6.	
3.		7.	
4.		8.	

PROCEDURE INFORMATION

Description of Procedure or Service	Date	Code	Charge
1. Office consult level IV	02-05-YYYY	99244	$95.00
2. X-ray wrist, complete	02-05-YYYY	73110	75.00
3. Application of cast, hand and lower forearm	02-05-YYYY	29085	50.00
4.			
5.			

SPECIAL NOTES:

Date of injury: 02/03/YYYY
Referred by Donald L. Givings, M.D. UPIN/SSN: 123-12-1234
Return visit: 2 weeks

PLEASE
DO NOT
STAPLE
IN THIS
AREA

CARRIER

[ ] [ ] PICA

HEALTH INSURANCE CLAIM FORM

PICA [ ] [ ]

1.	MEDICARE	MEDICAID	CHAMPUS	CHAMPVA	GROUP HEALTH PLAN	FECA BLK LUNG	OTHER	1a. INSURED'S I.D. NUMBER	(FOR PROGRAM IN ITEM 1)
	[ ] (Medicare #)	[ ] (Medicaid #)	[ ] (Sponsor's SSN)	[ ] (VA File #)	[ ] (SSN or ID)	[ ] (SSN)	[ ] (ID)		

2. PATIENT'S NAME (Last Name, First Name, Middle Initial)

3. PATIENT'S BIRTH DATE MM | DD | YY   SEX   M [ ] F [ ]

4. INSURED'S NAME (Last Name, First Name, Middle Initial)

5. PATIENT'S ADDRESS (No. Street)

6. PATIENT RELATIONSHIP TO INSURED
Self [ ] Spouse [ ] Child [ ] Other [ ]

7. INSURED'S ADDRESS (No. Street)

CITY   STATE

8. PATIENT STATUS
Single [ ]   Married [ ]   Other [ ]

Employed [ ]   Full-Time Student [ ]   Part-Time Student [ ]

CITY   STATE

ZIP CODE   TELEPHONE (Include Area Code)   (   )

ZIP CODE   TELEPHONE (INCLUDE AREA CODE)   (   )

9. OTHER INSURED'S NAME (Last Name, First Name, Middle Initial)

10. IS PATIENT'S CONDITION RELATED TO:

11. INSURED'S POLICY GROUP OR FECA NUMBER

a. OTHER INSURED'S POLICY OR GROUP NUMBER

a. EMPLOYMENT? (CURRENT OR PREVIOUS)
[ ] YES   [ ] NO

a. INSURED'S DATE OF BIRTH MM | DD | YY   SEX M [ ] F [ ]

b. OTHER INSURED'S DATE OF BIRTH MM | DD | YY   SEX M [ ] F [ ]

b. AUTO ACCIDENT?   PLACE (State)
[ ] YES   [ ] NO

b. EMPLOYER'S NAME OR SCHOOL NAME

c. EMPLOYER'S NAME OR SCHOOL NAME

c. OTHER ACCIDENT?
[ ] YES   [ ] NO

c. INSURANCE PLAN NAME OR PROGRAM NAME

d. INSURANCE PLAN NAME OR PROGRAM NAME

10d. RESERVED FOR LOCAL USE

d. IS THERE ANOTHER HEALTH BENEFIT PLAN?
[ ] YES   [ ] NO   If yes, return to and complete item 9 a – d.

READ BACK OF FORM BEFORE COMPLETING & SIGNING THIS FORM.
12. PATIENT'S OR AUTHORIZED PERSON'S SIGNATURE I authorize the release of any medical or other information necessary to process this claim. I also request payment of government benefits either to myself or to the party who accepts assignment below.

SIGNED _____ DATE _____

13. INSURED'S OR AUTHORIZED PERSON'S SIGNATURE I authorize payment of medical benefits to the undersigned physician or supplier for services described below.

SIGNED _____

PATIENT AND INSURED INFORMATION

14. DATE OF CURRENT: MM | DD | YY ◄ ILLNESS (First symptom) OR INJURY (Accident) OR PREGNANCY (LMP)

15. IF PATIENT HAS HAD SAME OR SIMILAR ILLNESS, GIVE FIRST DATE MM | DD | YY

16. DATES PATIENT UNABLE TO WORK IN CURRENT OCCUPATION
FROM MM | DD | YY   TO MM | DD | YY

17. NAME OF REFERRING PHYSICIAN OR OTHER SOURCE

17a. I.D. NUMBER OF REFERRING PHYSICIAN

18. HOSPITALIZATION DATES RELATED TO CURRENT SERVICES
FROM MM | DD | YY   TO MM | DD | YY

19. RESERVED FOR LOCAL USE

20. OUTSIDE LAB? $ CHARGES
[ ] YES   [ ] NO

21. DIAGNOSIS OR NATURE OF ILLNESS OR INJURY. (RELATE ITEMS 1, 2, 3, OR 4 TO ITEM 24E BY LINE)

1. ⌊___ . ___⌋   3. ⌊___ . ___⌋

2. ⌊___ . ___⌋   4. ⌊___ . ___⌋

22. MEDICAID RESUBMISSION CODE   ORIGINAL REF. NO.

23. PRIOR AUTHORIZATION NUMBER

24. A DATE(S) OF SERVICE						B Place of Service	C Type of Service	D PROCEDURES, SERVICES, OR SUPPLIES (Explain Unusual Circumstances)		E DIAGNOSIS CODE	F $ CHARGES	G DAYS OR UNITS	H EPSDT Family Plan	I EMG	J COB	K RESERVED FOR LOCAL USE
From			To					CPT/HCPCS	MODIFIER							
MM	DD	YY	MM	DD	YY											
1																
2																
3																
4																
5																
6																

25. FEDERAL TAX I.D. NUMBER   SSN [ ] EIN [ ]

26. PATIENT'S ACCOUNT NO.

27. ACCEPT ASSIGNMENT? (For govt. claims, see back)
[ ] YES   [ ] NO

28. TOTAL CHARGE $

29. AMOUNT PAID $

30. BALANCE DUE $

31. SIGNATURE OF PHYSICIAN OR SUPPLIER INCLUDING DEGREES OR CREDENTIALS (I certify that the statements on the reverse apply to this bill and are made a part thereof.)

SIGNED _____ DATE _____

32. NAME AND ADDRESS OF FACILITY WHERE SERVICES WERE RENDERED (If other than home or office)

33. PHYSICIAN'S, SUPPLIER'S BILLING NAME, ADDRESS, ZIP CODE & PHONE #

PIN# _____   GRP# _____

PHYSICIAN OR SUPPLIER INFORMATION

PLEASE PRINT OR TYPE

SAMPLE FORM 1500
SAMPLE FORM 1500 SAMPLE FORM 1500

DONALD L. GIVINGS, M.D.

11350 Medical Drive ■ Anywhere US 12345 ■ (101) 111-5555

EIN: 11-123456	SSN: 123-12-1234	MEDICARE: D1234
UPIN: DG1234	GRP: DG12345	MEDICAID: DLG1234
BCBS: 12345	TRICARE: 5555	

Encounter Form

PATIENT INFORMATION:

Name:	Marianna D. Holland
Address:	509 Dutch Street
City:	Anywhere
State:	US
Zip Code:	12345
Telephone:	(101) 333-5555
Gender:	Female
Date of Birth:	11-05-1977
Occupation:	
Employer:	Hair Etc.
Spouse's Employer:	

INSURANCE INFORMATION:

Patient Number:	17-c
Place of Service:	Office
Primary Insurance Plan:	Workers Shield
Primary Insurance Plan ID #:	BA6788
Group #:	
Primary Policyholder:	Marianna D. Holland
Policyholder Date of Birth:	11-05-1977
Relationship to Patient:	Self
Secondary Insurance Plan:	
Secondary Insurance Plan ID #:	
Secondary Policyholder:	

Patient Status ☒ Married   ☐ Divorced   ☐ Single   ☐ Student   ☐ Other

DIAGNOSIS INFORMATION

Diagnosis	Code	Diagnosis	Code
1. Fracture, nasal bones, closed	802.0	5.	
2.		6.	
3.		7.	
4.		8.	

PROCEDURE INFORMATION

Description of Procedure or Service	Date	Code	Charge
1. New patient OV level III	05-12-YYYY	99203	$80.00
2.			
3.			
4.			
5.			

SPECIAL NOTES:

Patient may return to work 5/16/YYYY
Return visit: PRN

PLEASE
DO NOT
STAPLE
IN THIS
AREA

CARRIER

☐☐ PICA

HEALTH INSURANCE CLAIM FORM

PICA ☐☐

1. MEDICARE	MEDICAID	CHAMPUS	CHAMPVA	GROUP HEALTH PLAN	FECA BLK LUNG	OTHER	1a. INSURED'S I.D. NUMBER	(FOR PROGRAM IN ITEM 1)
☐ (Medicare #)	☐ (Medicaid #)	☐ (Sponsor's SSN)	☐ (VA File #)	☐ (SSN or ID)	☐ (SSN)	☐ (ID)		

2. PATIENT'S NAME (Last Name, First Name, Middle Initial)

3. PATIENT'S BIRTH DATE MM ┆ DD ┆ YY   SEX   M ☐   F ☐

4. INSURED'S NAME (Last Name, First Name, Middle Initial)

5. PATIENT'S ADDRESS (No. Street)

6. PATIENT RELATIONSHIP TO INSURED   Self ☐   Spouse ☐   Child ☐   Other ☐

7. INSURED'S ADDRESS (No. Street)

CITY   STATE

8. PATIENT STATUS   Single ☐   Married ☐   Other ☐

CITY   STATE

ZIP CODE   TELEPHONE (Include Area Code) (   )

Employed ☐   Full-Time Student ☐   Part-Time Student ☐

ZIP CODE   TELEPHONE (INCLUDE AREA CODE) (   )

9. OTHER INSURED'S NAME (Last Name, First Name, Middle Initial)

10. IS PATIENT'S CONDITION RELATED TO:

11. INSURED'S POLICY GROUP OR FECA NUMBER

a. OTHER INSURED'S POLICY OR GROUP NUMBER

a. EMPLOYMENT? (CURRENT OR PREVIOUS)   YES ☐   NO ☐

a. INSURED'S DATE OF BIRTH MM ┆ DD ┆ YY   SEX   M ☐   F ☐

b. OTHER INSURED'S DATE OF BIRTH MM ┆ DD ┆ YY   SEX   M ☐   F ☐

b. AUTO ACCIDENT?   PLACE (State)   YES ☐   NO ☐

b. EMPLOYER'S NAME OR SCHOOL NAME

c. EMPLOYER'S NAME OR SCHOOL NAME

c. OTHER ACCIDENT?   YES ☐   NO ☐

c. INSURANCE PLAN NAME OR PROGRAM NAME

d. INSURANCE PLAN NAME OR PROGRAM NAME

10d. RESERVED FOR LOCAL USE

d. IS THERE ANOTHER HEALTH BENEFIT PLAN?   YES ☐   NO ☐   If yes, return to and complete item 9 a – d.

READ BACK OF FORM BEFORE COMPLETING & SIGNING THIS FORM.
12. PATIENT'S OR AUTHORIZED PERSON'S SIGNATURE I authorize the release of any medical or other information necessary to process this claim. I also request payment of government benefits either to myself or to the party who accepts assignment below.

SIGNED _____   DATE _____

13. INSURED'S OR AUTHORIZED PERSON'S SIGNATURE I authorize payment of medical benefits to the undersigned physician or supplier for services described below.

SIGNED _____

PATIENT AND INSURED INFORMATION

14. DATE OF CURRENT: MM ┆ DD ┆ YY   ILLNESS (First symptom) OR INJURY (Accident) OR PREGNANCY (LMP)

15. IF PATIENT HAS HAD SAME OR SIMILAR ILLNESS, GIVE FIRST DATE   MM ┆ DD ┆ YY

16. DATES PATIENT UNABLE TO WORK IN CURRENT OCCUPATION MM ┆ DD ┆ YY   FROM   TO   MM ┆ DD ┆ YY

17. NAME OF REFERRING PHYSICIAN OR OTHER SOURCE

17a. I.D. NUMBER OF REFERRING PHYSICIAN

18. HOSPITALIZATION DATES RELATED TO CURRENT SERVICES MM ┆ DD ┆ YY   FROM   TO   MM ┆ DD ┆ YY

19. RESERVED FOR LOCAL USE

20. OUTSIDE LAB?   YES ☐   NO ☐ $ CHARGES

21. DIAGNOSIS OR NATURE OF ILLNESS OR INJURY. (RELATE ITEMS 1, 2, 3, OR 4 TO ITEM 24E BY LINE)

1. ┆___ . ___
2. ┆___ . ___
3. ┆___ . ___
4. ┆___ . ___

22. MEDICAID RESUBMISSION CODE   ORIGINAL REF. NO.

23. PRIOR AUTHORIZATION NUMBER

24. A DATE(S) OF SERVICE						B Place of Service	C Type of Service	D PROCEDURES, SERVICES, OR SUPPLIES (Explain Unusual Circumstances)		E DIAGNOSIS CODE	F $ CHARGES	G DAYS OR UNITS	H EPSDT Family Plan	I EMG	J COB	K RESERVED FOR LOCAL USE
From			To					CPT/HCPCS	MODIFIER							
MM	DD	YY	MM	DD	YY											
1																
2																
3																
4																
5																
6																

25. FEDERAL TAX I.D. NUMBER   SSN ☐   EIN ☐

26. PATIENT'S ACCOUNT NO.

27. ACCEPT ASSIGNMENT? (For govt. claims, see back)   YES ☐   NO ☐

28. TOTAL CHARGE $

29. AMOUNT PAID $

30. BALANCE DUE $

31. SIGNATURE OF PHYSICIAN OR SUPPLIER INCLUDING DEGREES OR CREDENTIALS (I certify that the statements on the reverse apply to this bill and are made a part thereof.)

SIGNED _____   DATE _____

32. NAME AND ADDRESS OF FACILITY WHERE SERVICES WERE RENDERED (If other than home or office)

33. PHYSICIAN'S, SUPPLIER'S BILLING NAME, ADDRESS, ZIP CODE & PHONE #

PIN# _____   GRP# _____

PHYSICIAN OR SUPPLIER INFORMATION

PLEASE PRINT OR TYPE

SAMPLE FORM 1500
SAMPLE FORM 1500 SAMPLE FORM 1500

DONALD L. GIVINGS, M.D.

Encounter Form

11350 Medical Drive ■ Anywhere US 12345 ■ (101) 111-5555

EIN: 11-123456	SSN: 123-12-1234	MEDICARE: D1234
UPIN: DG1234	GRP: DG12345	MEDICAID: DLG1234
BCBS: 12345	TRICARE: 5555	

PATIENT INFORMATION:

Name:	Thomas J. Buffet
Address:	12 Hauser Drive
City:	Anywhere
State:	US
Zip Code:	12345
Telephone:	(101) 333-5555
Gender:	Male
Date of Birth:	12-03-1965
Occupation:	
Employer:	Start Packing Real Estate
Spouse's Employer:	

INSURANCE INFORMATION:

Patient Number:	17-d
Place of Service:	Office
Primary Insurance Plan:	Workers Guard
Primary Insurance Plan ID #:	WC4958
Group #:	
Primary Policyholder:	Thomas J. Buffet
Policyholder Date of Birth:	12-03-1965
Relationship to Patient:	Self
Secondary Insurance Plan:	
Secondary Insurance Plan ID #:	
Secondary Policyholder:	

Patient Status   ☒ Married   ☐ Divorced   ☐ Single   ☐ Student   ☐ Other

DIAGNOSIS INFORMATION

Diagnosis	Code	Diagnosis	Code
1. Ankle sprain, deltoid	845.01	5.	
2.		6.	
3.		7.	
4.		8.	

PROCEDURE INFORMATION

Description of Procedure or Service	Date	Code	Charge
1. New patient OV level II	10-10-YYYY	99202	$70.00
2.			
3.			
4.			
5.			

SPECIAL NOTES:

Patient may return to work tomorrow
Return visit: PRN

(SAMPLE ONLY - NOT APPROVED FOR USE)

CARRIER

HEALTH INSURANCE CLAIM FORM

PICA ☐☐☐   PICA ☐☐

| 1. MEDICARE ☐ (Medicare #) | MEDICAID ☐ (Medicaid #) | CHAMPUS ☐ (Sponsor's SSN) | CHAMPVA ☐ (VA File #) | GROUP HEALTH PLAN ☐ (SSN or ID) | FECA BLK LUNG ☐ (SSN) | OTHER ☐ (ID) | 1a. INSURED'S I.D. NUMBER (FOR PROGRAM IN ITEM 1) |

| 2. PATIENT'S NAME (Last Name, First Name, Middle Initial) | 3. PATIENT'S BIRTH DATE MM ┊ DD ┊ YY   SEX M ☐ F ☐ | 4. INSURED'S NAME (Last Name, First Name, Middle Initial) |

| 5. PATIENT'S ADDRESS (No. Street) | 6. PATIENT RELATIONSHIP TO INSURED Self ☐ Spouse ☐ Child ☐ Other ☐ | 7. INSURED'S ADDRESS (No. Street) |

| CITY | STATE | 8. PATIENT STATUS Single ☐ Married ☐ Other ☐ | CITY | STATE |

| ZIP CODE | TELEPHONE (Include Area Code) ( ) | Employed ☐ Full-Time Student ☐ Part-Time Student ☐ | ZIP CODE | TELEPHONE (INCLUDE AREA CODE) ( ) |

| 9. OTHER INSURED'S NAME (Last Name, First Name, Middle Initial) | 10. IS PATIENT'S CONDITION RELATED TO: | 11. INSURED'S POLICY GROUP OR FECA NUMBER |

| a. OTHER INSURED'S POLICY OR GROUP NUMBER | a. EMPLOYMENT? (CURRENT OR PREVIOUS) YES ☐ NO ☐ | a. INSURED'S DATE OF BIRTH MM ┊ DD ┊ YY   SEX M ☐ F ☐ |

| b. OTHER INSURED'S DATE OF BIRTH MM ┊ DD ┊ YY   SEX M ☐ F ☐ | b. AUTO ACCIDENT? PLACE (State) YES ☐ NO ☐ | b. EMPLOYER'S NAME OR SCHOOL NAME |

| c. EMPLOYER'S NAME OR SCHOOL NAME | c. OTHER ACCIDENT? YES ☐ NO ☐ | c. INSURANCE PLAN NAME OR PROGRAM NAME |

| d. INSURANCE PLAN NAME OR PROGRAM NAME | 10d. RESERVED FOR LOCAL USE | d. IS THERE ANOTHER HEALTH BENEFIT PLAN? YES ☐ NO ☐ If yes, return to and complete item 9 a – d. |

READ BACK OF FORM BEFORE COMPLETING & SIGNING THIS FORM.

12. PATIENT'S OR AUTHORIZED PERSON'S SIGNATURE I authorize the release of any medical or other information necessary to process this claim. I also request payment of government benefits either to myself or to the party who accepts assignment below.

SIGNED _____ DATE _____

13. INSURED'S OR AUTHORIZED PERSON'S SIGNATURE I authorize payment of medical benefits to the undersigned physician or supplier for services described below.

SIGNED _____

PATIENT AND INSURED INFORMATION

| 14. DATE OF CURRENT: MM ┊ DD ┊ YY   ILLNESS (First symptom) OR INJURY (Accident) OR PREGNANCY (LMP) | 15. IF PATIENT HAS HAD SAME OR SIMILAR ILLNESS, GIVE FIRST DATE MM ┊ DD ┊ YY | 16. DATES PATIENT UNABLE TO WORK IN CURRENT OCCUPATION MM ┊ DD ┊ YY   TO   MM ┊ DD ┊ YY FROM |

| 17. NAME OF REFERRING PHYSICIAN OR OTHER SOURCE | 17a. I.D. NUMBER OF REFERRING PHYSICIAN | 18. HOSPITALIZATION DATES RELATED TO CURRENT SERVICES MM ┊ DD ┊ YY   TO   MM ┊ DD ┊ YY FROM |

| 19. RESERVED FOR LOCAL USE | | 20. OUTSIDE LAB? $ CHARGES YES ☐ NO ☐ |

| 21. DIAGNOSIS OR NATURE OF ILLNESS OR INJURY. (RELATE ITEMS 1, 2, 3, OR 4 TO ITEM 24E BY LINE) 1. ┗___ . ___   3. ┗___ . ___ 2. ┗___ . ___   4. ┗___ . ___ | 22. MEDICAID RESUBMISSION CODE   ORIGINAL REF. NO. |
| | 23. PRIOR AUTHORIZATION NUMBER |

24. A DATE(S) OF SERVICE					B Place of Service	C Type of Service	D PROCEDURES, SERVICES, OR SUPPLIES (Explain Unusual Circumstances)		E DIAGNOSIS CODE	F $ CHARGES	G DAYS OR UNITS	H EPSDT Family Plan	I EMG	J COB	K RESERVED FOR LOCAL USE
From MM	DD	YY	To MM	DD	YY			CPT/HCPCS	MODIFIER							
1																
2																
3																
4																
5																
6																

| 25. FEDERAL TAX I.D. NUMBER   SSN ☐ EIN ☐ | 26. PATIENT'S ACCOUNT NO. | 27. ACCEPT ASSIGNMENT? (For govt. claims, see back) YES ☐ NO ☐ | 28. TOTAL CHARGE $ | 29. AMOUNT PAID $ | 30. BALANCE DUE $ |

| 31. SIGNATURE OF PHYSICIAN OR SUPPLIER INCLUDING DEGREES OR CREDENTIALS (I certify that the statements on the reverse apply to this bill and are made a part thereof.) SIGNED _____ DATE _____ | 32. NAME AND ADDRESS OF FACILITY WHERE SERVICES WERE RENDERED (If other than home or office) | 33. PHYSICIAN'S, SUPPLIER'S BILLING NAME, ADDRESS, ZIP CODE & PHONE # PIN# _____   GRP# _____ |

PHYSICIAN OR SUPPLIER INFORMATION

(SAMPLE ONLY - NOT APPROVED FOR USE)

PLEASE PRINT OR TYPE

SAMPLE FORM 1500
SAMPLE FORM 1500 SAMPLE FORM 1500

DONALD L. GIVINGS, M.D.

11350 Medical Drive ■ Anywhere US 12345 ■ (101) 111-5555

EIN: 11-123456   SSN: 123-12-1234   MEDICARE: D1234
UPIN: DG1234   GRP: DG12345   MEDICAID: DLG1234
BCBS: 12345   TRICARE: 5555

Encounter Form

PATIENT INFORMATION:

Name:	Priscilla R. Shepard
Address:	23 Easy Street
City:	Anywhere
State:	US
Zip Code:	12345
Telephone:	(101) 333-5555
Gender:	Female
Date of Birth:	07-15-1956
Occupation:	
Employer:	Ultimate Cleaners
Spouse's Employer:	

INSURANCE INFORMATION:

Patient Number:	17-e
Place of Service:	Mercy Hospital
Primary Insurance Plan:	Workers Prompt
Primary Insurance Plan ID #:	MA4958
Group #:	
Primary Policyholder:	Priscilla R. Shepard
Policyholder Date of Birth:	07-15-1956
Relationship to Patient:	Self
Secondary Insurance Plan:	
Secondary Insurance Plan ID #:	
Secondary Policyholder:	

Patient Status ☐ Married ☐ Divorced ☒ Single ☐ Student ☐ Other

DIAGNOSIS INFORMATION

Diagnosis	Code	Diagnosis	Code
1. Open wound shoulder, complicated	880.10	5.	
2.		6.	
3.		7.	
4.		8.	

PROCEDURE INFORMATION

Description of Procedure or Service	Date	Code	Charge
1. ER visit level III	07-16-YYYY	99283	$150.00
2.			
3.			
4.			
5.			

SPECIAL NOTES:

Patient was seen in the ER today. Injury occurred at work this morning.
Patient is to be admitted in the morning.

(SAMPLE ONLY - NOT APPROVED FOR USE)

CARRIER

HEALTH INSURANCE CLAIM FORM

[ ] [ ] PICA   PICA [ ] [ ]

| 1. MEDICARE   MEDICAID   CHAMPUS   CHAMPVA   GROUP HEALTH PLAN   FECA BLK LUNG   OTHER | 1a. INSURED'S I.D. NUMBER   (FOR PROGRAM IN ITEM 1) |

[ ] (Medicare #)   [ ] (Medicaid #)   [ ] (Sponsor's SSN)   [ ] (VA File #)   [ ] (SSN or ID)   [ ] (SSN)   [ ] (ID)

2. PATIENT'S NAME (Last Name, First Name, Middle Initial)

3. PATIENT'S BIRTH DATE   MM | DD | YY   SEX   M [ ]   F [ ]

4. INSURED'S NAME (Last Name, First Name, Middle Initial)

5. PATIENT'S ADDRESS (No. Street)

6. PATIENT RELATIONSHIP TO INSURED   Self [ ]   Spouse [ ]   Child [ ]   Other [ ]

7. INSURED'S ADDRESS (No. Street)

CITY   STATE

8. PATIENT STATUS   Single [ ]   Married [ ]   Other [ ]

CITY   STATE

ZIP CODE   TELEPHONE (Include Area Code) ( )

Employed [ ]   Full-Time Student [ ]   Part-Time Student [ ]

ZIP CODE   TELEPHONE (INCLUDE AREA CODE) ( )

9. OTHER INSURED'S NAME (Last Name, First Name, Middle Initial)

10. IS PATIENT'S CONDITION RELATED TO:

11. INSURED'S POLICY GROUP OR FECA NUMBER

a. OTHER INSURED'S POLICY OR GROUP NUMBER

a. EMPLOYMENT? (CURRENT OR PREVIOUS)   [ ] YES   [ ] NO

a. INSURED'S DATE OF BIRTH   MM | DD | YY   SEX   M [ ]   F [ ]

b. OTHER INSURED'S DATE OF BIRTH   MM | DD | YY   SEX   M [ ]   F [ ]

b. AUTO ACCIDENT?   PLACE (State)   [ ] YES   [ ] NO

b. EMPLOYER'S NAME OR SCHOOL NAME

c. EMPLOYER'S NAME OR SCHOOL NAME

c. OTHER ACCIDENT?   [ ] YES   [ ] NO

c. INSURANCE PLAN NAME OR PROGRAM NAME

d. INSURANCE PLAN NAME OR PROGRAM NAME

10d. RESERVED FOR LOCAL USE

d. IS THERE ANOTHER HEALTH BENEFIT PLAN?   [ ] YES   [ ] NO   If yes, return to and complete item 9 a – d.

READ BACK OF FORM BEFORE COMPLETING & SIGNING THIS FORM.
12. PATIENT'S OR AUTHORIZED PERSON'S SIGNATURE I authorize the release of any medical or other information necessary to process this claim. I also request payment of government benefits either to myself or to the party who accepts assignment below.

SIGNED _____ DATE _____

13. INSURED'S OR AUTHORIZED PERSON'S SIGNATURE I authorize payment of medical benefits to the undersigned physician or supplier for services described below.

SIGNED _____

PATIENT AND INSURED INFORMATION

14. DATE OF CURRENT: ILLNESS (First symptom) OR INJURY (Accident) OR PREGNANCY (LMP)   MM | DD | YY

15. IF PATIENT HAS HAD SAME OR SIMILAR ILLNESS, GIVE FIRST DATE   MM | DD | YY

16. DATES PATIENT UNABLE TO WORK IN CURRENT OCCUPATION   MM | DD | YY   FROM   MM | DD | YY   TO

17. NAME OF REFERRING PHYSICIAN OR OTHER SOURCE

17a. I.D. NUMBER OF REFERRING PHYSICIAN

18. HOSPITALIZATION DATES RELATED TO CURRENT SERVICES   MM | DD | YY   FROM   MM | DD | YY   TO

19. RESERVED FOR LOCAL USE

20. OUTSIDE LAB? $ CHARGES   [ ] YES   [ ] NO

21. DIAGNOSIS OR NATURE OF ILLNESS OR INJURY. (RELATE ITEMS 1, 2, 3, OR 4 TO ITEM 24E BY LINE)

1. |___| . |__|

3. |___| . |__|

2. |___| . |__|

4. |___| . |__|

22. MEDICAID RESUBMISSION CODE   ORIGINAL REF. NO.

23. PRIOR AUTHORIZATION NUMBER

24. A DATE(S) OF SERVICE		B Place of Service	C Type of Service	D PROCEDURES, SERVICES, OR SUPPLIES (Explain Unusual Circumstances)	E DIAGNOSIS CODE	F $ CHARGES	G DAYS OR UNITS	H EPSDT Family Plan	I EMG	J COB	K RESERVED FOR LOCAL USE
From MM DD YY	To MM DD YY			CPT/HCPCS MODIFIER							
1											
2											
3											
4											
5											
6											

25. FEDERAL TAX I.D. NUMBER   SSN [ ] EIN [ ]

26. PATIENT'S ACCOUNT NO.

27. ACCEPT ASSIGNMENT? (For govt. claims, see back)   [ ] YES   [ ] NO

28. TOTAL CHARGE $

29. AMOUNT PAID $

30. BALANCE DUE $

31. SIGNATURE OF PHYSICIAN OR SUPPLIER INCLUDING DEGREES OR CREDENTIALS (I certify that the statements on the reverse apply to this bill and are made a part thereof.)

SIGNED _____ DATE _____

32. NAME AND ADDRESS OF FACILITY WHERE SERVICES WERE RENDERED (If other than home or office)

33. PHYSICIAN'S, SUPPLIER'S BILLING NAME, ADDRESS, ZIP CODE & PHONE #

PIN# _____ GRP# _____

PHYSICIAN OR SUPPLIER INFORMATION

PLEASE PRINT OR TYPE

SAMPLE FORM 1500
SAMPLE FORM 1500 SAMPLE FORM 1500

231

DONALD L. GIVINGS, M.D.

11350 Medical Drive ■ Anywhere US 12345 ■ (101) 111-5555

EIN: 11-123456	SSN: 123-12-1234	MEDICARE: D1234
UPIN: DG1234	GRP: DG12345	MEDICAID: DLG1234
BCBS: 12345	TRICARE: 5555	

Encounter Form

PATIENT INFORMATION:

Name:	Priscilla R. Shepard
Address:	23 Easy Street
City:	Anywhere
State:	US
Zip Code:	12345
Telephone:	(101) 333-5555
Gender:	Female
Date of Birth:	07-15-1956
Occupation:	
Employer:	Ultimate Cleaners
Spouse's Employer:	

INSURANCE INFORMATION:

Patient Number:	17-f
Place of Service:	Mercy Hospital
Primary Insurance Plan:	Workers Prompt
Primary Insurance Plan ID #:	MA4958
Group #:	
Primary Policyholder:	Priscilla R. Shepard
Policyholder Date of Birth:	07-15-1956
Relationship to Patient:	Self
Secondary Insurance Plan:	
Secondary Insurance Plan ID #:	
Secondary Policyholder:	

Patient Status ☐ Married ☐ Divorced ☒ Single ☐ Student ☐ Other

DIAGNOSIS INFORMATION

Diagnosis	Code	Diagnosis	Code
1. Open wound shoulder, complicated	880.10	5.	
2.		6.	
3.		7.	
4.		8.	

PROCEDURE INFORMATION

Description of Procedure or Service	Date	Code	Charge
1. Initial visit level III	07-17-YYYY	99223	$150.00
2. Subsq. hosp. level II	07-18-YYYY	99232	$75.00
3. Subsq. hosp. level II	07-19-YYYY	99232	$75.00
4. Hosp. discharge, 45 min.	07-20-YYYY	99239	$75.00
5.			

SPECIAL NOTES:

Date of injury 07/16/YYYY

CARRIER

HEALTH INSURANCE CLAIM FORM

PICA ☐☐☐

☐☐ PICA

1. MEDICARE ☐ (Medicare #) MEDICAID ☐ (Medicaid #) CHAMPUS ☐ (Sponsor's SSN) CHAMPVA ☐ (VA File #) GROUP HEALTH PLAN ☐ (SSN or ID) FECA BLK LUNG ☐ (SSN) OTHER ☐ (ID)

1a. INSURED'S I.D. NUMBER (FOR PROGRAM IN ITEM 1)

2. PATIENT'S NAME (Last Name, First Name, Middle Initial)

3. PATIENT'S BIRTH DATE MM ┊ DD ┊ YY SEX M ☐ F ☐

4. INSURED'S NAME (Last Name, First Name, Middle Initial)

5. PATIENT'S ADDRESS (No. Street)

6. PATIENT RELATIONSHIP TO INSURED Self ☐ Spouse ☐ Child ☐ Other ☐

7. INSURED'S ADDRESS (No. Street)

CITY STATE

8. PATIENT STATUS Single ☐ Married ☐ Other ☐ Employed ☐ Full-Time Student ☐ Part-Time Student ☐

CITY STATE

ZIP CODE TELEPHONE (Include Area Code) ( )

ZIP CODE TELEPHONE (INCLUDE AREA CODE) ( )

9. OTHER INSURED'S NAME (Last Name, First Name, Middle Initial)

10. IS PATIENT'S CONDITION RELATED TO:

11. INSURED'S POLICY GROUP OR FECA NUMBER

a. OTHER INSURED'S POLICY OR GROUP NUMBER

a. EMPLOYMENT? (CURRENT OR PREVIOUS) YES ☐ NO ☐

a. INSURED'S DATE OF BIRTH MM ┊ DD ┊ YY SEX M ☐ F ☐

b. OTHER INSURED'S DATE OF BIRTH MM ┊ DD ┊ YY SEX M ☐ F ☐

b. AUTO ACCIDENT? PLACE (State) YES ☐ NO ☐

b. EMPLOYER'S NAME OR SCHOOL NAME

c. EMPLOYER'S NAME OR SCHOOL NAME

c. OTHER ACCIDENT? YES ☐ NO ☐

c. INSURANCE PLAN NAME OR PROGRAM NAME

d. INSURANCE PLAN NAME OR PROGRAM NAME

10d. RESERVED FOR LOCAL USE

d. IS THERE ANOTHER HEALTH BENEFIT PLAN? YES ☐ NO ☐ If yes, return to and complete item 9 a – d.

READ BACK OF FORM BEFORE COMPLETING & SIGNING THIS FORM.
12. PATIENT'S OR AUTHORIZED PERSON'S SIGNATURE I authorize the release of any medical or other information necessary to process this claim. I also request payment of government benefits either to myself or to the party who accepts assignment below.

SIGNED _____ DATE _____

13. INSURED'S OR AUTHORIZED PERSON'S SIGNATURE I authorize payment of medical benefits to the undersigned physician or supplier for services described below.

SIGNED _____

PATIENT AND INSURED INFORMATION

14. DATE OF CURRENT: ILLNESS (First symptom) OR INJURY (Accident) OR PREGNANCY (LMP) MM ┊ DD ┊ YY

15. IF PATIENT HAS HAD SAME OR SIMILAR ILLNESS, GIVE FIRST DATE MM ┊ DD ┊ YY

16. DATES PATIENT UNABLE TO WORK IN CURRENT OCCUPATION MM ┊ DD ┊ YY FROM TO MM ┊ DD ┊ YY

17. NAME OF REFERRING PHYSICIAN OR OTHER SOURCE

17a. I.D. NUMBER OF REFERRING PHYSICIAN

18. HOSPITALIZATION DATES RELATED TO CURRENT SERVICES MM ┊ DD ┊ YY FROM TO MM ┊ DD ┊ YY

19. RESERVED FOR LOCAL USE

20. OUTSIDE LAB? $ CHARGES YES ☐ NO ☐

21. DIAGNOSIS OR NATURE OF ILLNESS OR INJURY. (RELATE ITEMS 1, 2, 3, OR 4 TO ITEM 24E BY LINE)

1. └── . ──
2. └── . ──
3. └── . ──
4. └── . ──

22. MEDICAID RESUBMISSION CODE ORIGINAL REF. NO.

23. PRIOR AUTHORIZATION NUMBER

24. A DATE(S) OF SERVICE						B Place of Service	C Type of Service	D PROCEDURES, SERVICES, OR SUPPLIES (Explain Unusual Circumstances) CPT/HCPCS ┊ MODIFIER	E DIAGNOSIS CODE	F $ CHARGES	G DAYS OR UNITS	H EPSDT Family Plan	I EMG	J COB	K RESERVED FOR LOCAL USE
From MM	DD	YY	To MM	DD	YY										
1															
2															
3															
4															
5															
6															

25. FEDERAL TAX I.D. NUMBER SSN ☐ EIN ☐

26. PATIENT'S ACCOUNT NO.

27. ACCEPT ASSIGNMENT? (For govt. claims, see back) YES ☐ NO ☐

28. TOTAL CHARGE $

29. AMOUNT PAID $

30. BALANCE DUE $

31. SIGNATURE OF PHYSICIAN OR SUPPLIER INCLUDING DEGREES OR CREDENTIALS (I certify that the statements on the reverse apply to this bill and are made a part thereof.)

SIGNED _____ DATE _____

32. NAME AND ADDRESS OF FACILITY WHERE SERVICES WERE RENDERED (If other than home or office)

33. PHYSICIAN'S, SUPPLIER'S BILLING NAME, ADDRESS, ZIP CODE & PHONE #

PIN# _____ GRP# _____

PHYSICIAN OR SUPPLIER INFORMATION

(SAMPLE ONLY - NOT APPROVED FOR USE)

PLEASE PRINT OR TYPE

SAMPLE FORM 1500
SAMPLE FORM 1500 SAMPLE FORM 1500